Lecture Notes in Computer Science 7322

Commenced Publication in 1973
Founding and Former Series Editors:
Gerhard Goos, Juris Hartmanis, and Jan van Leeuwen

Editorial Board

David Hutchison
Lancaster University, UK

Takeo Kanade
Carnegie Mellon University, Pittsburgh, PA, USA

Josef Kittler
University of Surrey, Guildford, UK

Jon M. Kleinberg
Cornell University, Ithaca, NY, USA

Alfred Kobsa
University of California, Irvine, CA, USA

Friedemann Mattern
ETH Zurich, Switzerland

John C. Mitchell
Stanford University, CA, USA

Moni Naor
Weizmann Institute of Science, Rehovot, Israel

Oscar Nierstrasz
University of Bern, Switzerland

C. Pandu Rangan
Indian Institute of Technology, Madras, India

Bernhard Steffen
TU Dortmund University, Germany

Madhu Sudan
Microsoft Research, Cambridge, MA, USA

Demetri Terzopoulos
University of California, Los Angeles, CA, USA

Doug Tygar
University of California, Berkeley, CA, USA

Gerhard Weikum
Max Planck Institute for Informatics, Saarbruecken, Germany

Ioannis Askoxylakis   Henrich C. Pöhls
Joachim Posegga (Eds.)

Information Security Theory and Practice

Security, Privacy and Trust
in Computing Systems
and Ambient Intelligent Ecosystems

6th IFIP WG 11.2 International Workshop, WISTP 2012
Egham, UK, June 20-22, 2012
Proceedings

 Springer

Volume Editors

Ioannis Askoxylakis
FORTH-ICS
Vassilika Vouton, P.O. Box 1385, 711 10 Heraklion, Crete, Greece
E-mail: asko@ics.forth.gr

Henrich C. Pöhls
Joachim Posegga
University of Passau, Innstrasse 43, 94032 Passau, Germany
E-mail: {hp, jp} @sec.uni-passau.de

ISSN 0302-9743   e-ISSN 1611-3349
ISBN 978-3-642-30954-0   e-ISBN 978-3-642-30955-7
DOI 10.1007/978-3-642-30955-7
Springer Heidelberg Dordrecht London New York

Library of Congress Control Number: 2012939067

CR Subject Classification (1998): E.3, C.2, D.4.6, K.6.5, C.5.3, H.4

LNCS Sublibrary: SL 4 – Security and Cryptology

© IFIP International Federation for Information Processing 2012
This work is subject to copyright. All rights are reserved, whether the whole or part of the material is
concerned, specifically the rights of translation, reprinting, re-use of illustrations, recitation, broadcasting,
reproduction on microfilms or in any other way, and storage in data banks. Duplication of this publication
or parts thereof is permitted only under the provisions of the German Copyright Law of September 9, 1965,
in its current version, and permission for use must always be obtained from Springer. Violations are liable
to prosecution under the German Copyright Law.
The use of general descriptive names, registered names, trademarks, etc. in this publication does not imply,
even in the absence of a specific statement, that such names are exempt from the relevant protective laws
and regulations and therefore free for general use.

Typesetting: Camera-ready by author, data conversion by Scientific Publishing Services, Chennai, India

Printed on acid-free paper

Springer is part of Springer Science+Business Media (www.springer.com)

Preface

Future ICT technologies, like the concepts of Ambient Intelligence and Internet of Things, provide a vision of the Information Society where the emphasis is on surrounding people by intelligent interactive interfaces and objects and on environments that are capable of recognizing and reacting to the presence of different individuals in a seamless, unobtrusive, and invisible manner. The success of such future ICT technologies will crucially depend on their security properties, how privacy and individuals' rights will be protected, and how much individuals will trust the intelligent world that will surround them and through which they will move.

The 6th Workshop in Information Security Theory and Practice (WISTP 2012) addressed the security, privacy, and trust issues in computing systems and ambient intelligence ecosystems along with evaluating their impact on business, individuals, and society. WISTP 2012 was organized by the Royal Holloway University of London during June 20–22, 2012, in Egham, United Kingdom. The workshop received 36 submissions. Each submission was reviewed by at least three reviewers.

This volume contains the nine full papers and six short papers that were selected for presentation at WISTP 2012. Furthermore, the proceedings include the three keynotes given by Dieter Gollmann, Paul Kearney and Frank Piessens, to whom we are grateful.

There is a long list of people who also devoted their energy and provided active support to the successful organization of the workshop. We are grateful to the members of the Program Committee and the external reviewers for reviewing all submissions and selecting the ones with substantial contribution to the thematic area of the workshop. We gratefully acknowledge everyone involved in the successful organization process: the members of the Steering Committee, Claudio Ardagna, Angelos Bilas, Konstantinos Markantonakis, Jean-Jacques Quisquater, Damien Sauveron and Jianying Zhou for their advice, the General Chairs Gerhard Hancke, Konstantinos Markantonakis and Keith Mayes for their invaluable support in the organization of the workshop, Sara Foresti and Taeshik Shon for their efforts as Publicity Chairs and Emma Dobson for her support in the local organization.

Last but not least we are grateful to the authors for submitting their excellent research results and to all attendees that honored us with their presence. We hope that the workshop proceedings will be helpful for future research in the area of Information Security.

June 2012

Ioannis Askoxylakis
Henrich C. Pöhls
Joachim Posegga

Organization

General Chairs

Konstantinos Markantonakis   ISG-SCC, Royal Holloway University of
London, UK

Gerhard Hancke   ISG, Royal Holloway University of London, UK

Keith Mayes   ISG-SCC, Royal Holloway University of
London, UK

Local Organizers

Emma Dobson   ISG, Royal Holloway University of London, UK

Workshop/Panel/Tutorial Chair

Damien Sauveron   XLIM, University of Limoges, France

Publicity Chairs

Sara Foresti   Universitá degli Studi di Milano, Italy

Taeshik Shon   Ajou University, Korea

Program Chairs

Ioannis Askoxylakis   FORTH-ICS, Greece

Joachim Posegga   Institute of IT Security and Security Law
at the University of Passau, Germany

Program Committee

Claudio Ardagna   Universitá degli Studi di Milano, Italy

Lejla Batina   Radboud University Nijmegen,
The Netherlands

Angelos Bilas   FORTH-ICS and University of Crete, Greece

Levente Buttyan   Budapest University of Technology and
Economics, Hungary

Serge Chaumette   LaBRI and University of Bordeaux, France

Jorge Cueller   Siemens, Germany

Josep Domingo-Ferrer   Universitat Rovira i Virgili, Catalan, Spain

Jaap-Henk Hoepman	TNO and Radboud University Nijmegen, The Netherlands
Michael Huth	Imperial College London, UK
Martin Johns	SAP Research, Germany
Cagatay Karabat	TUBITAK BILGEM (The Scientific and Technological Research Council of Turkey), Turkey
Angelos Keromytis	Columbia University, USA
Kwok Yan Lam	National University of Singapore, Singapore
Peter Lipp	Technische Universität Graz, Austria
Javier Lopez	University of Malaga, Spain
Emmanuel Magkos	Ionian University, Greece
Mark Manulis	Technische Universität Darmstadt, Germany
Louis Marinos	European Network and Information Security Agency (ENISA), EU
Fabio Martinelli	IIT-CNR, Italy
Aikaterini Mitrokosta	EPFL, Switzerland
Jose Onieva	University of Malaga, Spain
Gerardo Pelosi	University of Bergamo, Italy
Svetla Petkova-Nikova	Katholieke Universiteit Leuven, Belgium
Henrich C. Pöhls	Institute of IT Security and Security Law at the University of Passau, Germany
Ilia Polian	University of Passau, Germany
Axel Poschmann	National University of Singapore, Singapore
Jean-Jacques Quisquater	DICE, Catholic University of Louvain, Belgium
Bill Roscoe	Department of Computer Science, UK
Kouichi Sakurai	Kyushu University, Japan
Pierangela Samarati	Universitá degli Studi di Milano, Italy
Christos Siaterlis	Joint Research Centre, EU
George Spanoudakis	City University of London, UK
Theo Tryfonas	University of Bristol, UK
Michael Tunstall	University of Bristol, UK
Ingrid Verbauwhede	Katholieke Universiteit Leuven, Belgium
Heung-Youl Youm	Soonchunhyang University, Korea

WISTP Steering Committee

Claudio Ardagna	Universitá degli Studi di Milano, Italy
Angelos Bilas	FORTH-ICS, University of Crete, Greece
Konstantinos Markantonakis	ISG-SCC, Royal Holloway University of London, UK
Jean-Jacques Quisquater	DICE, Catholic University of Louvain, Belgium
Damien Sauveron	XLIM, University of Limoges, France
Jianying Zhou	Institute for Infocomm Research, Singapore

External Reviewers

Alcaraz, Cristina	Nishide, Takashi
Alpár, Gergely	Ochoa, Martin
Beslay, Laurent	Palomba, Andrea
Braun, Bastian	Petroulakis, Nikolaos
Chen, Bangdao	Poll, Erik
Dimitriou, Giorgos	Roman, Rodrigo
Farras, Oriol	Samelin, Kai
Fragkiadakis, Alexandros	Schroepfer, Axel
Hanser, Christian	Singelee, Dave
Huaqun, Wang	Su, Chunhua
Jawurek, Marek	Suzaki, Tomoyasu
Karyotis, Vasileios	Tragos, Elias
Kótyuk, Gergely	Trujillo-Rasua, Rolando
Lueks, Wouter	Uhsadel, Leif
Moyano, Francisco	Whitnall, Carolyn
Naya-Plasencia, María	Zhao, Laiping

Table of Contents

Policy and Access Control

Multi-Party Computation

Cryptography (Short Papers)

Mobile Security

Recent Developments in Low-Level Software Security

Pieter Agten, Nick Nikiforakis, Raoul Strackx,
Willem De Groef, and Frank Piessens

IBBT-Distrinet, Katholieke Universiteit Leuven, Belgium
firstname.lastname@cs.kuleuven.be

Abstract. An important objective for low-level software security research is to develop techniques that make it harder to launch attacks that exploit implementation details of the system under attack. Baltopoulos and Gordon have summarized this as the *principle of source-based reasoning* for security: security properties of a software system should follow from review of the source code and its source-level semantics, and should not depend on details of the compiler or execution platform.

Whether the principle holds – or to what degree – for a particular system depends on the attacker model. If an attacker can only provide input to the program under attack, then the principle holds for any *safe* programming language. However, for more powerful attackers that can load new native machine code into the system, the principle of source-based reasoning typically breaks down completely.

In this paper we discuss state-of-the-art approaches for securing code written in C-like languages for both attacker models discussed above, and we highlight some very recent developments in low-level software security that hold the promise to restore source-based reasoning even against attackers that can provide arbitrary machine code to be run in the same process as the program under attack.

Keywords: software security, C language, full abstraction.

1   Introduction

Programming languages are supposed to provide developers with a high-level abstraction of the platform on which programs will eventually be executed. The programmer should be able to reason about his code at source-code level, and let the compiler and run-time system worry about the low-level execution platform details.

Unfortunately, programming languages fail to do this from the point of view of security. Attacks against software systems often depend in an essential way on details of the platform on which the software is executed, and one can for instance not understand the security consequences of a bug in the program without understanding many details of the execution platform.

I. Askoxylakis, H.C. Pöhls, and J. Posegga (Eds.): WISTP 2012, LNCS 7322, pp. 1–16, 2012.
© IFIP International Federation for Information Processing 2012

This is obviously the case for attacks that exploit memory errors in programs written in unsafe languages such as C and C++. Understanding low-level attacks such as stack smashing attacks, direct code injection attacks, jump-to-libc attacks or return-oriented programming requires one to understand many details of the compiler, operating system or processor architecture [14].

But it is also true for attacks against any software system – including software written in safe languages – where the attacker can interact with the program at the machine code level. For instance a malicious natively implemented function called from a Java program can attack the Java program in very powerful ways and such attacks wil again depend essentially on many details of the execution platform. In a similar way, a natively implemented browser extension can attack any web page visited, or a malicious kernel module can install a root kit.

An important objective for low-level software security research is to correct this situation, and restore what Baltopoulos and Gordon have called the *principle of source-based reasoning* for security [5]. It should be sound to reason about security properties of a software system on the level of source code. In this paper we discuss state-of-the-art approaches for both attacker models discussed above, and we highlight some very recent developments in low-level software security that hold the promise to restore source-based reasoning even against attackers that can inject arbitrary machine code.

The remainder of this paper is structured as follows. First, we illustrate low-level software attacks in both attacker models in Section 2. Next, we briefly discuss the state-of-the-art in securing C programs in the first attacker model where attackers can only provide input to the program. This is a well-understood problem with many mature solutions, and we provide an overview in Section 3. In Section 4, we turn to the more challenging attacker model, and we discuss two recent lines of research that make important steps forward against such attackers.

2   An Illustration of Low-Level Attacks

We distinguish two different but related attacker models. In the first model, that we call the *interactive attacker model*, an attacker can interact with the program under attack by providing input and reading output. An interactive attacker can for instance try to exploit a buffer overflow vulnerability if the program was written in an unsafe language, or could try to do SQL injection, or exploit a logic flaw against a program written in a safe language. The interactive attacker model is a reasonable model for the case where an attacker is trying to subvert a network service running on a hardened and well-protected server machine.

In the second model – the *in-process attacker model* – an attacker can load arbitrary machine code in the process executing the program under attack. This attacker can for instance scan memory for secrets, and overwrite control-flow data, or non-control data of the program under attack, even when the program was written in a safe language. The in-process attacker model is a reasonable model for the case where applications can be extended at run-time with (binary) plugins, or for the case where an application is built from components coming from different stakeholders.

An interactive attacker against a program written in an unsafe language can escalate to an in-process attacker by doing a code-injection attack as we will discuss below.

2.1 The Interactive Attacker Model

In this attacker model, the principle of source-based reasoning fails for unsafe languages such as C or C++. This is well-known and many papers give examples; we refer the reader to Erlingsson et al. [14] for an overview. Here is one simple example of a program in C for which the principle of source-based reasoning fails.

Example 1. In the presence of memory errors such as buffer overflows, an interactive attacker can modify variables in ways that can not be explained by the source code semantics, but that can only be explained by looking at details of the compiler and execution platform.

Consider the example vulnerable function `do_maintenance` of Code Listing 1. The purpose of the `do_maintenance` function is to read the username and password of the current user and if these credentials are valid then perform privileged operations. Source level reasoning can lead a programmer to believe that privileged operations can only be executed after a succesful call to `valid_credentials`.

However, the program has a buffer overflow vulnerability: the programmer has incorrectly used the size of the password buffer for reading in the username, thus allowing the attacker to overflow four characters past the username buffer. The source code semantics (in this case the C standard) says that further behaviour of the program is then *undefined*.

However, by relying on details of the compiler and execution platform, an attacker can perform a useful attack. Compilers will typically allocate the local variables of a function one after the other on the stack, and hence by overflowing the username, the attacker can modify the `authenticated` variable. Since any non-zero value for this variable will be interpreted as true, this will give the attacker access to the authenticated part of the program without the need of a valid username and password combination.

It is often the case that memory errors in a C program can allow an interactive attack to escalate to an in-process attack. The attacker achieves this by performing a so-called *code injection attack*.

Example 2. Code Listing 2 is vulnerable to a traditional code injection attack. The purpose of the program is to read a string from the user, perform a transformation on that string and then save it along with the original string, in an object-oriented programming style. Since there could be many transformations, the transformation function is called through a function pointer which is set by the programmer before the copying of the string. The code that reads the string from the execution environment is vulnerable to a buffer overflow since

Code Listing 1. Code snippet vulnerable to a non-control data attack

```
int do_maintenance () {
    int authenticated = 0;
    char username [24];
    char password [28];

    fgets(username, sizeof(password), stdin);
    fgets(password, sizeof(password), stdin);

    if (valid_credentials(username,password) == 1)
        authenticated = 1;

    if (authenticated){
        //Do privileged operations
    }
}
```

it doesn't perform any checks whether the src buffer is large enough to hold the contents of the command line argument. If the attacker provides a string that is longer than 128 bytes, the string will spill out to the dst buffer. If the provided string is longer than 256 bytes then the string will also overwrite the function pointer that is called in the next line. The attacker can simply enter his shellcode in the src buffer and overwrite the function pointer with the address of the buffer. Thus the program, instead of calling capitalize, will jump to the attacker-provided shellcode.

Again, the source code semantics would say that further execution of the program after overflowing of the buffer is undefined. But relying on many details of the compiler and execution platform (including the layout of variables in memory, and the fact that the program executes on a Von Neumann architecture where code and data are in the same memory) the attacker can actually have some of the data that he inputs to the program be interpreted as code. In other words, the interactive attack escalates to an in-process attack.

2.2   The In-Process Attacker Model

In this model, an attacker is given the ability to load and execute code in the same process as the program under attack. For instance, when a user installs a plug-in for an extensible program, the plug-in will traditionally run in the same process. Also, as discussed earlier, an interactive attacker can inject code in a process running a vulnerable C program.

Against an in-process attacker, the principle of source-based reasoning fails completely. Consider for instance a browser that can be extended with new features and functionality by loading native plug-ins. If the browser stores secret information such as cryptographic keys or passwords in memory, then a malicious plug-in can find and read all these secrets by scanning memory, even in the case

Code Listing 2. Code snippet vulnerable to a heap-based buffer overflow

```
struct data_node {
    char src [128];
    char dst [128];
    int (*transform_func)(char *, char*);
};
int main (int argc, char *argv[]) {
    struct data_node *n;
    int i;
    n = malloc(sizeof(struct data_node));
    n->transform_func = capitalize;

    for(i=0; argv[1][i] != '\0'; i++)
        n->src[i] = argv[1][i];

    (*n->transform_func)(n->src, n->dst);
}
```

where the browser stored these secrets in variables or fields that – according to the source code semantics – should be private.

Whereas the problem of restoring source-based reasoning for the interactive attacker is well understood, the same problem for the in-process attacker is much more challenging. Making source-based reasoning sound in the presence of in-process attacks is very much an open problem. Recent advancements however, allow a system to maintain certain security guarantees even when an attacker can execute arbitrary code. These advancements will be explored in Section 4, and may open up the possibility to restore the principle of source-based reasoning even against in-process attackers.

3 Countermeasures against the Interactive Attacker

Low-level software vulnerabilities in the interactive attacker model are essentially bugs in the program that allow an attacker to drive the program into a state where – according to the source programming language semantics – further behaviour of the program is *undefined*. In practice, this means that further behaviour depends on compiler, runtime system or operating system details, exactly the kind of thing that the principle of source-based reasoning argues against.

For the interactive attacker model, this is a well-understood and widely studied problem. Broadly speaking there are two types of solutions.

3.1 Safe Languages

From a programming language point of view, defenses against the interactive attacker are well understood. A programming language is *safe* if – informally speaking – it is completely defined by its programmer's manual [23]. This is of course just another way of phrasing the principle of source-based reasoning. Technically, safety is achieved by ruling out dangerous language features, and through a combination of compile-time and run-time checks. The objective is that any bug that could lead to implementation-dependent behaviour (such as accessing an array out of bounds, or dereferencing a dangling pointer) is either impossible to write in the language (e.g. dangling pointers do not exist in a language with automatic garbage collection), will be detected at compile time (e.g. casting an integer to a reference will be prohibited by the type checker), or will lead to well-defined error behaviour at run-time (e.g. throwing an exception on accessing an array out of bounds).

Many modern languages are safe, or at least provide very restricted access to unsafe features. Examples include Java, C#, Haskell, Scala and so forth. There is also a significant body of research on designing languages that are safe, but try to stay very close to C, so-called *safe dialects of C* [17,22].

Despite this important progress in language design, most software engineers do not expect the C language to disappear any time soon, and hence the proposal of new languages is only a partial solution.

3.2   More Defensive Execution of Unsafe Languages

A wide variety of techniques has been developed to execute unsafe languages more defensively [14,34,35]. Roughly speaking, these techniques can be grouped into two categories.

Additional Run-Time Checks. the idea here is to detect source-level undefined behaviour by means of run-time checks and to terminate the program. Proposed techniques range from simple heuristics, such as *canaries* to fairly complete *bounds-checking.*

The concept of canaries as a means of protection was first used by Stack-Guard [12]. StackGuard added a new random value on the stack between the return address and stored stacked pointer which the function checked before using the stored return address. If the canary was modified, that was a sign of a buffer overflow and thus the program was terminated before the possibly-modified return address was used. ProPolice [15] later re-implemented Stack-Guard and added a series of new features that increased the overall security of the stack, e.g. re-organizing the local variables and placing character buffers right next to the canary. ProPolice-like countermeasures are widely used in modern operating systems. Variations of the canary-principle have also been proposed to protect a program's heap [24,37] and individual program variables [31].

In bounds-checking, countermeasures attempt to give to the C and C++ programming language what they, by design, lack: memory safety. These countermeasures insert additional bounds-checks before critical operations. Depending on the frequency and types of checks, these checked programs can be significantly slower than their unchecked versions. Even though the latest proposed bounds checkers [3, 36] are many times faster than their older versions [18], they still impose a non-negligible performance overhead on running systems.

Finally, also techniques based on memory protection, such as setting data memory to be non-executable can be seen as additional run-time checks to terminate a program that has run into source-level undefined behaviour. Many modern operating systems will make for instance the stack and/or heap non-executable.

Randomizing or Obfuscating Execution Platform Details. The most popular instantiation of this principle is Address Space Layout Randomization (ASLR) which is currently implemented in all modern operating systems [7]. When a process is fully protected with ASLR, its stack, heap and libraries are always loaded in different memory offsets. The rationale is that even if an attacker can trigger a memory error, and hence has the power to overwrite program variables or hijack the control flow, he will not know where these variables are located or where he should make the CPU jump to.

Instruction Set Randomization (ISR) is also popular within this domain [6,19]. In ISR, each system or process has its own set of instructions so that attacker-injected code will not be meaningful for the CPU of the attacked process. Point-Guard [11] uses a similar principle to encrypt and decrypt all pointers within a program. If an attacker overwrites a critical pointer with his own data, the pointer, upon decryption, will be mangled, thus crashing the process instead of running the attacker's code.

Other instantiations of the randomization principle include the randomization of all data in a program's address space [8] and the randomization of the operating system's interface [10].

3.3 Conclusion

Hardening unsafe languages against the interactive attacker is a mature research area, but it is still active. The fact that the security community came up with ways to protect against the interactive attacker, fueled the evolution of attacking techniques which circumvented the proposed countermeasures. Several attacks were devised which circumvent ASLR [25, 27, 30]; return-to-libc [33] and return-oriented programming [26] defeat the non-executable stack or heap and indirect pointer overwrites can in some cases void the protection of canary-based systems [9]. Thus today, even though many of the originally-used attacking techniques no longer work, there are still scenarios which allow an interactive attacker to bypass modern countermeasures and compromise a vulnerable program.

4   Countermeasures against the In-Process Attacker

An attacker that can load and execute arbitrary machine code is very powerful, which makes protecting against this kind of attacker very challenging. Unfortunately, in-process attacks are also realistic, and so an important direction for low-level software security research is to protect against such attacks.

A first important class of approaches for defending against in-process attacks provides support for a trusted program to load untrusted machine code modules in its address space. A critical assumption for these approaches is that the trusted program can inspect or even modify the module before it enters the process. By combinations of code analysis and code rewriting, the newly loaded module can be sandboxed using techniques such as Software Fault Isolation [32]. These approaches are fundamentally *asymmetric*: they protect a trusted host program from untrusted modules, but modules are not protected in any way against the host. While such sandboxing is an effective technique to protect against dynamically loaded code that is potentially malicious, it can not guarantee for instance the secrecy of sensitive information in a module. Cryptographic keys used by a plug-in, for example, can still be accessed by the main application.

In order to restore the principle of source-based reasoning for both the host program as well as the module, more symmetric solutions are needed. In the last few years, two interesting lines of research results indicate potential directions. In the systems security research community, new security architectures have been developed that support the isolated execution of modules, protecting the module against its host. Research on security foundations on the other hand has shown how some of the existing low-level software security countermeasures can provide sufficiently strong protection to restore the principle of source-based reasoning, at least for simple source programming languages. We briefly discuss both research tracks.

4.1   Isolated Execution of Security-Critical Modules

Various security architectures have been developed the past few years that provide a more fine-grained protection than at the process level. The general idea is that security sensitive code and data from applications are identified and placed into different modules[1]. Each module has total control over the sensitive information it protects and specifies when and how information leaves the module. A cryptographic module for instance can prevent a private key from ever leaving the module unencrypted. Moreover, these architectures achieve this isolation with a very small trusted computing base (TCB). In particular, the TCB does *not* include the operating system.

We discuss three influential examples.

Flicker. McCune et.al. [21] proposed a security architecture based on the late launch and TPM functionality present on modern computer platforms. Using a late launch sequence, the CPU can be set in a known safe state, excluding the BIOS and operating system from the TCB. After a late launch, Flicker will initialize the system and execute the module. After termination of the module,

---

[1] The literature does not use a consistent name for this isolated code and data. Depending on the proposed security architecture, they are called AppCores [28], Piece of Application Logic (PALs) [20,21], workloads [4], Self-Protecting Modules (SPMs) [29] etc. We will use the name *module* to refer to the general concept.

the memory allocated for the module is cleared (with the exception of the return value) and the execution of the application is resumed.

The TPM chip is used to save sensitive information between the invocation of two (possibly different) modules. The TPM chip provides secure storage based on PCR registers. These registers contain a measurement of software that was loaded. Whenever software is loaded on the system, its cryptographic hash is calculated, appended with the contents of the PCR register and the register is overwritten. The contents of these registers can never be set to a specific value. However, they can be reset either through a reboot of the entire system or a late launch sequence, depending on the type of the PCR register. When sensitive data is stored on the TPM chip, the required content of the PCR registers on retrieval of the data can be specified. This allows modules to store sensitive data for themselves or for other modules of which the measurement is known.

Flicker relies on a TCB of only 250 lines of code. Relying heavily on the slow TPM chip unfortunately also results in a significant performance overhead.

TrustVisor. In subsequent work, McCune et.al. [20] reduced this overhead by several orders of magnitude. Using virtual machine extensions of recent processors, a small hypervisor guarantees the total isolated execution of modules. When a module is started, Flicker's late launch sequence is replaced with a hypervisor call ensuring that only the module is executed and cannot be interrupted. The hypervisor offers a software-based TPM implementation. It stores and retrieves a single cryptographic key from the TPM chip when the security architecture is loaded. This key can be used to store sensitive data on behalf of modules encrypted and signed on disk. As the hypervisor remains loaded in memory and is isolated from the rest of the system, the TPM chip has to be accessed only when the security architecture is loaded, resulting in a significant performance improvement over Flicker.

SICE. Azab et.al. proposed [4] yet another technique to provide complete isolation of modules (called workloads) based on system management mode (SMM). SMM typically is used for system management such as power management, system hardware control or proprietary OEM-designed code. Although it is not intended to be used for general-purpose system software, its easily isolated processor environment makes it an interesting choice for a security architecture.

When the execution of a workload is requested, a system management interrupt (SMI) is issued. This causes the processor to enter a known safe state and SICE is executed. Then an isolated execution environment is prepared and the workload is executed. The authors showed that SICE has a TCB of similar size as Flicker but without the significant overhead incurred by a late launch.

Conclusions. These security architectures show that it is feasible to build applications from components (modules) that live (at least conceptually) in the same process but are isolated at the machine code level, and this without relying on a trusted hosting application or operating system. The TCB is reduced to something between a few hundreds to a few thousands lines of code. Such

```
public class C {              public class C {
  private int f = 0;            private int f = 1;

  public C() {                  public C() {
    [...]                         [...]
  }                             }
}                             }
```

Fig. 1. Example of two contextually equivalent Java classes

low-level isolation mechanisms are an essential ingredient to provide strong protection against the in-process attacker, and hence are an important enabler for restoring the principle of source-based reasoning.

4.2 Fully Abstract Compilation

Low-level isolation mechanisms, such as Flicker, TrustVisor or SICE, are by themselves insufficient for making source-based reasoning sound. What is needed is a correct mapping of source-level protection mechanisms to low-level protection mechanisms.

Modern high-level programming languages such as Java, C#, ML or Haskell offer protection facilities such as abstract data types, the private field modifier, or module systems. These programming language concepts were designed to enforce software engineering principles such as information hiding and encapsulation. But these can also be used as building blocks to ensure security properties of programs. For instance, declaring a class instance variable private in Java protects the integrity and confidentiality of that field towards instances of other classes.

Unfortunately, these protection features are typically lost when the program is compiled. Suppose for instance that we compile a Java program to native machine code, then an in-process attacker can read or write any private variable, thus violating that variable's confidentiality and integrity. In other words, the principle of source-based reasoning fails.

However, recent research has shown that it is possible to maintain the security properties of a high-level program even after it is compiled into a lower-level language (such as native code). The way to formalize this notion of security is through *full abstraction*. Roughly speaking, compilation from a source language to a target language is fully abstract if the equivalence of source programs implies the equivalence of target programs and vice versa. That is, for full abstraction to hold, two source-level programs must be contextually equivalent if and only if their corresponding low-level translations are contextually equivalent as well. Two programs P_1 and P_2 are contextually equivalent if no third program P_T interacting with them can distinguish P_1 from P_2. At the high level, two programs can typically only interact through method calls and returns, while at the low level two programs can interact in less controlled ways, such as directly reading from or writing to each others memory locations.

The contextual equivalence of two programs can express important security properties. For instance, saying that the two classes shown in Fig.1 are contextually equivalent, is the same as saying that the value of a private instance variable in a Java class is confidential. This is obvious at the source-code level, but if we were to compile these two classes into native code using a standard compiler, their contextual equivalence would be lost. That is, the two resulting native code modules could be differentiated by a low-level test module M_T that runs in the same address space: M_T could simply inspect the memory location storing the value of f. The essence of a fully abstract compiler is that contextual equivalence is preserved at the low level. A fully abstract compilation scheme effectively reduces the power of an in-process attacker to that of a source code-level attacker. That is, any attack at the low level is also possible at the source code level. One can think of full abstraction as the formal equivalent in this setting to the principle of source-based reasoning.

Currently no production-class compiler for any programming language to machine code on any platform is even close to be fully abstract. However, recently two promising approaches have been proposed towards achieving full abstraction.

Techniques Based on Randomization. Abadi and Plotkin have shown full abstraction results for ASLR [1]. At the high level they consider a simple lambda-calculus language that uses an abstract *location* type for memory locations. Each location stores a single integer that can be read or written. Some locations are public while others are designated as private, with the intent that an attacker should not have direct access to the latter. A high-level program can preserve the confidentiality and integrity of a variable by simply not exposing that variable's location.

The low-level target language is similar to the high-level language but uses integers to address memory locations instead of the abstract location type. This enables attackers to probe arbitrary memory locations. The low-level language can be considered an abstract model of a real-world Von Neumann computer architecture, as each memory location can be addressed using an integer.

To translate from the high- to the low-level language, each abstract location must be mapped to a concrete integer address. ASLR is incorporated into the low-level model by mapping private locations to *random* low-level addresses. In their paper, Abadi and Plotkin show that the security properties provided by the high-level language continue to hold at the low level, albeit in a probabilistic sense. They prove this full abstraction result for two low-level memory models. In the first model, accesses to unused addresses in memory are fatal violations that terminate the program, while in the second model such accesses are not fatal. For the non-fatal memory access model, these results assume a bound on the number of erroneous accesses, for otherwise an attacker could iterate over all addresses.

While the lambda-calculus language used by Adadi and Plotkin is relatively simple, Jagadeesan et al. [16] have shown that the same results hold for a more complex language supporting dynamic memory allocation, first-class and higher-order references (references that can be compared and can hold other references) and control operators (the ability to perform callbacks to attacker-controlled code). These features increase the power of the attacker, as he now has an influence on the control flow of a program and can build up knowledge on the layout of memory by comparing public references. Furthermore, the extended language can model a number of system hardening principles such as instruction set randomization, enabling one to analyze their security properties in the presence of ASLR.

Even though these results are based on low-level languages that are only very rough models of a real-world low-level execution platform, they indicate that ASLR has the potential to be a very valuable technique for making the principle of source-based reasoning sound.

Techniques Based on Low-Level Memory Access Control. Agten et al. have recently shown that it is possible to rely on low-level memory access control techniques instead of randomization, to achieve full abstraction [2]. The high-level source language for which this has been shown is a small, single-threaded object-based language with a syntax similar to Java. It supports the basic constructs expected of a modern programming language, such as branches, loops, local variables and indirect method calls (by using typed function pointers). In this language, a program consists of a number of interacting objects, each of which consists of private fields and public methods.

The low-level target language is an assembly language for an x86-like computer architecture, consisting of a program counter, a register file (including a stack pointer register), a flags register and a memory space. This basic machine model does not suffice as the target language of a fully abstract compiler. In order to support full abstraction, a program counter-dependent memory access protection scheme is added as part of the target language. This protection scheme divides memory into *protected* and *unprotected* memory, the former of which is further divided into a *code* and a *data* section. Within the code section, a variable number of memory addresses are designated as *entry points*, which are the only points through which execution of code in protected memory can start. Table 1 shows the memory access control rules enforced by this protection scheme.

Table 1. Memory permissions enforced by the low-level language

from \ to	Protected			Unprotected
	Entry point	Code	Data	
Protected	r x	r x	r w	r w x
Unprotected	x			r w x

Like in any object-based language, in the high-level language, the internal representation of an object is hidden from outside of that object's definition. This means two high-level objects can be equivalent from an external point of view, even though they have a different internal implementation. This maps naturally to contextual equivalence.

In order to achieve full abstraction, we need to use a compiler that takes advantage of the memory protection features provided by the low-level machine model. First of all, the data and code of the compiled object must be placed into the data and code parts of protected memory respectively. Next, an entry point must be created for the first low-level instruction of each method. Because the protected memory can only be entered through an entry point, one additional *return entry point* must be created to support returning from a callback (i.e. a call from protected to unprotected memory). The address of this entry point should be used as the return address for all callbacks. To prevent private data leakage or control flow tampering through the stack, the protected module must use its own *secure stack* in protected data memory. Consequently, the runtime stack must be switched from the unprotected stack to the secure stack and vice versa on each entry to or exit from the protected module. Relevant parameters and control flow information must be moved between these stacks on entry and exit points. Private data can also leak through other channels, such as the register file or the flags register. The compiler must ensure that these registers are cleared when exiting the protected module. To further preserve control flow integrity, the compiler must verify the destination of any jump to an externally supplied address (such as a callback). A valid address is either the address of the first instruction of one the protected module's own methods or an address in unprotected memory. Finally, the compiler must also ensure that any parameter value or return value passed to the protected module has a corresponding high-level value. For instance, if a boolean `false` is mapped to low-level value 0 and `true` is mapped to 1, then the compiler must verify that boolean-typed parameters and return values are confined to these values at run time.

This compilation scheme, in combination with the program counter-dependent memory access control scheme of the low-level language, has been proved to be fully abstract. Hence, with this compilation scheme, the principle of source-based reasoning holds, even for the in-process attacker model.

Implementations. For this full abstraction result to have practical relevance, the program counter-dependent memory protection scheme must have an efficient real-world implementation. Both hardware and software implementations are possible. Strackx et al. [29] propose a hardware implementation for *self-protecting modules*, which uses a low-level memory protection scheme similar to the one needed to achieve full abstraction. El Defrawy et al. [13] have developed a hardware-based program counter-dependent memory protection scheme for their implementation of SMART, which is an architecture for establishing a dynamic root of trust in embedded devices. This protection scheme provides the necessary primitives to support full abstraction and can be implemented relatively easily on current low-end microcontrollers.

For software based implementations, an interesting avenue for future work is to investigate whether the security architectures discussed in Section 4.1 can be used as building blocks. It seems likely that the kind of isolation provided by these architectures can be used to provide a suitable low-level protection mechanism as required by the secure compiler proposed by Agten et al. [2].

5   Conclusions

The field of low-level software security is an exciting and high-impact area of research. For the interactive attacker model, several decades of research have resulted in a good understanding of the problems and solutions, and some of these solutions already have found their way into mainstream operating systems and compilers.

But some important and realistic attacks against software systems are not covered by the interactive attacker model, in particular those attacks where an attacker has the possibility to load arbitrary machine code in the same process as the software under attack. An important challenge for research in low-level software security is to address this new class of attacks modeled in the *in-process attacker model*. We have shown in this paper that several important first steps in defending against this style of attacker have been taken recently.

Acknowledgments. This research is partially funded by the Interuniversity Attraction Poles Programme Belgian State, Belgian Science Policy, IBBT, IWT, the Research Fund K.U.Leuven and the EU-funded FP7-project NESSoS. Pieter Agten holds a Ph. D. fellowship of the Research Foundation - Flanders (FWO).

References

1. Abadi, M., Plotkin, G.D.: On protection by layout randomization. In: CSF, pp. 337–351. IEEE Computer Society (2010)
2. Agten, P., Strackx, R., Jacobs, B., Piessens, F.: Secure compilation to modern processors. In: CSF (2012)
3. Akritidis, P., Costa, M., Castro, M., Hand, S.: Baggy bounds checking: An efficient and backwards-compatible defense against out-of-bounds errors. In: Proceedings of the 18th USENIX Security Symposium, Montreal, QC (August 2009)
4. Azab, A., Ning, P., Zhang, X.: Sice: a hardware-level strongly isolated computing environment for x86 multi-core platforms. In: Proceedings of the 18th ACM Conference on Computer and Communications Security, pp. 375–388. ACM (2011), http://www4.ncsu.edu/~amazab/SICE-CCS11.pdf
5. Baltopoulos, I.G., Gordon, A.D.: Secure compilation of a multi-tier web language. In: TLDI, pp. 27–38 (2009)
6. Barrantes, E.G., Ackley, D.H., Forrest, S., Palmer, T.S., Stefanović, D., Zovi, D.D.: Randomized instruction set emulation to disrupt binary code injection attacks. In: Proceedings of the 10th ACM Conference on Computer and Communications Security, Washington, D.C, pp. 281–289 (October 2003)
7. Bhatkar, S., DuVarney, D.C., Sekar, R.: Address obfuscation: An efficient approach to combat a broad range of memory error exploits. In: Proceedings of the 12th USENIX Security Symposium, Washington, D.C, pp. 105–120 (August 2003)
8. Bhatkar, S., Sekar, R.: Data Space Randomization. In: Zamboni, D. (ed.) DIMVA 2008. LNCS, vol. 5137, pp. 1–22. Springer, Heidelberg (2008)
9. Bulba, Kil3r: Bypassing Stackguard and Stackshield. Phrack 56 (2000)
10. Chew, M., Song, D.: Mitigating buffer overflows by operating system randomization. Tech. Rep. CMU-CS-02-197, Carnegie Mellon University (December 2002)

11. Cowan, C., Beattie, S., Johansen, J., Wagle, P.: PointGuard: protecting pointers from buffer overflow vulnerabilities. In: Proceedings of the 12th USENIX Security Symposium, Washington, D.C, pp. 91–104 (August 2003)
12. Cowan, C., Pu, C., Maier, D., Hinton, H., Walpole, J., Bakke, P., Beattie, S., Grier, A., Wagle, P., Zhang, Q.: StackGuard: Automatic adaptive detection and prevention of buffer-overflow attacks. In: Proceedings of the 7th USENIX Security Symposium (1998)
13. El Defrawy, K., Francillon, A., Perito, D., Tsudik, G.: Smart: Secure and minimal architecture for (establishing a dynamic) root of trust. In: Proceedings of the Network & Distributed System Security Symposium (NDSS), San Diego, CA (2012), http://francillon.net/~aurel/papers/2012_SMART.pdf
14. Erlingsson, U., Younan, Y., Piessens, F.: Low-level software security by example. In: Handbook of Information and Communication Security. Springer (2010)
15. IBM: Gcc extension for protecting applications from stack-smashing attacks, http://www.trl.ibm.com/projects/security/ssp/
16. Jagadeesan, R., Pitcher, C., Rathke, J., Riely, J.: Local memory via layout randomization. In: CSF, pp. 161–174. IEEE Computer Society (2011)
17. Jim, T., Morrisett, J.G., Grossman, D., Hicks, M.W., Cheney, J., Wang, Y.: Cyclone: A safe dialect of c. In: Proceedings of the General Track of the Annual Conference on USENIX Annual Technical Conference, ATEC 2002, pp. 275–288. USENIX Association, Berkeley (2002), http://dl.acm.org/citation.cfm?id=647057.713871
18. Jones, R.W.M., Kelly, P.H.J.: Backwards-compatible bounds checking for arrays and pointers in C programs. In: Proceedings of the 3rd International Workshop on Automatic Debugging, Linköping, Sweden, pp. 13–26 (1997)
19. Kc, G.S., Keromytis, A.D., Prevelakis, V.: Countering code-injection attacks with instruction-set randomization. In: Proceedings of the 10th ACM Conference on Computer and Communications Security, Washington, D.C, pp. 272–280 (October 2003)
20. McCune, J.M., Li, Y., Qu, N., Zhou, Z., Datta, A., Gligor, V., Perrig, A.: TrustVisor: Efficient TCB reduction and attestation. In: Proceedings of the IEEE Symposium on Security and Privacy (May 2010), http://www.ece.cmu.edu/~jmmccune/papers/MLQZDGP2010.pdf
21. McCune, J.M., Parno, B., Perrig, A., Reiter, M.K., Isozaki, H.: Flicker: An execution infrastructure for TCB minimization. In: Proceedings of the ACM European Conference in Computer Systems (EuroSys), pp. 315–328. ACM (April 2008), http://www.ece.cmu.edu/~jmmccune/papers/mccune_parno_perrig_reiter_isozaki_eurosys08.pdf
22. Necula, G.C., Condit, J., Harren, M., McPeak, S., Weimer, W.: Ccured: type-safe retrofitting of legacy software. ACM Trans. Program. Lang. Syst. 27(3), 477–526 (2005), http://doi.acm.org/10.1145/1065887.1065892
23. Pierce, B.C.: Types and Programming Languages. MIT Press (2002)
24. Robertson, W., Kruegel, C., Mutz, D., Valeur, F.: Run-time detection of heap-based overflows. In: Proceedings of the 17th Large Installation Systems Administrators Conference, pp. 51–60. USENIX Association (2003)
25. Roglia, G.F., Martignoni, L., Paleari, R., Bruschi, D.: Surgically returning to randomized lib(c). In: 25th Annual Computer Security Applications Conference (2009)

26. Shacham, H.: The geometry of innocent flesh on the bone: Return-into-libc without function calls (on the x86). In: Proceedings of the 14th ACM Conference on Computer and Communications Security, Washington, D.C, pp. 552–561 (October 2007)

27. Shacham, H., Page, M., Pfaff, B., Goh, E.J., Modadugu, N., Boneh, D.: On the Effectiveness of Address-Space Randomization. In: Proceedings of the 11th ACM Conference on Computer and Communications Security, Washington, D.C, pp. 298–307 (October 2004)

28. Singaravelu, L., Pu, C., Härtig, H., Helmuth, C.: Reducing tcb complexity for security-sensitive applications: three case studies. In: EuroSys 2006: Proceedings of the 1st ACM SIGOPS/EuroSys European Conference on Computer Systems 2006, pp. 161–174. ACM, New York (2006),
http://www.cs.kuleuven.ac.be/conference/EuroSys2006/
papers/p161-singaravelu.pdf

29. Strackx, R., Piessens, F., Preneel, B.: Efficient isolation of trusted subsystems in embedded systems. In: Jajodia, S., Zhou, J. (eds.) SecureComm 2010. LNICST, vol. 50, pp. 344–361. Springer, Heidelberg (2010)

30. Strackx, R., Younan, Y., Philippaerts, P., Piessens, F., Lachmund, S., Walter, T.: Breaking the memory secrecy assumption. In: EUROSEC, pp. 1–8 (2009)

31. Van Acker, S., Nikiforakis, N., Philippaerts, P., Younan, Y., Piessens, F.: Value-Guard: Protection of Native Applications against Data-Only Buffer Overflows. In: Jha, S., Mathuria, A. (eds.) ICISS 2010. LNCS, vol. 6503, pp. 156–170. Springer, Heidelberg (2010)

32. Wahbe, R., Lucco, S., Anderson, T.E., Graham, S.L.: Efficient software-based fault isolation. SIGOPS Oper. Syst. Rev. 27(5), 203–216 (1993),
http://doi.acm.org/10.1145/173668.168635

33. Wojtczuk, R.: Defeating solar designer non-executable stack patch. Posted on the Bugtraq mailinglist (January 1998),
http://www.securityfocus.com/archive/1/8470

34. Younan, Y., Joosen, W., Piessens, F.: Code injection in C and C++: A survey of vulnerabilities and countermeasures. Tech. Rep. CW386, Departement Computerwetenschappen, Katholieke Universiteit Leuven (2004)

35. Younan, Y., Joosen, W., Piessens, F.: Runtime countermeasures for code injection attacks against C and C++ programs. ACM Computing Surveys (to appear, 2012)

36. Younan, Y., Philippaerts, P., Cavallaro, L., Sekar, R., Piessens, F., Joosen, W.: Paricheck: an efficient pointer arithmetic checker for c programs. In: ASIACCS, pp. 145–156. ACM (2010),
http://dblp.uni-trier.de/db/conf/ccs/asiaccs2010.html#YounanPCSPJ10

37. Zeng, Q., Wu, D., Liu, P.: Cruiser: concurrent heap buffer overflow monitoring using lock-free data structures. In: Proceedings of the 32nd ACM SIGPLAN Conference on Programming Language Design and Implementation, PLDI 2011, pp. 367–377. ACM, New York (2011),
http://doi.acm.org/10.1145/1993498.1993541

Towards a C²I Platform for Combating the Cyber-Threat

Paul Kearney

Security Futures Practice, BT Innovate & Design
paul.3.kearney@bt.com

Abstract. In my talk, I outline a number of cyber-attacks that have been reported in recent years, and examine the vulnerability of organisations and critical infrastructure to them. I then discuss an approach to combating cyber-threats that integrates specialised tools within a managed service platform to create a command, control an intelligence (C2I) system used to co-ordinated defences against a diverse collection of resourceful and persistent opponents. The discussion is illustrated with examples from BT research and development projects. Such a system will have to be refreshed and up-graded regularly to keep pace with challenges such as:

- The escalating arms race against threat agents,
- Innovations in technology and business practice,
- Changing regulations and compliance demands,
- A cyber-Moore's Law that dictates a continual shrinking of required response times

Ultimately it will need to be adaptive and to learn from experience.

Keywords: Cybersecurity, Cyber-threat, Managed Security Service.

1 Extended Abstract

Cybersecurity is not a well-defined term. It has come to prominence in recent years due to use of the cyber prefix by the government, defence and law enforcement community to contrast new, ICT-enabled, forms of warfare, espionage, terrorism, activism and crime with their conventional, 'physical world' counterparts. However, the usage has caught on and cybersecurity is often applied more broadly and used as a trendy synonym for information and network security, etc.

In addressing cybersecurity we are primarily concerned with threats that are state sponsored and/or politically motivated. Criminal activities on a scale that threatens national economic or social well-being or the financial health of targeted organisations is also in scope. Such threats include: cyberwarfare, cyberespionage, cyberterrorism, and cyberactivism (aka 'Hacktivism'). Characteristics shared by many of the above include:

- They are well funded and have may have significant black-hat expertise;
- They play a long game, and attacks may be complex and stealthy, and hence difficult to detect and/or interpret;

I. Askoxylakis, H.C. Pöhls, and J. Posegga (Eds.): WISTP 2012, LNCS 7322, pp. 17–19, 2012.
© IFIP International Federation for Information Processing 2012

- Individuals responsible may be difficult to identify. Even if they are known it may be difficult to apply sanctions.

The term Advanced Persistent Threat (APT) has been coined as a short hand for threats with these characteristics. Reputedly the term originated within the US Department of Defence (DoD), but it has been taken up and popularised by McAfee and some other vendors, who use it in their marketing literature. Others dislike this name, preferring terms such as targeted threat, as attackers do not necessarily use advanced techniques.

In many ways there is nothing new about APTs, and there have been no major breakthroughs in combating them, so why is Cybersecurity the word of the moment? People have long talked about the feasibility and danger of politically-motivated and state-sponsored cyber-attacks, and speculated that stealthy, probing attacks have taken place. However, in recent years, there have been a number of incidents that indicate that those with the capability and motivation to carry out such attacks are actually willing to do so. Significant incidents include:

- The denial of service (DoS) attacks on Estonia and Georgia;
- Stuxnet: most likely a state-sponsored attack on Iran's nuclear processing capability. An example of a cyber-attack causing physical damage;
- Wikileaks: not only the original disclosure of confidential information, but also the cyberattacks of the supporters (primarily the Anonymous group) and opponents (e.g. HBGary) of Wikileaks on each other;
- A succession of attacks on Sony;
- Nightdragon: the name given by McAfee to a series of covert cyberattacks they believe were launched against several oil, energy and petrochemical companies;
- Operation Aurora / Hydraq: Aurora is McAfee's name for alleged targeted attacks (using the Hydraq Trojan) on the corporate infrastructures of Google and other large companies with the aim of stealing intellectual property and accessing the e-mail accounts of Chinese human rights activists;
- RSA SecurID: RSA has revealed little information on the recent security compromise of their SecurID authentication products, but claim it was the result of an APT. Some reports indicate that the initial penetration was via a phishing attack that planted backdoor software on an employee's PC;
- Fraudulent SSL certificates acquired from Comodo. Iran has been accused of being behind the attack.

In response to these and other trends, a number of governments, including those of the UK, US, France and Germany have proposed to established or strengthen their cybersecurity programmes.

The publicity received by the above-mentioned attacks and government programmes have established the cyber prefix in the popular psyche (one suspects Dr Who had something to do with it as well). Vendors have latched on to this, and as a result numerous information / network products have been re-branded 'with added cyber'. While undoubtedly, serious vendors and service providers are making gradual progress in combating cyber-threat, there is no new cyber-technology, but rather a continued incremental evolution of information / network techniques and tools.

So, while the definition of the term remains a little vague, we have the image that cybersecurity is about countering sophisticated, knowledgeable and committed opponents, whose goals, if achieved will result in significant negative Impact on the targeted organisation and those who depend on its services. We may also consider nations themselves and supra-national groupings as 'organisations', for whom cybersecurity is about countering threats to their sovereignty, economy, political systems and the rights, safety and well-being of their citizens.

In my talk, I outline a number of cyber-attacks that have been reported in recent years, and examine the vulnerability of organisations and critical infrastructure to them. I then discuss an approach to combating cyber-threats that integrates specialised tools within a managed service platform to create a command, control an intelligence (C^{2}I) system used to co-ordinated defences against a diverse collection of resourceful and persistent opponents. The discussion is illustrated with examples from BT research and development projects. Such a system will have to be refreshed and up-graded regularly to keep pace with challenges such as:

- The escalating arms race against threat agents;
- Innovations in technology and business practice;
- Changing regulations and compliance demands;
- A cyber-Moore's Law that dictates a continual shrinking of required response times.

Ultimately it will need to be adaptive and to learn from experience.

Veracity, Plausibility, and Reputation

Dieter Gollmann

Institute for Security in Distributed Applications,
Hamburg University of Technology,
21073 Hamburg, Germany
diego@tu-harburg.de

Abstract. The canonical IT security properties are geared towards infrastructure security. The task of an infrastructure security service is completed once data has been delivered to the application. When false data is submitted to the infrastructure, false data will be delivered securely. To secure an application, one thus may have to go beyond securing the infrastructure and in addition provide mechanisms for detecting false data. We propose *veracity* as a new security property relevant at the application level. We examine examples for veracity mechanisms from network management and conclude with a discussion of security in cyber-physical systems.

Keywords: Veracity, plausibility, reputation, security in cyber-physical systems.

1 Introduction

The standard textbook introduction to IT security starts by defining *confidentiality*, *integrity*, and *availability* as the three pillars of security. These properties refer to the protection of data, be it data in storage (a main topic in operating system security) or data in transit (communications security). In both instances, we are looking at security properties of IT *infrastructures*. The job of a security mechanism is done once memory management or file management has securely delivered data to an application. The job of a security protocol is done once data has been securely delivered to the recipient.

ISO 7498-2 had added the notions of *authentication* and *non-repudiation* to confidentiality, integrity, and availability. Authentication and non-repudiation potentially take us away from a pure IT-centric view of security. Take, for example, the following definition from [10]:

> *Peer entity authentication* is provided for use at the establishment of, or at times during, the data transfer phase of a connection to confirm the identities of one or more of the entities connected.

This definition may suggest that a relationship between aspects of cyberspace, here connections, and entities in physical space, here the peers (people, machines) connected, is being established. However, peer entity authentication establishes

I. Askoxylakis, H.C. Pöhls, and J. Posegga (Eds.): WISTP 2012, LNCS 7322, pp. 20–28, 2012.
© IFIP International Federation for Information Processing 2012

a link between connections and identities (names), i.e. it still describes a service within cyberspace. We have argued previously [9] that authentication services in general verify links between different aspects of the IT domain.

Similar observations apply to non-repudiation. The following definition is taken from ISO/IEC 10181-4.

> The goal of the *Non-repudiation* service is to collect, maintain, make available and validate irrefutable evidence concerning a claimed event or action in order to resolve disputes about the occurrence or non-occurrence of the event or action.

A sentence on the resolution of disputes strongly alludes to events outside the IT domain. However, cryptographic protocols cannot provide such a service on their own[1]. We would more appropriately refer to *unforgeable* evidence, and use non-repudiation for differentiating between the authentication services provided by symmetric key cryptography, where evidence can only be verified by a party in possession of the secret also used when creating the evidence, and the authentication services provided by public-key cryptography, where evidence can be verified with the help of a public verification key. Following this line of argument non-repudiation would be a security property within cyberspace[2].

The properties listed so far can be seen as security properties of an IT infrastructure. This state of affairs has a natural historical explanation. IT security has its root in the 1970s and 1980s when IT became a new infrastructure for data processing. Purists could justifiably complain that the term information technology was a misnomer as the services provided referred in the main to the storage and transmission of *data*, not to their interpretation. IT security services were provided primarily in *cyberspace*, and in cyberspace alone. When discussing such services, no statements are made about what happens after data have been delivered to the application consuming the data.

It is this latter aspect that this paper aims to explore. We begin by looking for security properties that reach into the application domain.

1.1 The Parkerian Hexad

Donn Parker's security framework [15] adds possession and utility to confidentiality, integrity, availability, and authenticity. *Possession* refers to control or ownership of data containers. This notion makes it possible to distinguish between violations of confidentiality, when information is disclosed to an adversary, and situations where the adversary has obtained a data container but cannot access the information within, e.g. because it is encrypted. *Utility* refers to usefulness (of data) for a given purpose. Possession and utility express relationships between cyberspace and applications in the physical world, as does integrity when interpreted in the meaning of *external consistency*.

---

[1] Consult, e.g., `http://world.std.com/~cme/non-repudiation.htm`

[2] As a historical footnote, [17] uses *veracity transaction receipts* as a synonym for unforgeable transaction receipts, i.e. for non repudiation. This paper will use the term veracity in a different meaning.

External consistency: The correspondence between the data object and the real world object it refers to [5].

1.2   Outlook

Security is moving to the application layer. This trend can be observed in computer security where the reference monitor is moving from the operating system into the browser and into web pages. This trend can be observed in communications security where security services are provided, for example, with the *http* protocol and in the layer above, such as in web services. The closer we move to the applications running on top of the IT infrastructure, the more urgently we need to ask whether the data provided by the infrastructure is actually fit for the intended purpose.

Utility addresses the issue whether the data received is presented in a useful format. We will pursue the question whether the data received truthfully captures the aspects of the physical world relevant for the application at hand. Section 2 will propose veracity as a new security property for cyber-physical systems. Section 3 gives three case studies that show how the veracity of assertions may be checked in network management. Section 4 deals briefly with plausibility and reputation. Section 5 discusses concepts from the business world intended for decreasing the likelihood of false assertions. Section 6 concludes with remarks on the security of cyber-physical systems.

2   Veracity

Assertions are statements about an aspect relevant in a given application domain. Assertions may, rightly or wrongly, be attributed to some entity in the application domain; authentication and non-repudiation verify the claimed origin of an assertion. Assertions may be true or false.

Veracity: The property that an assertion truthfully reflects the aspect it makes a statement about.

Authentication and non-repudiation do not verify the veracity of assertions. Veracity is not a property guaranteed by any of the familiar IT infrastructure security services. Veracity is not a property that can be provided by familiar IT infrastructures. Veracity refers to aspects outside the IT infrastructure: the adversary is not an entity launching an attack in the infrastructure but an entity making false assertions. The data are already false when passed to the infrastructure.

Veracity is not an entirely new notion. In the field of databases veracity corresponds to external consistency. For mobile agent systems Borselius gives the following definition [2]:

Veracity: The concept that an agent will not knowingly communicate false information.

Our definition is not restricted to assertions that are false on purpose but includes also assertions that are false by accident. This distinction does not matter for the application; the application would react to a false assertion in the same way in both cases. The distinction matters in the design of countermeasures. Borselius comments that veracity cannot be effectively enforced in mobile agent systems as *the required redundancy for such a [protection] system is likely to make the [mobile agent] system useless.*

Veracity can be achieved in two ways. We can protect the *sensor* making the observation reported in the assertion. The sensor must be tamper-resistant and it must not be possible to deceive the sensor by interfering with the observations it is expected to make. This approach may be applicable in scenarios where there is a sufficient degree of physical security.

Secondly, we can perform *consistency checks*. A consistency check may compare an assertion with a prediction made by a (local) *model* of the application. Alternatively, a consistency check may be performed on the facts reported in assertions made by several *witnesses*. Such schemes are only effective under the assumption that the adversary is unable to corrupt a sufficient number of assertions. This assumption moves us closer to research on reliability where mechanisms are designed on the basis that some but not all inputs are corrupted.

3   Veracity in Network Management

Although we have noted that there are no generic security mechanisms providing veracity services to applications running on top of familiar IT infrastructures, we can point to a few cases where there are checks on the veracity of assertions made in the context of network management.

3.1   DNS Rebinding

The Domain Name System (DNS) is a distributed directory service for binding host names to IP addresses. Most technical details of this service are not relevant for our discussion. The reader needs to be aware that *authoritative name servers* make assertions about such bindings for hosts in their zone, and that *resolving name servers* perform name resolution for their clients and cache bindings received with a time-to-live set by the authoritative name server. The resolving name server trusts the assertions received from the authoritative name server.

In DNS rebinding attacks the authoritative name server is telling lies. The adversary has its own domain with a corresponding authoritative name server and a host with a page containing a script that will issue requests to the victim's machine. The attack is launched via the browser of some unwitting user who has been lured to the adversary's web page.

When the user's browser resolves the adversary's host, the adversary's authoritative name server is consulted and binds the adversary's host first to the true IP address (so that the attack page can be loaded) but then also to the IP address of the victim's machine. (Details about when and how this is done

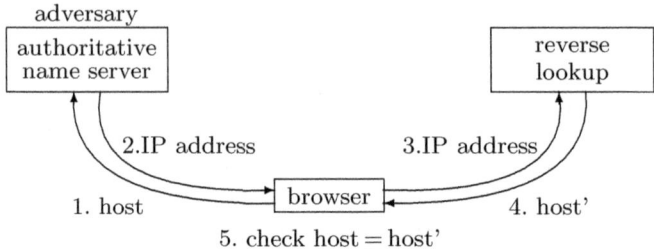

Fig. 1. Double checking the binding between host name an IP address

are again out of scope.) The same origin policy enforced by the user's browser permits scripts from the adversary's web page to connect back to the host they came from. When this host is bound to the victim's machine, requests sent to that machine will be passed on.

To defend against DNS rebinding, make it difficult for the adversary to get away with lies. Applying the same origin policy at the level of IP addresses fixes the original (true) IP address for the duration of its time-to-live in the cache [8], but this value is set by the authoritative name server. Pinning the original IP address for a period set by the browser delays the opportunity to substitute a false for a true assertion. The attack can become possible again if the browser can be induced to drop the pinning [12]. There are further problems when the same origin policy is relaxed and a script may connect to other sites authorized by the host the script originates from. Ultimately, we may resort to a consistency check and, similar to reverse DNS lookup, check that the host running on the given IP address is the one authorized by the policy (Fig. 1) [11].

3.2   Return Routability

In mobile IPv6 a node has a static home address in its home domain. The node is always addressable at this address. When a node has moved, messages sent to its home address will be forwarded by the home agent in an IPsec tunnel.

A node that has moved out of the home domain acquires a care-of address in its current domain. Correspondent nodes may be informed about the current care-of address as a performance optimization. This feature could be abused by a node claiming to be in a location it is not in and launching a denial-of-service attack by ordering a huge volume of data to be sent to that location. This attack cannot be prevented by authenticating the originator of the assertion (binding update) claiming that the node had moved to its new location. The assertion does come from the claimant.

The solution standardized in RFC 3775 and explained in [1] performs the following consistency check. The correspondent node sends two test messages to the claimant, one to its home address, from where it would be forwarded to the node by its home agent, the other directly to the care-of address given. Both test

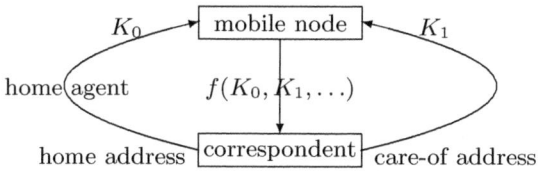

Fig. 2. Return routability: check that two challenges have arrived at the same location

messages contain a key transmitted in the clear. A node in the claimed location will receive both keys, which are required for creating a valid response (Fig. 2). When the correspondent node receives a valid response it concludes that the mobile node is in the location asserted (return routability).

This protocol relies on the assumption that the adversary is unable to obtain both keys. How this is achieved, e.g. by using IPsec between correspondent node and home agent, is outside the scope of the protocol. The security service provided could be denoted as *location authentication* [9] when we focus on the binding between home address and care-of address. Alternatively, we may view this mechanism as a veracity check on an assertion about a current care-of address.

3.3   Secure Network Coordinates

Network coordinate systems in the Internet, such as Vivaldi [7], assign synthetic coordinates to nodes. Coordinates are computed based on round trip times measured between some of the nodes. The coordinates are then used for predicting communication latency between other nodes. Such schemes can be subverted by parties making false assertions about round trip times. Such schemes can be secured by establishing the veracity of assertions. Proposed security mechanisms rely on:

- trusted surveyor nodes (witnesses) [13],
- models that capture some aspects of the physical domain, e.g. a triangle inequality test for round trip times as in PIC [6],
- a set of untrusted verification nodes that vote on the veracity of an assertion, as in Veracity [16]; each verification node has its own local model to decide whether to accept an assertion.

Models are used for detecting deviations from expected or from possible behaviour. An assertion making an impossible claim is clearly false. An assertion making an unexpected claim may be true. A false assertion may still report an expected value. We thus must not place too much reliance on the prediction of a single model. Security can be strengthened by employing several models. Assessing the strength of a combination of models requires some understanding of their dependencies.

4   Plausibility and Reputation

In contrast to the first two case studies where a single node reached a binary decision on the veracity of an assertion based on checks it could perform on its own, schemes in the third case study consider inputs from several witnesses and arrive at a decision about the *plausibility* of an assertion received.

> An assertion is *plausible* if it does not deviate too far from the values estimated by the models used.

Schemes that rely on witnesses can be undermined by witnesses that make false statements. Schemes can be designed so that they can handle a certain proportion of witnesses colluding in an attack. Security proofs will be based on the assumption that the adversary can compromise only a limited number of witnesses.

The *constrained-collusion Byzantine failure model* [4] may serve as an example. A fraction f, $0 \leq f < 1$, of the N nodes in a system may be faulty (compromised). Faulty nodes can behave arbitrarily. Faulty nodes can be partitioned into disjoint coalitions bounded in size by cN, $1/N \leq c \leq f$. For $c < f$ there are multiple independent coalitions; for $c = f$ all faulty nodes may collude.

Witness selection has an impact on how easy it is for the adversary to predict which witnesses to compromise so that a collusion attack is effective. Veracity, for example, uses a deterministic selection scheme based on hash chains [16]. For security arguments based on statistical independence assumptions, the case needs to be made that such assumptions can be substantiated in practice.

Schemes that rely on witnesses may be augmented by features that try to detect and exclude witnesses making false statements. *Reputation systems* employ witnesses on witnesses, i.e. entities that make statements (reputation ratings) about the veracity of statements made by other witnesses. CONFIDANT, for example, applies this approach to source routing in mobile ad-hoc networks [3]. A security analysis of a reputation system must now in turn consider the impact of false reputation ratings.

5   Fostering Veracity in Business Processes

Commercial applications are a further area to turn to for cues on how veracity may be checked and maintained. The Clark-Wilson model captures established business practices and proposes *separation of duties* as a design principle *to control fraud and error*, i.e. for maintaining external consistency [5]. A process is split into parts that must be executed by different entities. We may view the different entities involved as witnesses with respect to the actions of their predecessors. A related design principle requires that a quorum of entities approves a transaction before it can go ahead.

These principles are similar to those deployed for ensuring veracity in network management. Multiple entities are involved so that a collusion by a small subset can be detected.

6   Securing Cyber-Physical Systems

The "applications" in Section 3 had been network management functions. These applications were still within the IT domain but we can generalize the fundamental principles observed to securing cyber-physical systems.

Consider an applications with observations and effects in the physical world, relying on services provided in "cyberspace" by an IT infrastructure. An adversary can attack the application by feeding it with data causing undesired effects. Stuxnet may serve as an illustrative example [14]. Securing the IT infrastructure protects against an adversary who can manipulate data as it is processed in the infrastructure, but not against an attacker who can feed manipulated data to the infrastructure, possibly by manipulating the sensors that supply the data. To quote from [14]:

> *Manipulations of a controller have less to do with the confidentiality, integrity, and availability of information and more to do with the performance and output of a physical production process.*

Defences outside cyberspace may focus on the sensors and controllers that provide the interface between physical space and cyberspace. Defensive measures include:

- physically tamper-resistant sensors and controllers,
- attestation of the software configurations of programmable devices, maybe on the basis of Trusted Platform Modules, together with secure update procedures,
- controlling the environment of sensors so that an adversary cannot induce a truthful reporting of distorted facts that would promote the adversary's objectives.

Defences that secure devices can be implemented more easily in closed, controlled environments. When such defences are not feasible, countermeasures can take the form of plausibility checks on inputs received and plausibility checks on actions performed. Plausibility checks rely on models of the physical system that capture the expected behaviour of the application. In the most simple case, we could model that two sensors observe the same quantity so that their readings should be the same within the bounds of measurement errors. We may further model the relationship between different quantities to check the consistency of a collection of observations. We may also use models to check the consistency between predicted and observed behaviour.

Security analysis is performed in a threat model where not all components in the system are trusted. Concepts from Byzantine fault tolerance become relevant in this context. The efficiency of security mechanisms may improve when suitable independence assumptions can be made. It must, however, be noted that provably secure systems are ever so often broken by violating some of the assumptions of the security proof; independence assumptions would appear to present an attractive target.

References

1. Aura, T., Roe, M., Arkko, J.: Security of Internet location management. In: Proceedings of the 18th Annual Computer Security Applications Conference, pp. 78–87 (December 2002)
2. Borselius, N.: Mobile agent security. Electronics & Communication Engineering Journal 14(5), 211–218 (2002)
3. Buchegger, S., Boudec, J.Y.L.: Performance analysis of the CONFIDANT protocol. In: MobiHoc, pp. 226–236 (2002)
4. Castro, M., Druschel, P., Ganesh, A.J., Rowstron, A.I.T., Wallach, D.S.: Secure routing for structured peer-to-peer overlay networks. In: OSDI (2002)
5. Clark, D.R., Wilson, D.R.: A comparison of commercial and military computer security policies. In: Proceedings of the 1987 IEEE Symposium on Security and Privacy, pp. 184–194 (1987)
6. Costa, M., Castro, M., Rowstron, A.I.T., Key, P.B.: PIC: Practical internet coordinates for distance estimation. In: ICDCS, pp. 178–187 (2004)
7. Dabek, F., Cox, R., Kaashoek, M.F., Morris, R.: Vivaldi: a decentralized network coordinate system. In: ACM SIGCOMM, pp. 15–26 (2004)
8. Dean, D., Felten, E.W., Wallach, D.S.: Java security: from HotJava to Netscape and beyond. In: Proceedings of the 1996 IEEE Symposium on Security and Privacy, pp. 190–200 (1996)
9. Gollmann, D.: Authentication by correspondence. IEEE Journal on Selected Areas in Communications 21(1), 88–95 (2003)
10. International Organisation for Standardization: Basic Reference Model for Open Systems Interconnection (OSI) Part 2: Security Architecture, Genève, Switzerland (1989)
11. Jackson, C., Barth, A., Bortz, A., Shao, W., Boneh, D.: Protecting browsers from DNS rebinding attacks. In: Proceedings of the 14th ACM Conference on Computer and Communications Security, pp. 421–431 (2007)
12. Johns, M.: (Somewhat) breaking the same-origin policy by undermining DNS pinning. Posting to the Bug Traq mailing list (August 2006),
   http://www.securityfocus.com/archive/107/443429/30/180/threaded
13. Kaafar, M.A., Mathy, L., Barakat, C., Salamatian, K., Turletti, T., Dabbous, W.: Securing internet coordinate embedding systems. In: ACM SIGCOMM (August 2007)
14. Langner, R.: Stuxnet: Dissecting a cyberwarfare weapon. IEEE Security & Privacy 3(9), 49–51 (2011)
15. Parker, D.B.: Toward a new framework for information security. In: Bosworth, S., Kabay, M. (eds.) Computer Security Handbook, ch. 5, 4th edn. John Wiley & Sons (2002)
16. Sherr, M., Blaze, M., Loo, B.T.: Veracity: Practical secure network coordinates via vote-based agreements. In: USENIX Annual Technical Conference (USENIX-ATC). USENIX (June 2009)
17. Simmons, G.J., Purdy, G.B.: Zero-Knowledge Proofs of Identity and Veracity of Transaction Receipts. In: Günther, C.G. (ed.) EUROCRYPT 1988. LNCS, vol. 330, pp. 35–49. Springer, Heidelberg (1988)

Another Fallen Hash-Based RFID Authentication Protocol

Julio Cesar Hernandez-Castro[1], Pedro Peris-Lopez[2], Masoumeh Safkhani[3], Nasour Bagheri[4], and Majid Naderi[3]

[1] School of Computing, Portsmouth University, UK
Julio.Hernandez-Castro@port.ac.uk
[2] Computer Science Department, Carlos III University of Madrid, Spain
pperis@inf.uc3m.es
[3] Electrical Eng. Department, Iran University of Science and Technology, Tehran, Iran
{M_Safkhani,M_Naderi}@iust.ac.ir
[4] Electrical Engineering Department, Shahid Rajaee Teacher Training University, Tehran, Iran
NBagheri@srttu.edu

Abstract. In this paper, we scrutinize the security of an RFID protocol [9], which has been recently proposed, and show important vulnerabilities. Our first attack is a passive one that can disclose all secret information stored on the tags' memory. We only need to eavesdrop one session of the protocol between a tag and a legitimate reader (connected to the back-end database) and perform $O(2^{17})$ off-line evaluations of the *PRNG*-function – while the authors wrongly claimed the complexity of any such attack would be around 2^{48} operations. Although the extracted information is enough to launch other relevant attacks and thus to completely rule out any of the protocol's security claims, we additionally present several attacks using alternative strategies that show the protocol is flawed in more than one way and has many exploitable weaknesses. More precisely, we present a tag impersonation attack that requires the execution of only two runs of the protocol, and has a success probability of 1. It must be noted that this attack is, however, not applicable to the original protocol that the authors attempted to improve so, in a way, their improvement is not such. Finally, we show two approaches to trace a tag, as long as it has not updated its secret values. For all the above, we conclude that the improved protocol is even less secure than the original proposal, which is also quite insecure, and cannot be recommended.

Keywords: RFID, EPC-C1G2, Authentication, Secret Disclosure, Impersonation, Traceability.

1 Introduction

Radio Frequency Identification (RFID) is a wireless technology which can be employed to identify or track objects in various applications. Some common applications are animal tracking, retail, supply chain management in wholesale stores, library access control, toll payments, theft prevention, human implants, and e-passports. A typical RFID system includes a reader and a number of tags, which may range from the high

I. Askoxylakis, H.C. Pöhls, and J. Posegga (Eds.): WISTP 2012, LNCS 7322, pp. 29–37, 2012.
© IFIP International Federation for Information Processing 2012

end battery-powered ones with Wi-Fi capabilities, to the low-cost that are quite constrained in resources and have no internal power, harvesting it from the readers. The tag generally includes some information related to the tag holder, and can be read/modified by the reader, which is normally securely connected to a back-end database through classical means (e.g. SSL). This technology is expected to replace barcodes in grocery and retail stores in the near future.

However, despite the multiple benefits mentioned above, security and privacy are the main concerns that slow down the rapid and widespread deployment of this technology. For instance, regarding these security concerns, only the authorized readers should be able to read or modify the information stored on the tags, only valid tags should be authenticated by a legitimate reader and it should be infeasible for a fake tag to impersonate a legitimate one. To address these multiple security and privacy requirements, several RFID mutual authentication protocols and their security analysis have already been proposed in literature, e.g. [7, 10, 11, 14]. In addition, there are several interconnected standards for RFID systems, and among them EPC global and ISO have played a major role. The Electronic Product Code Class-1 Generation-2 specification [6, 8] (EPC-C1G2 in short) was announced in 2004 by EPC Global and ratified by ISO [12]. However, later security analysis carried out on the EPC-C1 G2 specification demonstrated several security concerns [1, 13]. Researchers, motivated by this, have proposed many EPC-compliant schemes –in an attempt to correct the weaknesses of the standard and improve its security– and have analyzed the security of these new schemes [2–5, 9, 15]. Among them, one of the most recent proposals is a protocol proposed by Habibi *et al.* [9], which is an improvement to the Yeh *et al.* 's protocol [15]. Specifically, the authors analyzed the security of Yeh *et al.* 's protocol and proposed an improved version as a repair for the attacks they found. This new proposal is the main concern of this paper.

In this paper, we show that Habibi *et al.* did not succeed in their attempt, and the proposed protocol is at least as insecure as its predecessor. More precisely, they decreased the security margin of the original protocol rather than improve it, because it is possible to apply an efficient tag impersonation on the revised protocol which is not applicable to the original protocol. In addition to that, all the security problems of the original protocol remain unsolved.

Paper Organization: In § 2 some preliminaries and notations are introduced. We describe the improved Yeh *et al.* 's protocol proposed by Habibi *et al.* in § 3. A secret information disclosure attack is presented in § 4. § 5 and § 6 describe tag impersonation and traceability attacks, respectively. Finally, in § 7 we extract some interestings conclusions.

2 Preliminaries

Throughout the paper, we use the following notation:

- EPC_s: The 96 bits of EPC code are divided into six 16-bit blocks, and then these six blocks are XORed to form EPC_s.
- $DATA$: The corresponding information for the tag, kept in the back-end database.

- K_i: The 16-bit authentication key stored in the tag to be authenticated by the back-end database at the $(i + 1)^{th}$ phase of authentication.
- P_i: The 16-bit access key stored in the tag to authenticate the back-end database at the $(i + 1)^{th}$ phase of authentication.
- K_{old} and K_{new}: The old and new authentication keys, respectively, stored in the back-end database.
- P_{old} and P_{new}: The old and new access keys, respectively, stored in the back-end database.
- C_i: The 16-bit index of the record of the ith tag's information in the back-end database, stored in the tag.
- C_{old} and C_{new}: The old and new back-end database indexes for the ith tag, respectively, stored in the back-end database .
- X: The value kept as either *new* or *old* to show which key in the record of the back-end database is matched with the ones on the tag.
- $B \longleftarrow A$: Assign the value of A to B.
- N_T and N_R: 16-bit random numbers (nonces) that are generated by the tag and the reader, respectively.
- $\oplus$: Exclusive-OR operation.
- RID: The reader identification number.
- $PRNG$: a 16-bit pseudo-random number generator.
- $H(.)$: A secure cryptographic hash function.

3   Protocol Description

In this section we give a brief description of Habibi *et al.* 's protocol – see the original paper [9] for further details. This protocol has two phases: an initialization phase and an $(i + 1)^{th}$ authentication phase, which are described as follows:

Initialization Phase: In this phase, the manufacturer generates random values for K_0, P_0 and C_0 respectively and sets the values of the record in the tag, i.e., $K_i = K_0$, $P_i = P_0, C_i = C_0$ and the corresponding record in the back-end database $K_{old} = K_{new} = K_0, P_{old} = P_{new} = P_0, C_{old} = C_{new} = 0$.

Authentication Phase: The authentication phase of Habibi *et al.* 's protocol, in its $(i + 1)^{th}$ run, depicted in Fig. 1 in Appendix, is as follow:

1. The reader generates a random number N_R and sends it to the tag.
2. The tag receives N_R, generates a random number N_T, computes M_1, D, E as shown below and finally sends M_1, D, C_i and E to the reader:
   $M_1 \longleftarrow PRNG(EPC_s \oplus N_R \oplus N_T) \oplus K_i$ and $D \longleftarrow N_T \oplus K_i$ and $E \longleftarrow N_T \oplus PRNG(C_i \oplus K_i)$.
3. Once the reader receives the message, it computes $V = H(RID \oplus N_R)$ and forwards M_1, D, C_i, E, N_R, V to the back-end database.
4. The back-end database receives M_1, D, C_i, E, N_R and V. After receiving these values, it proceeds as follows:
   - For each RID stored in the database (DB), it computes $H(RID \oplus N_R)$ and compares it with the received V to verifies the reader legitimacy.

- If $C_i = 0$, which means that it is the first access to the tag, it proceeds as follows, iteratively:
  - Picks up an entry (K_{old}, P_{old}, C_{old}, K_{new}, P_{new}, C_{new}, RID, EPS_s, $DATA$) stored in database.
  - Verifies whether $M_1 \oplus K_{old} \stackrel{?}{=} PRNG(EPC_s \oplus N_R \oplus D \oplus K_{old})$ or $M_1 \oplus K_{new} \stackrel{?}{=} PRNG(EPC_s \oplus N_R \oplus D \oplus K_{new})$. If "Yes" marks X as old or new provided that the verification process is satisfied based on the new record or the old record.
- Otherwise, it uses C_i as an index to find the corresponding record in the database and verify whether $PRNG(EPC_s \oplus N_R \oplus D \oplus K_X) \oplus K_X \stackrel{?}{=} M_1$. If "No" the protocol aborts.
- Verify whether $N_T \oplus PRNG(C_X \oplus K_X) \stackrel{?}{=} E$. If "No" the protocol aborts.
- Computes M_2 and $Info$ as follows and forwards them to the reader:
  $M_2 \longleftarrow PRNG(EPC_s \oplus N_T) \oplus P_X$ and $Info \longleftarrow DATA \oplus RID$
- If $X = new$, updates the database as follows:
  $K_{old} \longleftarrow K_{new}$, $K_{new} \longleftarrow PRNG(K_{new})$, $P_{old} \longleftarrow P_{new}$,
  $P_{new} \longleftarrow PRNG(P_{new})$, $C_{old} \longleftarrow C_{new}$, $C_{new} \longleftarrow PRNG(N_T \oplus N_R)$.
- Else, $C_{new} \longleftarrow PRNG(N_T \oplus N_R)$.

5. Once the reader receives the message, it extracts $DATA$ as $Info \oplus RID$ and forwards M_2 to the tag.
6. Once the tag receives the message, it proceeds as follows:
   - Verifies whether $PRNG(EPC_s \oplus N_T) \stackrel{?}{=} M_2 \oplus P_i$. If "No" the protocol aborts.
   - Authenticates the back-end database.
   - Updates the contents kept inside as $K_{i+1} \longleftarrow PRNG(K_i)$,
     $P_{i+1} \longleftarrow PRNG(P_i)$ and $C_{i+1} \longleftarrow PRNG(N_T \oplus N_R)$.

It must be noted that the only difference between the above protocol and the original protocol, proposed by Yeh $et\ al.$ [15], is that in the original protocol M_1 is computed as $M_1 = PRNG(EPC_s \oplus N_R) \oplus K_i$.

4   Secret Information Disclosure Attack

In this section we present an efficient and passive attack that retrieves any secret information in the tag, including EPC_s, K_i and P_i. The main observation, which is the milestone of the given attack, is the fact that given $Y = PRNG(X)$ and the assumptions that the $PRNG$-function is a public function, and the length of Y and X is 16-bit, then it is possible to do an exhaustive search and find X as a pre-image of Y in the cost of at most 2^{16} off-line evaluations of $PRNG$. Following this observation, and given the fact that the tag T_i communicates with a legitimate reader R_i, an adversary ($\mathcal{A}$) can disclose all the secret parameters of T_i as follows:

1. Eavesdrops one session of the protocol and stores all the exchanged messages:
   $N_R, C_i, M_1 = PRNG(EPC_s \oplus N_R \oplus N_T) \oplus K_i, D = N_T \oplus K_i, E = N_T \oplus PRNG(C_i \oplus K_i)$
   and $M_2 = PRNG(EPC_s \oplus N_T) \oplus P_X$.

2. $\forall\, i = 0,\, \ldots,\, 2^{16} - 1$ does as follows:
   - $K_i \longleftarrow i$ and $N_T \longleftarrow D \oplus K_i$,
   - If $E = N_T \oplus PRNG(C_i \oplus K_i)$ then return K_i and N_T.
3. For the returned values of K_i and N_T from Step 2 and $\forall\, i = 0,\, \ldots,\, 2^{16} - 1$ does as follows:
   - $EPC_s \longleftarrow i$,
   - If $M_1 = PRNG(EPC_s \oplus N_R \oplus N_T) \oplus K_i$ then return EPC_s.
4. For the returned values of K_i and N_T from Step 2 and EPC_s from Step 3 assigns $M_2 \oplus PRNG(EPC_s \oplus N_T)$ to P_i and returns the following values:
   $P_{old} = P_i$, $P_{new} = PRNG(P_i)$, $K_{old} = K_i$, $K_{new} = PRNG(K_i)$, $C_{old} = C_i$.

The complexity of the given attack is limited to eavesdropping one session of the protocol between a tag and a legitimate reader, and perform 2^{17} evaluations of the *PRNG*-function. However, the adversary succeeds in its attack if it comes up with only one pre-image in each of Steps 2 and 3 of the given attack (it must be noted that the existence of at least one pre-image in each step is guaranteed). Otherwise, it should repeat the attack several times to come up with an unique solution. To increase the efficiency of the proposed attack, the adversary can block M_2 in the last Step of the protocol to avoid the updating of the secret values. In this case two runs of the protocol should be fairly enough to extract all given parameters.

Given all secret values of the tag, it would be easy to launch other relevant attacks with a success probability of 1, and the cost of one execution of the protocol (e.g. traceability, tag impersonation, reader impersonation and de-synchronization).

Remark 1. It must be noted that a similar attack was applied by Habibi *et al.* [9] on the original protocol of Yeh *et al.* and the improved protocol was proposed to overcome this weaknesses. In their security analysis the authors claimed that the complexity of disclosing the secret information in their improved protocol is 2^{48} evaluations of the *PRNG* function. Nevertheless, we present an efficient attack which retrieves all secret parameters with a cost of 2^{17} evaluations, which explicitly contradicts their claims.

Although the above attack ruins all the security properties objectives of the protocol, we continue presenting other attacks based on different strategies.

5 Tag Impersonation Attack

Tag impersonation attack is a forgery attack that leads to the identification of spoofed tags by a legitimate reader. In this section we show how an adversary can deceive the reader to authenticate it as a legitimate tag. In the given tag impersonation attack, the adversary, which is an active adversary, can do as follows:

Phase 1 (Learning): The adversary eavesdrops one successful run of the protocol and stores the messages exchanged between the reader and the legitimate tag including N_R, M_1, D, C_i and E.

At the end of this phase the records linked to this tag in the back-end database include $(K_{old}, P_{old}, C_{old}, K_{new}, P_{new}, C_{new}, RID, EPS_s, DATA)$ and the tag record includes $(K_{new}, P_{new}, C_{new}, EPS_s)$, where: $K_{new} = PRNG(K_{old})$, $P_{new} = PRNG(P_{old})$, $C_{new} = PRNG(N_T \oplus N_R)$, $M_1 = PRNG(EPC_s \oplus N_R \oplus N_T) \oplus K_{old}$, $D = N_T \oplus K_{old}$ and $E = N_T \oplus PRNG(C_{old} \oplus K_{old})$.

Phase 2 (Impersonation): To impersonate the legitimate tag, the adversary waits until the reader initiates a new protocol session, where:

1. The reader generates a random number N_R' and sends it to the tag.
2. After receiving N_R', the adversary replies with M_1', D', C_i' and E' where:
   $M_1' = M_1 = PRNG(EPC_s \oplus N_R' \oplus N_T) \oplus K_{old}$, $C_i' = C_{old}$, $D' = D \oplus N_R \oplus N_R' = N_T \oplus K_i \oplus N_R \oplus N_R'$ and $E' = E \oplus N_R \oplus N_R' = N_T \oplus PRNG(C_{old} \oplus K_{old}) \oplus N_R \oplus N_R'$.
3. Once the reader receives the message, it computes $V = H(RID \oplus N_R')$ and forwards M_1', D', C_i', E', N_R' and V to the back-end database.
4. Once the back-end database receives the message, it proceeds as follows:
   - For each stored RID in the database, computes $H(RID \oplus N_R)$ and compares it with the received V. Since the adversary has not manipulated the exchanged message from the reader to the back-end database, the back-end database authenticates the reader.
   - We assume that $C_i' \neq 0$, then back-end database uses $C_i' = C_i$ as an index to find the corresponding record in the database. The record would be found in its records for the field C_{old}. Therefore the back-end database marks X as *old*.
   - Verifies whether $PRNG(EPC_s \oplus N_R' \oplus D' \oplus K_{old}') \oplus K_{old} \overset{?}{=} M_1'$, where:
     $PRNG(EPC_s \oplus N_R' \oplus D' \oplus K_{old}) \oplus K_{old} =$
     $PRNG(EPC_s \oplus N_R' \oplus D \oplus N_R \oplus N_R' \oplus K_{old}) \oplus K_{old} =$
     $PRNG(EPC_s \oplus N_R \oplus D \oplus K_{old}) \oplus K_{old} = M_1 = M_1'$.

   - Verifies whether $N_T' \oplus PRNG(C_{old}' \oplus K_{old}') \overset{?}{=} E'$, where:
     $N_T' = D' \oplus K_{old} = N_T \oplus N_R \oplus N_R' \Rightarrow N_T' \oplus PRNG(C_{old} \oplus K_{old}) =$
     $N_T \oplus N_R \oplus N_R' \oplus PRNG(C_{old} \oplus K_{old}) = E'$.

   - Authenticates the adversary as a legitimate tag and computes M_2' and $Info$ as follows, and forwards them to the reader:
     $M_2' \longleftarrow PRNG(EPC_s \oplus N_T') \oplus P_{old}'$ and $Info \longleftarrow DATA \oplus RID$
   - Since $X = old$, updates the back-end database as follows:
     $C_{new}' \longleftarrow PRNG(N_T' \oplus N_R')$.
5. Once the reader receives the message, it extracts $DATA$ and forwards M_2 to the expected tag, which is the adversary.

Following the given attack, the adversary is authenticated by the back-end database as a legitimate tag with a probability of 1, while the complexity of the attack is only two protocol runs with negligible time and memory requirements. It is worth to note that the given attack is not applicable to the original protocol of Yeh *et al.* and the complexity of the best known tag impersonation attack against the original protocol is 2^{16} evaluations of $PRNG$ function [9]. It shows that Habibi *et al.* have decreased the security of the original protocol while trying to improve it – at least from this attack's point of view.

6   Traceability Attack

In this section, we show that the improved Yeh *et al.* 's protocol, like the original protocol, puts at risk the location privacy of tags' holders because it is possible to track tags with a probability of 1 – between two successful runs of the authentication protocol. The following properties of the protocol are enough to trace a given tag T_i, as long as it has not updated its internal values:

1. When the reader or possibly the adversary $\mathcal{A}$, which supplants a legal reader in a mutual authentication session, sends a random number N_R to the tag, it will answer with M_1, C_i, where C_i is the tag's index in the back-end database and will remain fixed as long as the tag does not participate in another successful protocol run to update its internal values.
2. Given that the tag's reply to the reader's (or adversary) query includes D and E, where $D = N_T \oplus K_i$ and $E = N_T \oplus PRNG(C_i \oplus K_i)$. It can be seen that if $\mathcal{A}$ computes Y as follows:
   $Y \longleftarrow D \oplus E = N_T \oplus K_i \oplus N_T \oplus PRNG(C_i \oplus K_i) = K_i \oplus PRNG(C_i \oplus K_i)$
   then Y only depends on K_i and C_i and these ones will remain fixed as long as the tag does not execute a new updating phase. Hence, Y can be used as a value to perfectly trace T_i.

It must be noted that this attack also works against the original protocol of Yeh *et al.*

7   Conclusions

In this paper we analyzed the security of the improved Yeh *et al.* 's protocol, designed to be compliant with the EPC-C1G2 standard, and being one of the most recent proposed protocols in this area. Our main attack is a passive full disclosure attack which can retrieve efficiently all the secret parameters of the tag. The cost of this attack is the eavesdropping of one protocol session and the performing of $O(2^{17})$ off-line evaluations of the *PRNG*-function – while Habibi *et al.* claimed $O(2^{48})$ evaluations are needed for any such attack. This attack is so powerful that it ruins all the security properties claimed by the proposed scheme. To complete this analysis, and following different strategies, we also present tag impersonation and traceability attacks that prove that these protocols are flawed in more than one way and probably do not admit an easy fixing. Summarizing, in this paper we show how the improved protocol proposed by Habibi *et al.* is more insecure that the one they tried to correct, which is regrettably a too common occurrence in the area.

References

1. Bailey, D.V., Juels, A.: Shoehorning Security into the EPC Tag Standard. In: De Prisco, R., Yung, M. (eds.) SCN 2006. LNCS, vol. 4116, pp. 303–320. Springer, Heidelberg (2006)
2. Burmester, M., de Medeiros, B.: The Security of EPC Gen2 Compliant RFID Protocols. In: Bellovin, S.M., Gennaro, R., Keromytis, A.D., Yung, M. (eds.) ACNS 2008. LNCS, vol. 5037, pp. 490–506. Springer, Heidelberg (2008)

3. Burmester, M., de Medeiros, B., Munilla, J., Peinado, A.: Secure EPC Gen2 Compliant Radio Frequency Identification. In: Ruiz, P.M., Garcia-Luna-Aceves, J.J. (eds.) ADHOC-NOW 2009. LNCS, vol. 5793, pp. 227–240. Springer, Heidelberg (2009)
4. Chen, C.-L., Deng, Y.-Y.: Conformation of EPC Class-1 Generation-2 standards RFID system with mutual authentication and privacy protection. Eng. Appl. of AI 22(8), 1284–1291 (2009)
5. Chien, H.-Y., Chen, C.-H.: Mutual authentication protocol for RFID conforming to EPC Class-1 Generation-2 standards
6. Class-1 Generation-2 UHF air interface protocol standard version 1.2.0, EPCGlobal (2008), http://www.epcglobalinc.org/standards/
7. Duc, D.N., Kim, K.: Defending RFID authentication protocols against DoS attacks. Computer Communications 34(3), 384–390 (2011)
8. EPC Tag data standard version 1.6, EPCGlobal (2011), http://www.epcglobalinc.org/standards/
9. Habibi, M.H., Alagheband, M.R., Aref, M.R.: Attacks on a Lightweight Mutual Authentication Protocol under EPC C-1 G-2 Standard. In: Ardagna, C.A., Zhou, J. (eds.) WISTP 2011. LNCS, vol. 6633, pp. 254–263. Springer, Heidelberg (2011)
10. Hung-Yu, C.: SASI: A New Ultralightweight RFID Authentication Protocol Providing Strong Authentication and Strong Integrity. IEEE Transactions on Dependable and Secure Computing 4(4), 337–340 (2007)
11. Chien, H.Y.: Secure access control schemes for RFID systems with anonymity. In: Proceedings of MDM, p. 96 (2006)
12. Information technology Radio frequency identification for item management. Part 6: parameters for air interface communications at 860 MHz to 960MHz- (2005), http://www.iso.org
13. Peris-Lopez, P., Hernandez-Castro, J.C., Estevez-Tapiador, J.M., Ribagorda, A.: RFID specification revisited. In: The Internet of Things: From RFID to The Next-Generation Pervasive Networked Systems, pp. 6:311–6:346. Taylor & Francis Group (2008)
14. Weis, R.-D.E.S., Sarma, S.: Security and privacy aspects of low-cost radio frequency identification systems. In: Proceedings of WiCom, pp. 2078–2080 (2007)
15. Yeh, T.-C., Wang, Y.-J., Kuo, T.-C., Wang, S.-S.: Securing RFID systems conforming to EPC Class-1 Generation-2 standard. Expert Syst. Appl. 37(12), 7678–7683 (2010)

Appendix

A   Habibi *et al.*'s Protocol Description

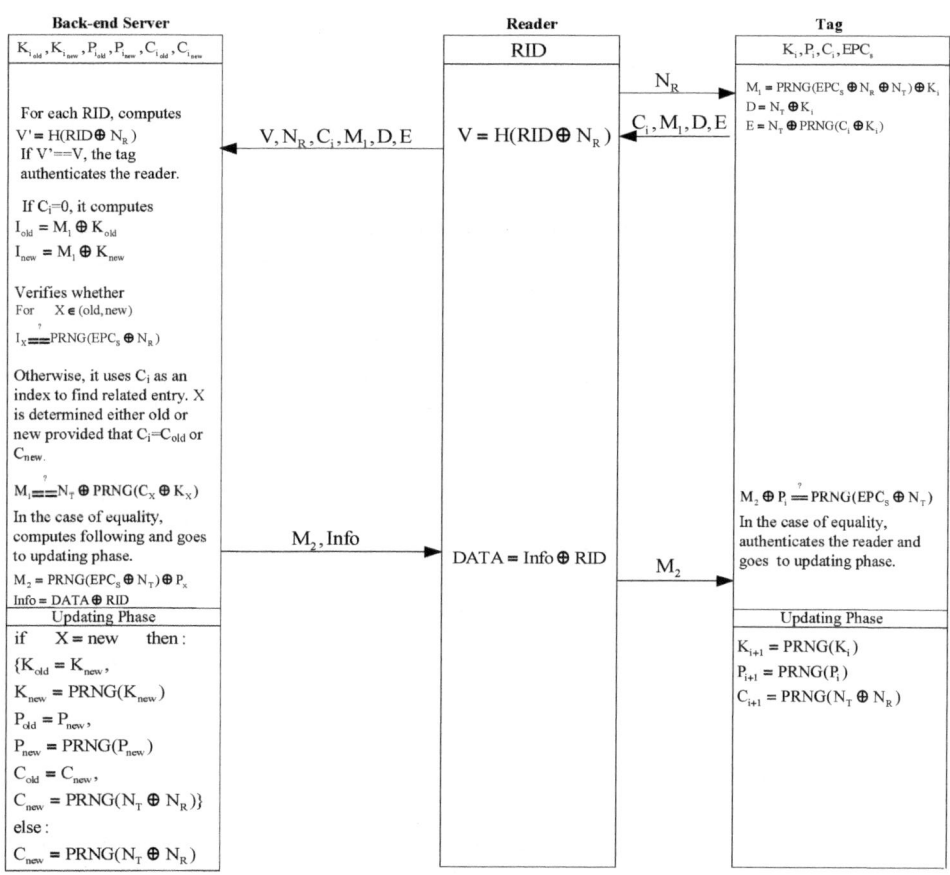

Fig. 1. Improvement of Yeh *et al.*'s Authentication Protocol by Habibi *et al.* [9]

HTTP Botnet Detection Using Adaptive Learning Rate Multilayer Feed-Forward Neural Network

G. Kirubavathi Venkatesh and R. Anitha Nadarajan

Department of Mathematics and Computer Applications
PSG College of Technology, Coimbatore, India
g.kiruba@gmail.com, anitha_nadarajan@mail.psgtech.ac.in

Abstract. Botnets have become a rampant platform for malicious attacks, which poses a significant threat to internet security. The recent botnets have begun using common protocols such as HTTP which makes it even harder to distinguish their communication patterns. Most of the HTTP bot communications are based on TCP connections. In this work some TCP related features have been identified for the detection of HTTP botnets. With these features a Multi-Layer Feed Forward Neural Network training model using Bold Driver Back-propagation learning algorithm is created. The algorithm has the advantage of dynamically changing the learning rate parameter during weight updation process. Using this approach, Spyeye and Zeus botnets are efficiently identified. A comparison of the actively trained neural network model with a C4.5 Decision Tree, Random Forest and Radial Basis Function indicated that the actively learned neural network model has better identification accuracy with less false positives.

Keywords: HTTP Botnet, Multilayer Feed-forward Neural Network, Bold Driver Back propagation algorithm.

1 Introduction

Botnets are organized networks of infected (Zombie) machines running bot codes, categorized by their use of a command and control (C&C) channel. Using the command and control of botnet, a botmaster can control a large group of compromised bots and then perform malicious attacks [1]. At early times, C&C communications were based on Internet Relay Chat (IRC) protocol. The attacker used to actively issue commands on the special channel of IRC server to all the bots. Recently, HTTP becomes a more popular communication protocol for bots. These web-based C&C bots try to blend into normal HTTP traffic, which makes them more difficult to be identified, since HTTP is a commonly used network communication protocol in many applications. The HTTP bots frequently request and download commands from web servers under the attacker's control. As a result, detecting bots with web-based controlling is more intricate than bots with IRC-based controlling. This paper identifies the anomaly in web flow behaviors of HTTP botnets, extracts some TCP related features and uses neural network with bold driver back propagation

I. Askoxylakis, H.C. Pöhls, and J. Posegga (Eds.): WISTP 2012, LNCS 7322, pp. 38–48, 2012.
© IFIP International Federation for Information Processing 2012

algorithm [2] to detect botnets. Neural networks have been successfully used in several applications like classification of internet users [3], intrusion detection at the host level [4-5] due to their advantages like parallel processing of information, capacity to recognize patterns of information in the presence of noise and handle non-linearity, capacity to classify information and quick adaptability of system dynamics. Also with the same features, training models like Decision tree, random forest and radial basis function have been created and tested for botnet detection. Extensive experimental results show that the neural network model is efficient and can detect HTTP bots with low false positive rate.

The rest of the paper is organized as follows: Section 2 presents the related work in botnet detection systems and Section 3 describes the proposed detection approach in detail. Section 4 gives the experimental results and Section 5 presents the performance evaluation of the proposed system. Finally, Section 6 concludes the paper.

2   Related Work

Botnets are now recognized as one of the most serious security threats. Detecting and tracking botnet is considered to be highly complicated and a daunting task and as a result it has become a major research topic in recent years. One of the earliest methods to detect botnet was based on the honeypots. Many researchers have used honeypots to detect botnets, but could not detect bot infection at all times. Freiling et al. [6], used honeypots to track botnets in the network and generated an early report for understanding the consequences of botnets. Goebel et al. [7] proposed a well-known signature based botnet detection technique called Rishi. Anomaly based detection approaches try to detect botnets based on a number of traffic anomalies such as high network latency, high volumes of traffic, traffic on unusual ports and unusual system behavior that could show existence of bots in the network. Binkley et al. [8] proposed an effective algorithm that combines TCP-based anomaly detection with IRC tokenization and IRC message statistics to create a system that can clearly detect client botnets. However, this approach could be easily defeated by simply using a trivial cipher to encode the IRC commands. Karasaridis et al. [9] presented an algorithm for detection and characterization of botnets using passive analysis based on flow data in transport layer and it could detect encrypted botnet communications also.

DNS-based detection techniques are based on particular DNS information generated by a botnet. Dagon [10] proposed a mechanism to identify botnet C&C servers by detecting domain names with abnormally high or temporarily concentrated dynamic DNS query rates, but this method generated many false positives. Masud et al. [11] proposed robust and effective flow based botnet traffic detection by mining multiple log files. They introduced multiple log correlation for C&C traffic detection and categorized the entire flow to identify botnet.

Chia et al. [12] proposed a novel method to detect HTTP bots based on timeslot, mutual authentication and clustering analysis. This method provided an efficient and practical approach to identify web-bots hiding in HTTP protocol. Since most of the web-based bots communicate with TCP connection, Wang B et al. [13] extracted key statistical features such as request bytes, response bytes, number of efficient packets and classified them using X-means clustering algorithm and this method was computationally light with good detection accuracy. The limitation of this work is that the proposed method will fail if the bot master uses random delay technique to break the periodicity. Guofei Gu et.al. [14], proposed BotMiner which clustered similar communication traffic and similar malicious traffic, and performed cross cluster correlation to identify the hosts that share both similar communication patterns and similar malicious activity patterns. Nogueira et.al. [23] proposed a botnet detection approach based on the identification of traffic patterns and used an Artificial Neural Network to identify the licit and illicit patterns. In this paper, a multi-layer neural network is trained with some TCP connection based features for the detection of HTTP botnets. Extensive experimental results show that the proposed method is efficient and can detect HTTP bots with low false positive rate.

3   Proposed Botnet Detection System

The proposed botnet detection uses a Multilayer Feed-forward Neural Network with adaptive learning rate. Since HTTP botnets communicate with TCP connection, in this paper we have extracted TCP connection related features. To increase the dynamic range of learning rate coefficient, bold driver back-propagation algorithm is used. The block diagram of the proposed system is given in Fig. 1.

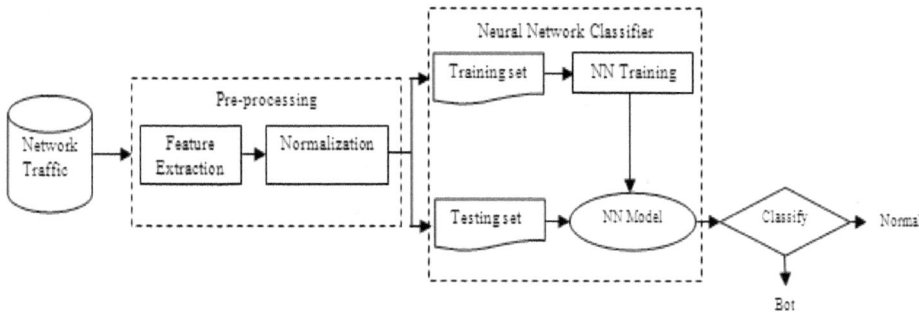

Fig. 1. Block diagram of the proposed system

3.1   Feature Extraction

Web botnets do not maintain a connection with C&C server, but they periodically download the instructions using web requests on a regular interval from the web server which is under the attacker control. Since, most of the communications between the web botnets is based on TCP connection, relative and direct features of TCP connections are extracted from the network traffic. Tu Xu et.al [25] have used some relative features like one-way connection density, ratio of TCP packets etc to efficiently identify DDoS attack. In this work, we use some of the relative features used by Tu Xu et.al for the detection of HTTP botnet. When the infected bot communicate with the web server which is under the control of the attacker, the number of half open connections will increase and hence one way connection ratio and Ratio of incoming and outgoing TCP packets are suitable features to reflect this scenario. In normal traffic, randomness will be there in the number of SYN flag, FIN flag and PSH flag send by a host, but when a bot communicates with a C&C server periodically there is a pattern and these counts will be high and almost a fixed one. Hence the SYN, FIN and PSH flag counts in the TCP packets send by the bot are considered as features.

In this work, the following TCP features are used for efficient detection of HTTP botnet.

- $One-way\ connection$ ratio of TCP $= \dfrac{\text{Number of one-way connection TCP packets}}{\text{Number of TCP packets}} * 100$

- Ratio of Incoming Outgoing TCP packets $= \dfrac{\text{Number of Incoming TCP packets}}{\text{Number of Outgoing TCP packets}}$

- Ratio of TCP packets $= \dfrac{\text{Number of TCP packets}}{\text{Total } number \text{ of packets}}$

- SYN Flag Count – the number of TCP packets with SYN flag set
- FIN Flag Count – the number of TCP packets with FIN flag set
- PSH Flag Count – the number of TCP packets with PSH Flag set

The selected features of TCP connections give considerable information associated with the presence of web-based botnet.

3.2   Normalization

During training of the neural network, higher valued input variables may tend to suppress the influence of smaller ones. Also, if the raw data is directly applied to the network, there is a risk of the simulated neurons reaching the saturated conditions. If the neurons get saturated, then the changes in the input value will produce a very small change or no change in the output value. This affects the network training to a great extent. To minimize the effects of magnitudes among inputs as well as to prevent saturation of the neuron activation function, the input data is normalized before being presented to the neural network. One way to normalize a feature x is using Min-Max normalization[15].

$$x^{'} = \frac{x - \min_x}{\max_x - \min_x} \tag{1}$$

where $x^{'}$ is the normalized value and $\min_x$, $\max_x$ are minimum and maximum values of features.

3.3   Classification Using Neural Network

Multilayer Feed-forward networks [16-17] are appropriate for solving problems where all the information can be presented to the neural network at once. In the training phase, a training set is presented as input to the neural network which iteratively adjusts network weights and biases in order to produce an output that matches, within a certain degree of accuracy, a previously known result. In the testing phase, a new input is presented to the network and a result is obtained based on the network parameters that were calculated during the training phase. In this work, the network is trained with bold-driver back propagation learning algorithm, which is an appropriate learning algorithm for training multilayer feed-forward networks for vector classification. The input layer will have 6 neurons, corresponding to the dimensionality of the input vectors, and the output layer will have one neuron. The number of neurons in the hidden layer is empirically selected such that the performance function, which is the mean square error for feed-forward networks, is minimized. Each neuron i in the input layer has a signal x_i as network's input and each neuron j in the hidden layer receives the signal $In(j)$ given by

$$In(j) = \theta_j + \sum_{i=1}^{n} x_i \, w_{ij} \tag{2}$$

where w_{ij} is the weight between the input layer and hidden layer and θ_j is the bias in the hidden layer. Then the signal $In(j)$ is passed through sigmoid activation function to produce f(In(j)). The output of the output layer is calculated as

$$y_k = \theta_k + \sum_{j=1}^{m} w_{jk} \, f(In(j)) \tag{3}$$

The output value will be compared with the target and error will be estimated. The bold driver back propagation learning algorithm is used to speed up the convergence of network, in which, the weights are updated after the presentation of all input patterns and the learning rate η is varied with each weight update with the rule,

$$w(t+1) = w(t) - \eta(t) \left[\sum_i \frac{\partial E(t)}{\partial w(t)} \right] + \alpha \Delta w(t) \tag{4}$$

where η is the learning rate, α is the momentum term $(0 < \alpha < 1)$.

Also we have used C4.5 decision tree, Random Forest and Radial Basis Function classifiers for the detection of botnets with the same set of features and a comparison is made between their performances. C4.5 Decision tree is an entropy based approach in which the attribute with the highest information gain ratio is the one used to make the decision [18]. Random Forest (RF) [19] is a multi-class prediction algorithm that can be used to predict either a categorical or a continuous response. Radial Basis Function (RBF) neural network is another type of feed-forward neural network and it performs the classification by measuring distances between inputs and the centers of the RBF hidden neurons [20]. Jiang et al. [21] and Zhang et al. [22] compared the RBF and MLFF-BP networks for misuse and anomaly detection on the KDD99 dataset. Their experiments have shown that for misuse detection, BP has a slightly better performance than RBF in terms of detection rate and false positive rate.

4   Experimental Results and Analysis

Botnet setup is created in our SSE lab Network that simulates the behavior of the existing real time HTTP botnet. We have used seven systems (1-BotMaster, 5- Zombies and 1-Command & Control Server) for our experimental purpose (Fig. 2). The physical topology is star and the speed of the Ethernet cable is 100baseTX.

TCP connections features are extracted from the network traffic by sampling at an interval of 5 seconds. The bot traces have been collected for 2 hours a day for five days in a week. In a similar manner, normal web traffic has been collected from the National Knowledge Network with the bandwidth of 100Mbps/s. The working mechanism is mentioned as below:

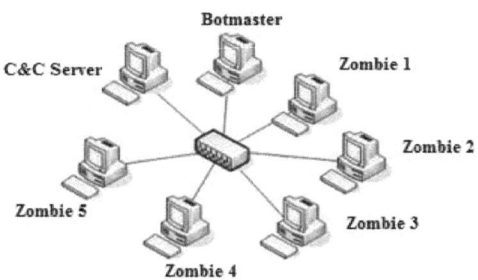

Fig. 2. Experimental Setup

Botmaster sends the Trojan or backdoor to these zombies using email spamming technique. Using the backdoor, botmaster installs the HTTP bot binaries in these machines. Now the victim machine will periodically communicate with the Command & Control server and follows the instructions from the botmaster without the know-ledge of the user. In this work, Spyeye [23] and Zeus [24] bots are used and table 1 shows the information of the bot traces collected. The traces are analyzed for the se-lected features with normal web traffic and botnet flow. The neural network is trained with 10250 normal samples, 8500 Zeus bot samples and 8250 Spyeye bot samples. The learning rate of the neural network is varied from 0.4 to 0.7. Fig.3 (a) shows the one way connection ratio of TCP Connection feature for Normal and Spyeye flow and Fig. 3(b) shows that of normal and Zeus. The graph clearly depicts that for normal flow the value of one way ratio is small, while for botnet flow it is comparatively large.

Table 1. Traces of different Web-based Botnets

Bot Fam-	Trace Size	Packets number
Zeus-1	5.85 MB	53,220
Zeus-2	4.13 MB	37,252
Spyeye-1	25.17 MB	1,75,870
Spyeye-2	3.90 MB	35,180

In case of Ratio of Incoming Outgoing TCP packets, from Fig. 4(a) we can see that for normal flow, there is an irregular deviation while in case of Spyeye it main-tains similarity in the connections. Fig. 4(b) shows the feature for normal and Zeus flow.

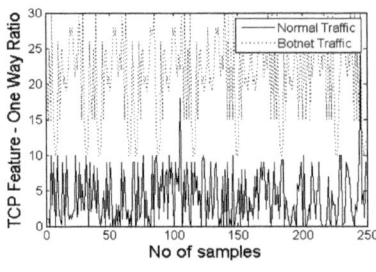
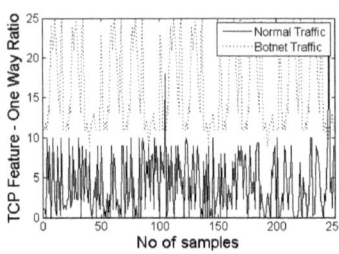

(a) For Normal and Spyeye flow   (b) For Normal and Zeus flow

Fig. 3. One-way connection ratio of TCP packets

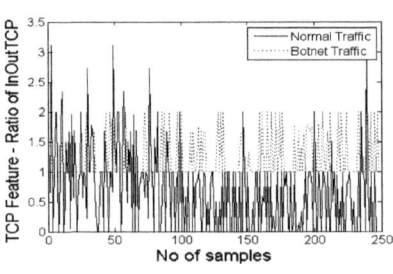
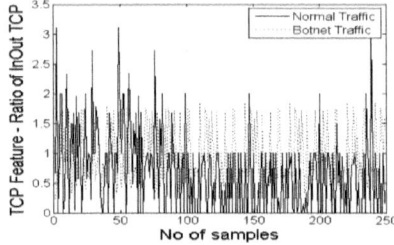

a) For Normal and Spyeye flow   (b) For Normal and Zeus flow

Fig. 4. Ratio of Incoming Outgoing TCP packets

Fig. 5(a) shows PSH feature for Normal and Spyeye flow. In case of PSH, normal traffic and botnet traffics are mixed. Normal traffic flows have randomness, while web botnet maintains some similarity in connections. Fig. 5(b) displays PSH feature for Normal and Zeus flow. Testing is done with 5200 normal samples, 3100 zeus bot samples and 3200 sypeye bot samples. For testing, both trained and untrained data have been used. For the best network performance, an optimal number of hidden neurons must be properly determined using the trial and error procedure. We experimented with 4 neurons to 18 neurons in the hidden layer. With 18 neurons in the hidden layer; the correct identification accuracy is increased within the minimum number of epochs. Table 2 gives the correct identification percentage of different botnets.

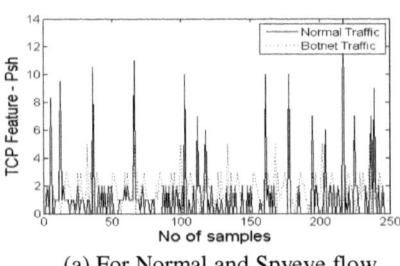
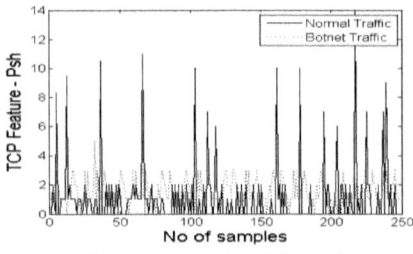

(a) For Normal and Spyeye flow   (b) For Normal and Zeus flow

Fig. 5. TCP PUSH Flag

Table 2. Identification accuracy of web botnet traffic profiles

Traffic traces	No. of Neurons in input layer	No. of Neurons in the hidden layer	Correct Identification
Spyeye-1	6	18	99.03%
Spyeye-2	6	18	99.02%
Zeus-1	6	18	99.01%
Zeus-2	6	18	99.04%

5   Performance Evaluation

The proposed method has been evaluated with different classifiers. The performance of the neural network model is compared with that of C4.5 decision tree, Random Forest and Radial Basis Function algorithm.

To evaluate the performance of neural network recognition system, measures like accuracy, precision, recall and F-measure are calculated as bellow:

$$Accuracy(A) = \frac{Number\ of\ correctly\ classified\ patterns}{Total\ number\ of\ patterns}$$

Precision is a measure of what fraction of test data is detected as attack are actually from the attack classes.

$$Precision(P) = \frac{TP}{TP + FP}$$

Recall measures the fraction of attack class that was correctly detected.

$$Recall\ (R) = \frac{TP}{TP + FN}$$

F-Measure is a measure of test's accuracy, which measures the balance between precision and recall.

$$F - Measure = \frac{2 \times Precision \times Recall}{Precision + Recall}$$

Table 3 gives the accuracy of the botnet detection system using various classifiers with the same set of TCP features and the performance measures of the proposed detection system for Spyeye Botnet and Zeus botnet. It shows Multilayer Feed Forward Neural Network with Bold driver back propagation learning algorithm gives the better accuracy compared with other methods.

The proposed model's performance is compared with some of the existing botnet detection techniques and table 4 shows the comparison results. Another performance indicator is the ROC curve. The ROC curve shows the tradeoff between the detection rate and false-positive rate under various detection algorithms. Our detection methodology achieves a detection rate of 99% with less than 1% of false positive. This result proves the effectiveness of the proposed detection mechanism.

Table 3. Performance Measures of Spyeye and Zeus Botnet

Method	Botnet	Precision	Recall	F-Measure	Accuracy
Decision Tree		0.968	0.931	0.949	96.5333
Random Forest	Spyeye	0.968	0.934	0.950	96.667
RBF		0.976	0.927	0.950	96.5333
Proposed Model		0.964	0.983	0.973	99.03
Decision Tree		0.956	0.930	0.941	96.1333
Random Forest		0.952	0.930	0.940	96.00
RBF	Zeus	0.959	0.922	0.940	95.8667
Proposed Model		0.948	0.992	0.969	99.04

Table 4. Comparison of Performance

Method	Average Detection Accuracy
Gu et al (2008) BotMiner [14]	96.825
Anotnio, Nogueira et al (2010) [23]	94.9175
Proposed NN Model	99.025

Fig. 6 shows the ROC curve for Spyeye botnet whereas Fig. 7 shows that of Zeus botnet. From the figures we can conclude that the proposed method outperforms other classifiers.

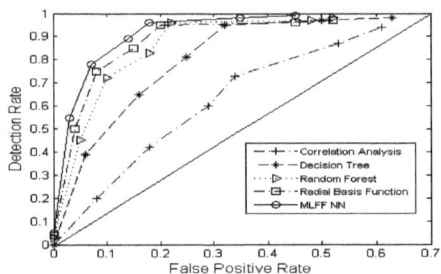

Fig. 6. ROC curve for Spyeye Botnet   **Fig.7.** ROC curve for Zeus Botnet

6   Conclusion

In this work, we propose a new method to identify HTTP-based botnet by using the network behavior of botnet. On observation of activities of web-based botnet, we notice that most of the communications of web-based botnets are based on TCP connections. The TCP connection behavior shared by web-based botnets have been extracted, used as features and a neural network model is created and it is able to detect the HTTP botnet traffic. The proposed detection method's performance is compared with that of some more classifiers like Decision Tree C4.5, Random forest, Radial Basis function network. The results obtained showed that the proposed method using neural network is able to achieve good identification results with less false positive. Another advantage of the proposed model is that it can detect HTTP botnets even if the communications are encrypted.

Acknowledgement. This work is a part of the Collaborative Directed Basic Research on Smart and Secure Environment project, funded by NTRO, Govt. of India.

References

1. Lai, G.H., Chen, C.M., Tzeng, R.Y., Laih, C.S., Faloutsos, C.: Botnet Detection by Abnormal IRC Traffic Analysis. In: Proceedings of the Fourth Joint Workshop on Information Security, JWIS (2009)
2. Sarkar, D.: Methods to speed up error back-propagation learning algorithm. ACM Computing Surveys 27(4), 519–542 (1995)
3. Nogueira, A., de Oliveira, M.R., Salvador, P., Valadas, R., Pacheco, A.: Classification of internet users using discriminant analysis and neural networks. In: First Conference on Traffic Engineering for the Next Generation Internet, pp. 341–348 (April 2005)
4. Debar, H., Becker, M., Siboni, D.: A neural network component for an intrusion detection system. In: Proceedings of the ACM/IEEE Symposium on Research in Security and Privacy, Los Almitos, CA, May 4-6, pp. 240–250 (1992)
5. Salvador, P., Nogueira, A., Franca, U., Valadas, R.: Framework for Zombie Detection Using Neural Networks. In: Proceedings of the Fourth International IEEE Conference on Internet Monitoring and Protection ICIMP 2009, pp. 14–16 (2009)
6. Freiling, F.C., Holz, T., Wicherski, G.: Botnet Tracking: Exploring a Root-Cause Methodology to Prevent Distributed Denial-of-Service Attacks. In: di Vimercati, S.d.C., Syverson, P.F., Gollmann, D. (eds.) ESORICS 2005. LNCS, vol. 3679, pp. 319–335. Springer, Heidelberg (2005)
7. Goebel, J., Holz, T.: Rishi: Identify bot contaminated hosts by irc nickname evaluation. In: Proceedings of USENIX HotBots 2007 (2007)
8. Binkley, J.R., Singh, S.: An algorithm for anomaly based botnet detection. In: Proceedings of the 2nd Conference on Steps to Reducing Unwanted Traffic on the Internet (SRUTI 2006), San Jose, CA (July 2006)
9. Karasaridis, A., Rexroad, B., Hoeflin, D.: Wide-scale botnet detection and characterization. In: First Workshop on Hot Topics in Understanding Botnets (HotBots 2007), Cambridge, MA (April 2007)
10. Dagon, D.: Botnet Detection and Response. In: Operations, Analysis and Research Center Workshop (July 2005)
11. Masud, M.M., Al-khateeb, T., Khan, L., Thuraisingham, B., Hamlen, K.W.: Flow- based identification of Botnet traffic by mining multiple log files. In: Proceedings of the International Conference on Distributed Framework & Application, Penang, Malaysia (2008)
12. Chen, C.-M., Ou, Y.-H., Tsai, Y.-C.: Web Botnet Detection based on Flow Information. In: International Computer Symposium 2010, pp. 381–384. IEEE (2010)
13. Wang, B., Li, Z., Li, D., Liu, F., Chen, H.: Modeling Connections Behavior for WebBased Bots Detection. In: IEEE International Conference on e-Business and Information System Security, EBISS 2010, Wuhan, pp. 1–4 (2010)

14. Gu, G., et al.: BotMiner: Clustering Analysis of Network traffic for protocol and structure independent botnet detection. In: Proceedings of 17th Conference on Security Symposium, pp. 139–154. ACM Digital Library (2008)
15. Shalabi, A.L., Shaaban, Z.: Normalization as a preprocessing engine for data mining and the approach of preference matrix. In: Proceedings of the International IEEE Conference on Dependability of Computer Systems, 2006, pp. 207–214 (2006)
16. Moradi, M., Zulkernine, M.: A neural network based system for intrusion detection and classification of attacks. In: Proceedings of the 2004 IEEE International Conference on Advances in Intelligent Systems - Theory and Applications, Luxembourg-Kirchberg, Canada, November 15-18 (2004)
17. Kukiełka, P., Kotulski, Z.: Analysis of Different Architectures of Neural Networks for Application in Intrusion Detection Systems. In: Proceedings of the IEEE International Multi Conference on Computer Science and Information Technology, pp. 807–811 (2008)
18. Abbes, T., Bouhoula, A., Rusinowitch, M.: Protocol Analysis in Intrusion Detection Using Decision Tree. In: Proceedings of the IEEE International Conference on Information Technology: Coding and Computing (ITCC 2004), pp. 404–408 (April 2004)
19. Zhang, J., Zulkernine, M., Haque, A.: Random-Forests-Based Network Intrusion Detection System. IEEE Transactions on Systems, Man, and Cybernetics 38(5), 649–659 (2008)
20. Rapaka, A., Novokhodko, A., Wunsch, D.: Intrusion detection using radial basis function network on sequence of system calls. In: Proceedings of the IEEE International Joint Conference on Neural Networks (IJCNN 2003), Portland, OR, USA, July 20-24, vol. 3, pp. 1820–1825 (2003)
21. Jiang, J., Zhang, C., Kamel, M.: RBF-based real-time hierarchical intrusion detection systems. In: Proceedings of the IEEE International Joint Conference on Neural Networks (IJCNN 2003), Portland, OR, USA, July 20-24, vol. 2, pp. 1512–1516. IEEE Press (2003)
22. Zhang, C., Jiang, J., Kamel, M.: Comparison of BPL and RBF Network in Intrusion Detection System. In: Wang, G., Liu, Q., Yao, Y., Skowron, A. (eds.) RSFDGrC 2003. LNCS (LNAI), vol. 2639, p. 466–470. Springer, Heidelberg (2003)
23. Anotnio, N., Salvador, P., Blessa, F.: A Botnet Detection System Based on Neural Networks. In: Proceedings of Fifth International Conference on Digital Telecommunications, pp. 57–62 (2010)
24. Binsalleeh, H., Ormerod, T., Bouhtouta, A., Sinha, P., Youssef, A., Debbabi, M., Wang, L.: On the Analysis of the Zeus Botnet Crimeware Toolkit. In: Proceedings of the IEEE Eighth Annual Conference on Privacy, Security and Trust, PST, Ottawa, Canada, August 17–19 (2010)
25. Xu, T., He, D., Luo, Y.: DDoS attack detection based on RLT features. In: Proceedings of International Conference on Computational Intelligence and Security, pp. 697–700 (2007)

How to Break EAP-MD5

Fanbao Liu and Tao Xie

School of Computer, National University of Defense Technology, Changsha, 410073,
Hunan, P.R. China
liufanbao@gmail.com

Abstract. We propose an efficient attack to recover the passwords, used
to authenticate the peer by EAP-MD5, in the IEEE 802.1X network.
First, we recover the length of the used password through a method
called length recovery attack by on-line queries. Second, we crack the
known length password using a rainbow table pre-computed with a fixed
challenge, which can be done efficiently with great probability through
off-line computations. This kind of attack can also be implemented successfully even if the underlying hash function MD5 is replaced with SHA-
1 or even SHA-512.

Keywords: EAP-MD5, IEEE 802.1X, Challenge and Response, Length
Recovery, Password Cracking, Rainbow Table.

1 Introduction

IEEE 802.1X [6] is an IEEE Standard for port-based Network Access Control, which provides an authentication mechanism to devices wishing to attach
to a Local Area Network (LAN) or Wireless Local Area Network (WLAN).
IEEE 802.1X defines the encapsulation of the Extensible Authentication Protocol (EAP) [4] over IEEE 802 known as "EAP over LAN" (EAPoL). IEEE 802.1X
authentication involves three parties: a peer, an authenticator and an authentication server. The peer is a client device that wishes to attach to the LAN/WLAN.
The authenticator is a network device, such as a Wireless Access Point (WAP),
and the authentication server is typically a host running software supporting
the Remote Authentication Dial In User Service (RADIUS) and EAP protocols. EAP-MD5 [4], first used as Challenge-Handshake Authentication Protocol
(CHAP) [13] in Point-to-Point Protocol (PPP) [12,9] network for peer authentication, is a hash-based challenge and response protocol. EAP-MD5 applies the
secret prefix approach of hashing [14] to generate response $R = \mathrm{MD5}(P||C)$,
where P is the shared password and C is the challenge.

In EAP-MD5 based wireless network, the peer provides user name and the
shared password, which is further hashed after appending the challenge sent
by the authentication server, to the authenticator to get right to access the
network. The authenticator forwards the peer's credentials to the authentication
server, only if the server determines the peer's credentials are valid, and then
the authenticator will allow the peer to access the network.

I. Askoxylakis, H.C. Pöhls, and J. Posegga (Eds.): WISTP 2012, LNCS 7322, pp. 49–57, 2012.
© IFIP International Federation for Information Processing 2012

EAP-MD5 provides the peer authentication but without mutual authentication, it is prone to attacks as man-in-the-middle (MITM). The shared password between the peer and the authentication server is always chosen by the peer, who prefers to choose a simple and memorable one, as a result, EAP-MD5 is also vulnerable to dictionary attack just like other systems with human memorable passwords.

Our Contributions. We firstly propose an efficient method to break EAP-MD5 by efficiently cracking the shared password.

Based on the length recovery attack to MD4 [15], we apply this kind of attack after minor modification to recover the length of password used in EAP-MD5, with which we can reduce most of the extra costs of length guessing during password cracking.

Further, based on the rainbow table and the chosen challenge attack, we generate a series of rainbow tables using a fixed challenge combined with all password candidates with fixed lengths.

We look up the received response from the corresponding rainbow table to recover the known length password.

This paper is organized as follows. We introduce some preliminaries and background in section two. We present some related work about EAP-MD5 and password cracking in second three. We introduce an efficient password cracking method to EAP-MD5 in detail in section four. We conclude the paper in the last section.

2   Preliminaries

2.1   Brief Description of MD5

MD5 [11,17,7,8] is a typical Merkle-Damgård structure hash function, which takes a variable-length message M as input and outputs a 128-bit hash value. M is first padded to be multiples of 512 bits, a '1' added at the tail of M, followed by '0's until the bit length becomes 448 on modulo 512, finally, the length of the unpadded message M is inserted to the last 64 bits. Let $t = |M'|/512$, the padded M' is further divided into chunks of 512-bit blocks $(M_0, M_1, \ldots, M_{t-1})$.

The MD5 compression function (CF) takes M_i and a 128-bit chaining variable H_i, initialized to H_0, as input, and outputs H_{i+1}. For example, $H_1 = CF_{H_0}(M_0)$, and the hash result of MD5 is computed as (1).

$$\text{MD5}(M) = H_t = CF_{H_{t-1}}(M_{t-1}) \tag{1}$$

However, we omit the details of CF, since it is irrelevan t to this paper, for more details please refer [11].

Padding Rule. For two arbitrary distinct messages M and M', if their lengths $|M| = |M'|$, then, the padding bits of these two messages are just the same. Since

MD5, MD4 and SHA-1 et al. share the same padding procedure, the padding rule is also applicable to them.

Extension Attack. For an unknown message M and the corresponding hash $R = MD5(M)$. With the known length of M, compute the padding bits *pad* for M, then for arbitrary message x, compute the padding bits *pad1* for $M\|pad\|x$, then we can generate the hash value for $M\|pad\|x$ from computing $CF_R(x\|pad1)$, without any knowledge of M except its length.

2.2   EAP-MD5

Extensible Authentication Protocol (EAP) [4] is an authentication framework frequently used in 802.1X wireless networks and PPP connections. EAP provides some common functions and negotiation of authentication methods called EAP methods, such as EAP-MD5.

EAP-MD5 [4] is analogous to CHAP [13]. EAP-MD5 differs from other EAP methods in that it only provides peer authentication.

The authentication of EAP-MD5 in 802.1X network involves three parts, the peer, the wireless access point (WAP, the authenticator) and the RADIUS server (the authentication server). The peer first sends an "EAPoL-start" packet to the WAP, and after then the WAP replies an "EAP-Request/ID" to ask for the peer's ID. After the WAP and RADIUS server both receive the peer's ID, the WAP forwards the EAP-MD5 random challenge string including a 1-byte *id* and a variable length C, sent by the RADIUS server, to the peer. If the response R sent by the peer is valid, then the peer is authorized to use the network, otherwise, reject. At random interval, the server redoes the authentication, by sending different challenges, to limit the time of exposure to any single attack.

The peer authentication process of EAP-MD5 in IEEE 802.1X is shown in Fig. 1.

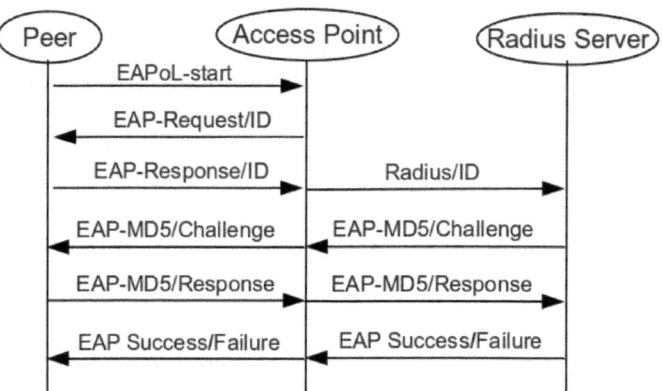

Fig. 1. The peer authentication of EAP-MD5

The response R of EAP-MD5 is calculated with MD5 using a 1-byte session identifier *id* and a challenge C both sent by the authentication server, combined with the shared password P. The calculation is shown in (2), where $||$ means concatenation.

$$R = \text{MD5}(id||P||C) \tag{2}$$

With randomly chosen id and C, EAP-MD5 provides protection against playback attack launched by malicious peer.

3   Related Work

3.1   EAP-MD5-Pass Attack

In 2008, Wright demonstrated that a program utility eapmd5pass [16] could crack the passwords used in EAP-MD5 of the wireless network. The utility includes a eavesdropping and a dictionary attack tools against the EAP-MD5 protocol. However, the successful ratio of eapmd5pass totally depends on the used dictionary and the complexity of the password.

3.2   Rainbow Table

Rainbow tables contain a connection between a hash value and its corresponding password P, for passwords hashed by $H(P)$, where H is a hash function. By having this connection pre-calculated for all possible hash values, a quick search through the table for a desired hash value can reveal the password.

In 1980, Hellman [5] proposed a time-memory trade-off when applying a cryptanalytic attack. Hellman used hash chains, which is time consuming, to decrease the memory requirements. In the way of hash chain, only the first and the last elements of the chain are stored in the memory, which saves memory at the cost of extra cryptanalysis time. Further, additional memory trade-off can be achieved by reducing the hash values to "keys" with the help of a reduction function. Instead of using a single reduction function R, Oechslin [10] suggested using a sequence of related reduction functions R_1 up to R_{k-1}, in 2003. Oechslin called the new chains rainbow chains, and the tables containing these chains rainbow tables. Since then, this method has been widely used and implemented in many popular password recovery tools [2,3,1], to break passwords hashed by the scheme of $h(P)$.

4   Breaking EAP-MD5

Since MD5 and MD4 share the same padding procedure, the length recovery attack to $\text{MD4}(P||C)$ [15] is also applicable to EAP-MD5. After the length of the used password is recovered, we search the corresponding rainbow table for the received response, which is generated by using a pre-chosen challenge. So, we divide the password cracking of EAP-MD5 into two parts, the first is to recover the length of the used password, and the second is to crack the password with already known length, using rainbow table technologies, based on fixed length passwords, and pre-chosen challenges.

4.1   On-Line Length Recovery Attack to EAP-MD5

In the wireless network, we can easily collect enough information, by eavesdropping, about the access point and the peer, such as a pair of (C, R), id, the MAC addresses of both, the user name and SSID of the access point, et al. We can generate faked packets, through masquerading as the access point, and send them to the peer; the peer will take it for granted that the packets are sent from the very access point, for he doesn't authenticate the access point. We omit the role of the authentication server, since it only interacts with the access point WAP.

We implement the length recovery attack to EAP-MD5 with pre-chosen challenge by masquerading as the access point (the authenticator), in the wireless network shown as follows.

1. Pre-choose a fixed id and a fixed challenge C.
2. Eavesdrop from the network and find a communicating pair, a peer and a server (the authenticator, access point). Collect information about them.
3. Masquerade as the server, send the pre-chosen id and C to the peer. Get the corresponding response $R = \mathrm{MD5}(id||P||C)$ from the peer, and reply an affirmative signal.
4. Initiate the length l of the password P with the guessing $l = 1$ character.
5. Generate the padding pad for $id||P||C$ with the guessing length l of the password.
6. Generate $C' = C||pad||r$, where r is a randomly generated string, and send C' with the known id to the peer by masquerading as the access point.
7. Receive R' from the peer, reply an affirmative signal. Generate $pad1$ for C' and check if $R' = \mathrm{CF}_R(r||pad1)$ holds. If so, l is the very length. Otherwise, set $l = l + 1$, go to step 5.

Packet Injection. We send the faked packet with the challenge information C, by masquerading as the access point. Since the peer doesn't authenticate the access point S in EAP-MD5, it will responds any packet from the pretended server S'. Both S and S' will receive response R'. Since S doesn't send C', it will silently discard the response R'. We let the pretending S' reply an affirmative signal to the peer to end this verification session.

To recover the password length l, we need to send $l + 1$ faked packets with different challenges and $l + 1$ packets of affirmation. The time of the length recovery attack to EAP-MD5 is negligible, since the server has full control over the time intervals to send challenge to verify the peer, and the peer will reply any challenge at any time from the claimed server.

4.2   Off-Line Fixed Length Password Cracking with Password Pre-computation

Passwords Pre-computation. We can utilize the security hole that challenges can be sent by unauthenticated server, to launch a password pre-computation cracking. The overall strategy is shown as follows.

1. Passwords pre-computation.
   (a) We first choose a string, satisfying all the restrictions placed on the EAP-MD5 challenges, as a fixed challenge C. And choose a byte as the fixed id.
   (b) Set the length of password candidates be $l = 5$.[1]
   (c) Use the fixed challenge C and the fixed id, we compute the corresponding hash values of all possible passwords Ps with fixed length l in the form of $MD5(id||P||C)$, and resort those results in a rainbow table[2].
   (d) Check if $l = 8$ holds, if so, go to step 2a. Otherwise, set $l = l + 1$, go to step 1c.
2. Break passwords in EAP-MD5.
   (a) Launch an on-line length recovery attack with the fixed challenge C and id. We can immediately get the very length of the user's password, which is discussed in last subsection.
   (b) We look up in the corresponding pre-computed rainbow table, generated in the phase of passwords pre-computation, for the first received response R replying from the peer, according to the already recovered password length. If it hits, we get the peer's very password.

Given a simple example of one password pre-computation attack to EAP-MD5, we choose a string "<jantie_lee@mukouren.com>" as a fixed challenge C. We also choose "x" as the fixed id. There are 95 printable characters to be used as password candidates in total, including digits, punctuations and letters with lower and upper cases. Then for a password with exact six characters, there may be $95^6 \approx 2^{39}$ password candidates. We compute the hash results of $R = MD5(x||P||< jantie\_lee@mukouren.com>)$, using all 2^{39} passwords with six characters in the brute force strategy, and get all corresponding "responses", eventually, then resort these results into a rainbow table.

Finally, we listen to the network and find a communicating pair. We impersonate the server and send the pre-chosen id "x" and the *challenge string* "<jantie_lee@mukouren.com>" to the peer, for recovering his password's length.

After the length of the peer's password is recovered, we look up in the corresponding rainbow table or a common table for the first received response. Obviously, if the peer uses a password with six characters, we can immediately get the very answer, for we have pre-computed all possible passwords.

Response Checking. To check whether a given hash value is in the pre-computed rainbow table, we first generate a chain from this value. For each password that we encounter in the chain, we check to see if it is at the end of the chain. When we find a match, we know that the hash is part of this chain. Thus we generate the complete chain again and get the very password.

The Rainbow Table. We use the rainbow tables to pre-compute all hashes of the possible passwords with fixed lengths, based on the pre-chosen challenge and

---

[1] We can directly generate a table mapping all possible candidates whose lengths are less than 5.

[2] We do not "store" their corresponding hash results, since those results are reduced by the reduction functions.

id. Here, we implement the rainbow table of passwords with six characters, which takes about 3 days to be completed on an ordinary PC with Intel 2.G CPU. The details of complexity of such rainbow table are shown in Table 1, where s means second. We also evaluate the overall complexity of generating rainbow tables of passwords with seven and eight characters, respectively. It seems infeasible to complete the rainbow table of passwords with eight characters on an ordinary PC. However, if utilize the parallelism computing with one thousand PCs, this work can be done soon. More important, an attacker of EAP-MD5 may only want to use the network as a legal user, hence, he needs to break a peer's passwords less than eight characters.

Table 1. The Complexity of Generating the Rainbow Table of MD5($id\|P\|C$)

Char Set	Characters	Passwords Space	Rainbow Table Size	Hit Time
95	8	$95^8 \approx 2^{52}$	576 GB	1108 s
95	7	$95^7 \approx 2^{45}$	64 GB	829 s
95	6	$95^6 \approx 2^{39}$	9 GB	18 s

Overall Complexity. The overall complexity of such attack consists of three parts, the off-line pre-computation, the on-line query and the off-line table looking up. The time of the on-line query is negligible, since we have full control over the time intervals to challenge the peer. The time of the off-line table looking up varies from seconds to minutes. The complexity of the rainbow table pre-computation depends on the chosen length of the passwords and the pre-chosen challenge. Since EAP-MD5 employs human-memorable passwords, it means that we can compute all of the passwords within eight characters to cover most of the ordinary using passwords. Moreover, we point out that once the pre-computations are done, thus rainbow tables can always be reused for this kind of attack. In [16], to crack a password, the repeated dictionary attack must be performed each time. Hence, the attack in [16] is not a reusable one. More important, we will not try to crack passwords with more characters than these in our pre-computed rainbow tables, hence, our attack is a clever one.

Nowadays, the computation technology is dramatically improving, which includes the memory and storage enlargement, CPU processing speed increasing, and the network computing strengthening. Parallel computing allows anybody owning a modern personal computer in a network to break such cryptographic systems, which were believed to be secure.

5 Conclusion

In this paper, we propose an efficient and universal way to break EAP-MD5. We first recover the length of the used password by on-line queries, and then we apply the advantage of rainbow table to crack the known length password off-line. Though the 802.1X wireless network may not use this authentication method any more, the operating systems supporting EAP-MD5 are vulnerable to this kind of attack. This attack is also applicable even the underlying hash function of EAP-MD5 is replaced with SHA-1 or even SHA-2, since these hash functions share the same padding rule and have the same weakness.

Acknowledgement. We thank the anonymous reviewers for their valuable comments. This work was partially supported by the program "Core Electronic Devices, High-end General Purpose Chips and Basic Software Products" in China (No. 2010ZX01037-001-001), and supported by the 973 program of China under contract 2007CB311202, and by National Science Foundation of China through the 61070228 project.

References

1. OphCrack, `http://ophcrack.sourceforge.net/`
2. Rainbow Tables, `http://rainbowtables.shmoo.com/`
3. RainbowCrack, `http://project-rainbowcrack.com/`
4. Aboba, B., Blunk, L., Vollbrecht, J., Carlson, J., Levkowetz, H.: Extensible Authentication Protocol (EAP). RFC 3748 (Proposed Standard) (June 2004), `http://www.ietf.org/rfc/rfc3748.txt`, (updated by RFC 5247)
5. Hellman, M.: A cryptanalytic time-memory trade-off. IEEE Transactions on Information Theory 26(4), 401–406 (1980)
6. IEEE: IEEE 802.1x: IEEE Standards for Local and Metropolitan Area Networks: Port based Network Access Control (2001)
7. Liu, F.: On the security of digest access authentication. In: Proc. 14th IEEE Int. Conf. on Computational Science and Engineering, CSE 2011 and 11th Int. Symp. on Pervasive Systems, Algorithms, and Networks, I-SPAN 2011 and 10th IEEE Int. Conf. on IUCC 2011, pp. 427–434 (2011)
8. Liu, F., Liu, Y., Xie, T.: Fast Password Recovery Attack: Application to APOP. Cryptology ePrint Archive, Report 2011/248 (2011), `http://eprint.iacr.org/`
9. Liu, F., Xie, T., Feng, Y., Feng, D.: On the Security of PPPoE Network. Security and Communication Networks, p. n/a (2012), `http://dx.doi.org/10.1002/sec.512`
10. Oechslin, P.: Making a Faster Cryptanalytic Time-Memory Trade-Off. In: Boneh, D. (ed.) CRYPTO 2003. LNCS, vol. 2729, pp. 617–630. Springer, Heidelberg (2003)
11. Rivest, R.: The MD5 Message-Digest Algorithm. RFC 1321 (Informational) (April 1992), `http://www.ietf.org/rfc/rfc1321.txt` (updated by RFC 6151)
12. Simpson, W.: The Point-to-Point Protocol (PPP). RFC 1661 (Standard) (July 1994), `http://www.ietf.org/rfc/rfc1661.txt` (updated by RFC 2153)
13. Simpson, W.: PPP Challenge Handshake Authentication Protocol (CHAP). RFC 1994 (Draft Standard) (August 1996), `http://www.ietf.org/rfc/rfc1994.txt` (updated by RFC 2484)

14. Tsudik, G.: Message authentication with one-way hash functions. SIGCOMM Comput. Commun. Rev. 22, 29–38 (1992)
15. Wang, L., Ohta, K., Kunihiro, N.: Password recovery attack on authentication protocol MD4 (Password||Challenge). In: Proceedings of the 2008 ACM Symposium on Information, Computer and Communications Security, ASIACCS 2008, pp. 3–9. ACM, New York (2008)
16. Wright, J.: EAPMD5PASS-AUDITING EAP-MD5 (2003),
    http://www.willhackforsushi.com
17. Xie, T., Liu, F., Feng, D.: Could The 1-MSB Input Difference Be The Fastest Collision Attack For MD5?. Cryptology ePrint Archive, Report 2008/391 (2008),
    http://eprint.iacr.org/

Privacy Preserving Social Network Publication on Bipartite Graphs

Jian Zhou*, Jiwu Jing, Ji Xiang, and Lei Wang

The State Key Laboratory of Information Security,
Graduate University of Chinese Academy of Sciences, China
{jzhou,jing,jixiang,lwang}@is.ac.cn

Abstract. In social networks, some data may come in the form of bipartite graphs, where properties of nodes are public while the associations between two nodes are private and should be protected. When publishing the above data, in order to protect privacy, we propose to adopt the idea generalizing the graphs to super-nodes and super-edges. We investigate the problem of how to preserve utility as much as possible and propose an approach to partition the nodes in the process of generalization. Our approach can give privacy guarantees against both static attacks and dynamic attacks, and at the same time effectively answer aggregate queries on published data.

Keywords: data publishing, privacy preservation, bipartite graph, generalization.

1 Introduction

Due to the rapid growth in the number of services and applications that leverage social networks, privacy in social networks becomes a serious concern, particularly when social network data is published. Recently, there have been many works devoting to the privacy preserving publication of social network data.

Among these works, [1] studied a particular type of network data that can be modeled as bipartite graphs: there are two types of entities, and an association only exists between two entities of different types. One typical example is customers and products bought from a pharmacy. The association between two nodes is considered to be private and needs to be protected while properties of entities are public. For example, the set of customers of a pharmacy may not be considered particularly sensitive, and the set of products which it sells may also be public knowledge. However, the set of products bought by a particular customer is considered private, and should not be revealed.

Rather than masking or altering the graph structure, their methodology focuses on masking the mapping from entities to nodes. The approach not only

---

* This work was supported by National Natural Science Foundation of China (Grant No. 70890084/G021102, and 61003274) and Knowledge Innovation Program of Chinese Academy of Sciences (Grant No. YYYJ-1013).

I. Askoxylakis, H.C. Pöhls, and J. Posegga (Eds.): WISTP 2012, LNCS 7322, pp. 58–70, 2012.
© IFIP International Federation for Information Processing 2012

ensures the privacy is protected, but also allows a wide variety of ad hoc analyses and novel valid uses of the data. More details about the work of [1] are described in Section 2.

However, their approach only performs well against *static attacks*, where the adversary solely uses the published data. In *dynamic attacks* where the adversary has some background knowledge such as existing associations or degrees of nodes, privacy issues may arise.

Following the work of [1], we propose an improved approach to publish an anonymized version of a given bipartite graph via generalization. Our work and contributions include:

- We investigate how to measure and optimize the utility when generalizing social network data that can be modeled as a bipartite graph.
- We propose an approach to partition the nodes in order to preserve as much utility as possible under a given level of privacy.
- In order to identify our approach, we compare it with the naive one called *Simple Generalization*. Although both maintain privacy against static attacks and dynamic attacks, our approach can answer a broad class of queries more accurately. All experiments are carried out with real social network data.

The remainder of the paper is organized as follows: in Section 2 we introduce some important notions. In Section 3 we investigate how to optimize utility and propose our approach. In Section 4, we demonstrate our approach by experimental study using some real social network data. In Section 5, we introduce some related works. At last, in Section 6 we make a conclusion and discuss some open problems.

2   Preliminaries

The social network data we investigate are those that can be represented in the form of large, sparse bipartite graphs G = (V,W,E). That is, the bipartite graph G consists of $|V|$ nodes of one type, $|W|$ nodes of a second type, and a set of $|E|$ edges $E \subseteq V \times W$. 'Sparse' indicates the edges account for a tiny portion of all possible ones, which holds in many real social networks. We want to protect the associations between nodes rather than the information of nodes themselves. For example, in Figure 2, information such as C1 is a 26-year-old male or P2 is an OTC drug is public knowledge. In contrast, information such as C1 bought P2 is considered to be sensitive. Thus, the final published data should guarantee those sensitive information can't be deduced. As in prior work, we are only concerned with attacks making positive inferences rather than those making negative inferences. For example, it is not allowed that an adversary could deduce C1 bought P2, but we don't guarantee the information such as C1 did not buy P1 is protected. Meanwhile, there is another requirement the published data should satisfy: it can be utilized for analyzing or mining. In our scenario, it should be able to answer a broad class of queries based on standard SQL aggregates (sum, count, avg, min, max) with relatively acceptant bias. In [1], the author listed three typical types of queries with increasing complexity.

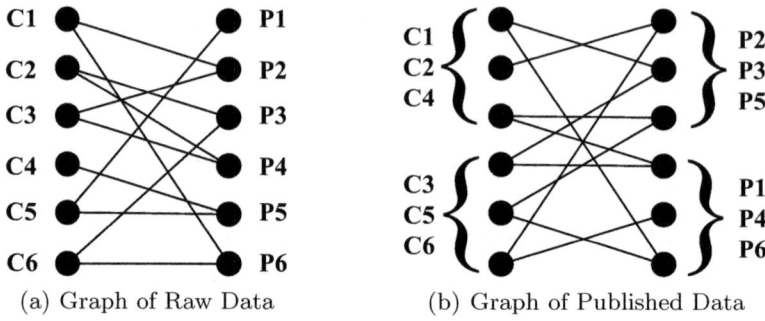

(a) Graph of Raw Data   (b) Graph of Published Data

Fig. 1. Safe Grouping

- Type 0 - Graph structure only: compute an aggregate over all neighbors of nodes in V that satisfy some P_n (i.e., predicates over solely graph properties of nodes).
  E.g.: Count the average number of products bought by each customer.
- Type 1 - Attribute predicate on one side only: Compute an aggregate for nodes in V satisfying P_a (i.e., predicates over attributes of the entities); Compute an aggregate on edges to nodes in V satisfying P_n from nodes in W satisfying P_a.
  E.g.: Find the average number of male customers buying only a single product.
- Type 2 - Attribute predicate on both sides: Compute an aggregate for nodes in V satisfying P_a to nodes in W satisfying P_a'.
  E.g.: Find total number of OTC products bought by customers aged from 20 to 30.

A novel approach is proposed in [1] to anonymize the data. As illustrated in Figure 1, they partition nodes into groups but preserve the structure of the graph exactly. Thus analysis principally based on the graph structure is correct. On the other hand, privacy is ensured because given a group of nodes, there is a secret mapping from these nodes to the corresponding group of entities. It is impossible for an adversary to learn, within a group, which node corresponds to which entity solely based on the published data. A (k, l)-grouping means that V is split into size k groups, W into size l groups. It is convenient to offer a tradeoff between privacy and utility by setting the values of k and l.

However, if we just simply group the nodes, an adversary may be able to deduce some associations due to the uniformly dense interaction pattern between two groups. E.g., if a published graph happens to contain complete subgraph between group $\{v1, v2, v3\}$ and group $\{w1, w2, w3\}$, an adversary can immediately infer all the connections between these six nodes. In order to avoid such attacks caused by lack of diversity [2], the notion of *safe grouping* is proposed. Denote by H the function mapping nodes into groups, we say H_V is a safe grouping of V if it satisfies:

$$\forall v_i \neq v_j \in V : H_V(v_i) = H_V(v_j) \Rightarrow \nexists w \in W : (v_i, w) \in E \wedge (v_j, w) \in E$$

A (k, l)-grouping is safe if both H_V and H_W are safe groupings. Intuitively, for either type of nodes, a safe grouping ensures any two nodes in the same group have no common neighbors of the other type. Safe grouping not only ensures a level of sparsity between groups, but also restricts the pattern of allowed links. The author proved that based on the anonymized data via safe groupings, an adversary can make a correct inference with the probability no more than $1/max(k, l)$.

A greedy algorithm which we called *Simple Safe Grouping* is also provided to find safe groupings in practice in [1]. In order to find a safe k-grouping of V, for each node $v \in V$ in turn, the algorithm tries to find the first existing group that satisfies: first, the number of nodes in it is fewer than k; second, the condition of safety won't be breached when v joins. If such a group is successfully found, add v to it. Otherwise, a new group is started, containing v alone. After processing all nodes, there may be a few groups with fewer than k nodes. The algorithm collects those nodes together, increases the allowed group size by one, and begins the next round. The algorithm continues until each node is placed in a group with the size no less than k or some large group size is reached. The process of finding a safe l-grouping of W is the same as V, and they are totally independent. Although this method is possible to fail, it is easy to find safe groupings for those sparse bipartite graphs.

3   Bipartite Graph Generalization

3.1   Motivation

Although the approach described in Section 2 is resilient to static attacks, where the adversary tries to deduce explicit associations solely by analyzing the published information. However, in dynamic attack models where an adversary already knows some background knowledge, he may be able to identify the relevant nodes, and further infer additional associations. Background knowledge may be available through sources external to the released data or obtained by intruding into the network. For example, considering the published data shown in Figure 2, the adversary is able to identify the nodes using various background knowledge. Note that dashed lines represent edges to other groups, which do not affect this example.

– *learned link attack*: If the adversary learns C1 bought P2, he can use the fact that there is only one edge between the group of C1 and the group of P2 to identify C1 and P2 with nodes in the anonymized graph. This attack is also discussed in [1]. Although the author proved that their approach could mitigate the damage, it still suffers from such attack.

– *learned degree attack*: If the adversary learns C4 bought 3 products meaning
the degree of C4 is 3, which is unique in the group of C4, he can easily
identity C4 with the node representing it.

So, if the adversary learns C1 bought P2 and C4 bought 3 products, he can
infer that C4 bought P2, no matter how many other nodes are in the groups.
In fact, any structural background information can be possibly leveraged by the
adversary to compromise the privacy. The adversary can easily de-anonymize a
node with a unique subgraph around it.

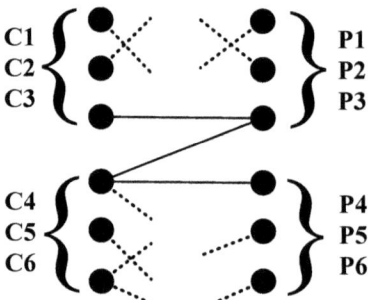

Fig. 2. Attack Examples

In order to preclude such attacks, we consider the generalization technique,
which partitions nodes and edges into groups called super-nodes and super-edges.
Compared with [1], we only release the number of edges between each subset
instead of the full edge information. Using the generalization technique, it is
impossible for the adversary to distinguish between individuals in the same group
even he has some structural background knowledge. For a super-node containing
k nodes, the probability of any one being the target is at most $1/k$. As described
in Section 2, in order to defend against the attacks caused by lack of diversity, we
should still follow the condition of safety such that for a (k, l)-grouping there are
at most $min(k, l)$ edges between two groups. For a super-node containing at least
k nodes, as the probability of any one node being the target is at most $1/k$, which
has been proved in [3], the probability of correctly guessing the existence of an
edge in the original data is bounded by $min(k, l)/kl = 1/max(k, l)$. Therefore,
the privacy is guaranteed against powerful dynamic attacks, let alone static
attacks.

In detail, generalization approaches can be divided into two steps: first, partition the nodes into groups; second, merge grouped nodes into super-nodes and
incident edges into super-edges, then give each an aggregate description. In our
approach, each super-node is labeled with all information of nodes in it and
each super-edge is labeled with the number of edges between two super-nodes.
Step two is quite simple and direct, so the core of generalization is how to partition the nodes in order to retain utility. A natural method is to use Simple

Safe Grouping. However, this greedy algorithm is aim to find a safe grouping as quickly as possible. In fact, for a sparse bipartite graph, there are many possible safe groupings and our target is to find such one that the loss of utility is as little as possible after generalization.

3.2 Algorithm Description

First of all, we should provide an approach to measure utility. We adopt the same method as [3] which evaluates utility by possible worlds. Possible worlds are those consistent with the data published. A possible world could be interpreted as an input that will result in the anonymization being produced. Assuming that all possible worlds are treated equally, the smaller the size of possible worlds introduced via generalization is, the better the utility is.

From the perspective of a single safe group G_i with k_i nodes in it, if G_i connects to n groups of the other type and the number of edges between them is $c_{i1}, c_{i2}, \ldots, c_{in}$ respectively, because each node in G_i has at most one edge to another group of the other type, the size of possible worlds induced by G_i is:

$$|W(G_i)| = \prod_{j=1}^{n} \binom{k_i}{c_{ij}}$$

Note that in our work we are only concerned with structural configurations and consider two isomorphic possible worlds as different ones, which is also implied by [3]. Therefore, in order to reduce the size of possible worlds, for any safe group g, we propose two rules:

- **R1**: The number of groups that g connects to should be minimized.
- **R2**: Under the precondition of R1, the number of edges between two groups should be either maximized or minimized.

Due to the symmetric property, in order to better find safe groupings consistent with $R1$ and $R2$, we only consider (k, k)-groupings in our work. Figure 3 illustrates the ideal safe grouping, where for any two safe groups, the number

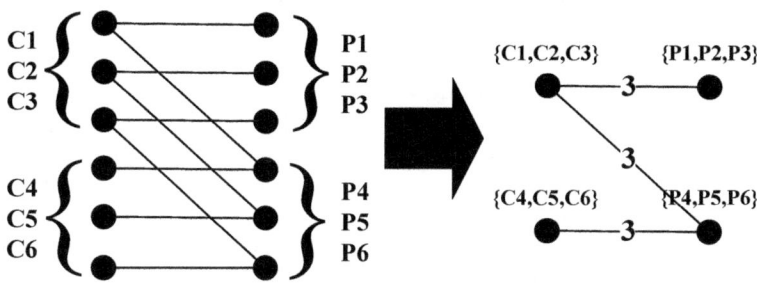

Fig. 3. Ideal Safe Grouping

of edges between them is either zero or maximum. In this ideal situation, the process of merging edges doesn't introduce any additional possible worlds. However, in most cases, this ideal safe grouping doesn't exist. Instead, based on $R1$ and $R2$, we propose an improved safe grouping algorithm to partition nodes.

Algorithm 1: ImprovedSafeGrouping

    Input: $G = (V, W, E), k$

1 **begin**

2   Sort V by degree in descending order

3      $VG \leftarrow$ Find a Safe Grouping of V

4   **foreach** $w \in W$ **do**

5         $VG_W(w) \leftarrow \{vg \in VG | \exists v \in vg : (v, w) \in E\}$

6   **end**

7      $WG \leftarrow \varnothing; RC \leftarrow \varnothing; C \leftarrow W$

8   **while** $|C| > 0$ **do**

9         $c \leftarrow$ select the one with the maximum degree from C

10        $wg \leftarrow \varnothing \cup c$ /*Create a new group*/

11        $C \leftarrow C - c$

12   **for** $i \leftarrow 0$ *to* $k - 1$ **do**

13           $c \leftarrow SelectGroupMember(G, VG, wg, C)$

14   **if** $c = \varnothing$ **then** break;

15           $wg \leftarrow wg \cup c$

16           $C \leftarrow C - c$

17   **end**

18   **if** $|wg| < k$ **then** $RC \leftarrow RC \cup \{w \in wg\}$

19   **else** $WG \leftarrow WG \cup wg$

20   **end**

21   **while** $|RC| > 0$ **do**

22   **foreach** $wg \in WG$ **do**

23           $c \leftarrow SelectGroupMember(G, VG, wg, RC)$

24           $wg \leftarrow wg \cup c$

25           $RC \leftarrow RC - c$

26   **end**

27   **end**

28 **end**

For a bipartite graph $G = (V, W, E)$, we first sort V by degree in descending order before finding a safe grouping because of two reasons: first, putting nodes with similar degree in one group are more likely to lead to less super-edges in generalized graph, which is helpful to reduce the number of groups involved to form possible worlds; second, sorting by node degree will greatly improve accuracy on queries involving node degree as illustrated in [1]. Then we partition V into groups VG using Simple Safe Grouping. Because of the symmetry, it is also available to deal with W first. In our work, we first partition the type of nodes with less number as this provides more opportunity to construct better groups of the other type. When the number is approximate, we can randomly

---

Algorithm 2: SelectGroupMember

Input: $G = (V, W, E), VG(/*\text{groups of V}*/)$, wg (/*a temporary group of
W*/) , C (/*nodes not processed*/)

Output: c (/*the node selected to insert into wg*)

1 **begin**
2      $SC \leftarrow \{c \in C | \nexists v \in V, w \in wg : (v, w) \in E \wedge (v, c) \in E\}$ /*Obtain
Candidates*/
3   **if** $|SC| = 0$ **then return** $\varnothing$
4   **foreach** $c \in SC$ **do**
5          $weight(c) \leftarrow 0$
6   **foreach** $vg \in \{g \in VG | \exists v \in g : (v, c) \in E\}$ **do**
7              $x \leftarrow |\{a \in wg | vg \in VG_W(a)\}|$
8   **if** $x > 0$ **then**
9                  $weight(c) \leftarrow weight(c) + 1 + \delta(x)$
10   **else**
11                 $weight(c) \leftarrow weight(c) - 1$
12   **end**
13   **end**
14     $c \leftarrow$ select the one with the maximum weight from SC
15   **return** c
16 **end**

---

choose one type. Next, we partition W according to VG. This is the crucial difference between our approach and the original one. The original algorithm deals with V and W in the same way and they are totally independent from each other, while in our algorithm, the result of partitioning W is influenced by VG. The process of partition W is described as follows:

1. Create a new group.
2. Pick nodes satisfying the condition of safety to fill the group until its size reaches k or there is no candidate. On each turn, the node is picked according to VG and those already picked.
3. Repeat step 1 and step 2 until all nodes in W have been processed.

The key point when partitioning W is how to pick nodes to fill a new group. In most cases, there are quite a lot of nodes satisfying the condition of safety and we should try to pick those who connect to the same set of VG as much as possible. We first pick the node with the maximum degree from the candidate list to add to a new group g. We deal with the nodes with higher degree first because they have more important affects on utility. We then record the groups that g has already connected to as $VG_{WG}(g)$ and depend on it to assign each candidate a weight indicating the priority it should be picked. Denote by $VG_W(w)$ the groups the node w connects to, the weight of a candidate c can be expressed by $weight(c) = \sum_{vg \in VG_W(c)} (\sigma(c, vg) + \delta(c, vg))$, where $\sigma(c, vg)$ is consistent with $R1$ and $\delta(c, vg)$ is consistent with $R2$. For each group vg in $VG_W(c)$, we in turn test whether it occurs in $VG_{WG}(g)$. If the answer is yes, the value of

$\sigma(c, vg)$ is set to 1, implying that we don't need to introduce an additional group. Otherwise it is set to -1. In fact, $\sum \sigma(c, vg)$ can be seen as the overlap degree between $VG_W(c)$ and $VG_{WG}(g)$. On the other hand, $\delta(c, vg)$ could be any function that increases with the increase of the number of edges between vg and g, and satisfies $|\sum \delta(c, vg)| < 1$, which ensures $R1$ precedes $R2$. The introduction of $\delta(c, vg)$ makes the scheme prefer to form a dense connection and a sparse connection rather than two average connections. On each turn, we pick the one with the maximum weight to add to the group. Then, we update weights of all candidates and continue.

After processing all nodes in W, there may also be some groups with fewer than k nodes in it. We collect them together and deal with them by expanding the allowed group size, which is similar to the original algorithm. However, those nodes are quite few when bipartite graphs are sparse enough and we can try to place them in the groups with as few edges as possible. Therefore, although there may be some groups whose size is $k + 1$ or even $k + 2$, the effect on utility is negligible.

From the perspective of object processed, the original algorithm deals with nodes in turn while we deal with groups in turn. In the original algorithm, the author tries to place a given node in some group. Different from it, in our algorithm, we are given a group, and try to fill it with some nodes. So our algorithm provides an opportunity to form a desired group not only satisfying the condition of safety but also retaining the data utility as much as possible.

4   Experimental Study

4.1   Experimental Framework

In order to demonstrate the efficacy of our approach, we perform our experiments on two real social network data sets that can be represented by bipartite graphs. The first data set (HEP-Th) presents information on papers in theoretical high-energy physics, which is derived from the abstract and citation files provided for the 2003 KDD Cup competition and could be retrieved from `http://kdl.cs.umass.edu/databases/hepth-data.xml.gz`. The data set contains $|V| = 9,200$ distinct authors, $|W| = 29,555$ distinct papers and $|E| = 58,515$ edges. The second data set (Epinions) is collected by Paolo Massa in a 5-week crawl from the shopping web site Epinions.com [4]. Because the original data set is rather huge, we extracted part of it, which contains $|V| = 1,000$ distinct customers, $|W| = 8,477$ distinct products and $|E| = 12,522$ edges.

As in prior work, there are too many possible queries on bipartite graphs. In order to efficiently evaluate the utility of the anonymized data, we specifically study the accuracy of three sample queries with different properties, which is the same as [1]. The three queries are:

- **Query A**: Find the average number of papers of any author satisfying predicate P_a. This is a type-1 query with an attribute predicate only. We vary the selectivity of P_a from 0.1 to 0.9. Higher selectivity means fewer eligible nodes.

- **Query B**: Find the total number of single author papers satisfying P_a. This is also a type-1 query with both attribute predicates and structural predicates. The selectivity of P_a is varied as above.
- **Query C**: Find the total number of papers satisfying P_a having authors who satisfy P'_a. This is a type-2 query. We vary the selectivity of both P_a and P'_a.

Given a predicate, whether a node is qualified is synthetic in our work. Meanwhile, we assume those eligible ones are uniform distributed. We do not introduce any type-0 queries because the results of type-0 queries are usually single values. In fact, a typical type-0 query can be regarded as a special case of Query A when P_a equals 1.0. So the results of Query A are enough to evaluate the accuracy of type-0 queries by the trends.

We use the approach called *Sampling Consistent Graphs* [5] to answer these queries on anonymized data. The approach randomly samples a graph that is consistent with the anonymized data, and uses this sample to perform the analysis. One could repeat this several times to get an approximate expected answer. To clearly show the trends, we repeat each experiment over ten random choices of predicates and extract ten samples from each anonymized data. For each query, if the correct answer on original data is Q and the expected answer on anonymized data is u, we are able to calculate the expected error $|u - Q|/Q$. We use this expected error to precisely evaluate utility. Smaller values of the expected error indicate better utility.

4.2 Experimental Results

We compare our approach called *Improved Generalization* with *Simple Generalization* that first partitions the nodes using Simple Safe Grouping and then aggregates nodes and edges. Figure 4 and Figure 5 plot the expected error vs. selectivity of P_a under the two approaches, respectively on the HEP-Th data set and the Epinions data set. In these figures, we perform the approaches using a $(10, 10)$ safe grouping. When using other appropriate values of group size, there are a few differences, however, the trends are the same.

Both Improved Generalization and Simple Generalization are robust against static attacks and dynamic attacks as described in 3.1. In other words, they

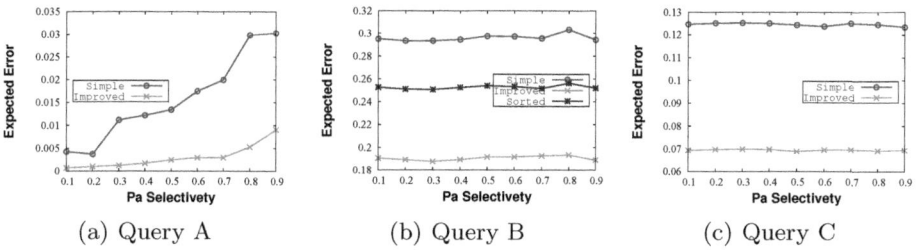

(a) Query A   (b) Query B   (c) Query C

Fig. 4. Expected Error on HEP-Th

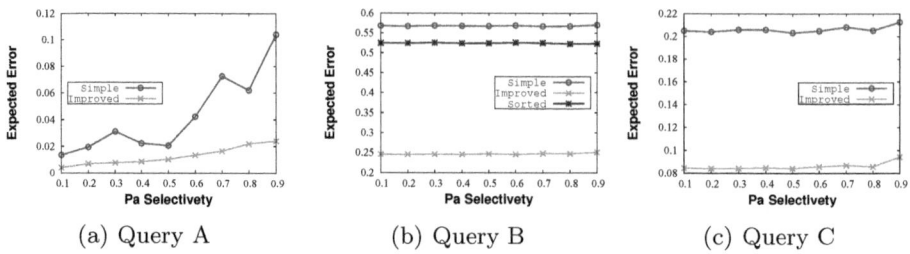

Fig. 5. Expected Error on Epinions

guarantee the same level of privacy. However, the utility of our approach is much better than Simple Generalization, as shown in Figure 4 and Figure 5, and the accuracy of answering queries is almost doubled. Because query B involves a structural predicate, sorting the data by degree before finding a safe grouping is helpful to answer such queries. So we also compare our approach with the sorted one that first sorts nodes by degree in descending order, then performs Simple Generalization. In fact, in Algorithm 1, we also sort V in the beginning. It can be seen from Figure 4(b) and Figure 5(b) that our approach still performs better. For Query C, the selectivity of P'_a is set to 0.5. Experimental results for other values of P'_a are similar. Particularly, the expected error using Improved Generalization is bounded by 0.25 in our experiments, which is accurate enough for most analyses.

5   Related Work

In recent years, there have been many works trying to anonymize and publish social network data under various scenarios, which should guarantee both privacy and utility. Generally speaking, the approaches of preserving privacy in social networks can be divided into three categories. One is K-anonymity [6] privacy preservation [3, 7–9], which ensures in the anonymized graph there are at least k nodes indistinguishable with each other in terms of some types of structural patterns. Another approach is edge randomization [10–12] where the privacy is protected in a probabilistic manner. This approach modifies graph structure by randomly adding/deleting edges or switching edges on the premise of preserving certain aggregate characteristics. These works all focus on simple graphs and need to modify the graph structure via a sequence of edge deletions and additions.

Different from the above two approaches, the generalization approach we adopt in our work simply groups nodes and edges. The idea of generalization was previously proposed in anonymizing tabular data and was adopted by [5] and [3] respectively to anonymize rich interaction graphs and simple graphs, which is different from our work. Moreover, [5] just simply partitioned the nodes into groups without considering the problem of how to improve utility. [3] searched the approximate optimal partitioning using simulated annealing [13]. However, we require additional structure of the partitions to ensure safe groupings.

Besides, there are some works investigating how to publish social network data that can be represented by some interesting graph models, which usually contain much richer information in addition to the simple graph structure. [14] considered the graphs, in which there are multiple types of edges but only one type of nodes and edges are classified as either sensitive or non-sensitive. The author proposed a greedy algorithm to construct anonymous graphs, which can protect privacy of the sensitive relationships while are still useful. Different from most ongoing works focusing on un-weighted social networks, [15] and [16] studied the situations where the network edges as well as the corresponding weights are considered to be private.

6 Conclusion and Discussion

When publishing social network data on bipartite graphs, in order to make it resilient against both static attacks and dynamic attacks, we propose to anonymize the data based on the idea of generalization. We investigate how to measure and optimize the utility and then propose an approach to produce the published data. Compared with the Simple Generalization approach, our approach improves utility greatly.

In our algorithm, we first partition nodes of one type using Simple Safe Grouping, and then partition nodes of the other type according to the result. We also consider the method that constructs a group of V and a group of W in turn. However, the weight of a candidate indicating how much utility it preserves is hard to evaluate. From the perspective of efficiency, our approach needs to calculate the weight of each candidate every time a new group member is to be picked, so our approach is less efficient than Simple Generalization and is time-consuming when the social network contains a large amount of nodes. However, it can be seen as a tradeoff between algorithm efficiency and utility. Moreover, utility is paid much more attention in most cases when publishing social network data.

References

1. Cormode, G., Srivastava, D., Yu, T., Zhang, Q.: Anonymizing bipartite graph data using safe groupings. The VLDB Journal 19, 115–139 (2010)
2. Machanavajjhala, A., Kifer, D., Gehrke, J., Venkitasubramaniam, M.: l-diversity: Privacy beyond k-anonymity. ACM Transactions on Knowledge Discovery from Data (TKDD) 1, 3 (2007)
3. Hay, M., Miklau, G., Jensen, D., Towsley, D., Li, C.: Resisting structural re-identification in anonymized social networks. The VLDB Journal 19, 797–823 (2010)
4. Massa, P., Avesani, P.: Trust-aware bootstrapping of recommender systems. In: ECAI, vol. 6, pp. 29–33. Citeseer (2006)

5. Bhagat, S., Cormode, G., Krishnamurthy, B., Srivastava, D.: Class-based graph anonymization for social network data. Proceedings of the VLDB Endowment 2, 766–777 (2009)
6. Sweeney, L.: k-anonymity: A model for protecting privacy. International Journal on Uncertainty Fuzziness and Knowledgebased Systems 10, 557–570 (2002)
7. Zhou, B., Pei, J.: Preserving privacy in social networks against neighborhood attacks. In: Proceedings of the 2008 IEEE 24th International Conference on Data Engineering, pp. 506–515. IEEE Computer Society, Washington, DC (2008)
8. Zou, L., Chen, L., Özsu, M.T.: k-automorphism: a general framework for privacy preserving network publication. Proc. VLDB Endow. 2, 946–957 (2009)
9. Cheng, J., Fu, A., Liu, J.: K-isomorphism: privacy preserving network publication against structural attacks. In: Proceedings of the 2010 International Conference on Management of Data, pp. 459–470. ACM (2010)
10. Hanhijärvi, S., Garriga, G.C., Puolamäki, K.: Randomization techniques for graphs. In: Proceedings of the 9th SIAM International Conference on Data Mining, SDM 2009, pp. 780–791 (2009)
11. Ying, X., Wu, X.: Randomizing social networks: a spectrum preserving approach. In: SDM, 739–750 (2008)
12. Ying, X., Wu, X.: Graph generation with prescribed feature constraints. In: SDM, pp. 966–977 (2009)
13. Russell, S., Norvig, P.: Artificial intelligence: A modern approach. Section15 (2003)
14. Zheleva, E., Getoor, L.: Preserving the Privacy of Sensitive Relationships in Graph Data. In: Bonchi, F., Malin, B., Saygın, Y. (eds.) PInKDD 2007. LNCS, vol. 4890, pp. 153–171. Springer, Heidelberg (2008)
15. Liu, L., Wang, J., Liu, J., Zhang, J.: Privacy preservation in social networks with sensitive edge weights. In: 2009 SIAM International Conference on Data Mining (SDM 2009), Sparks, Nevada, pp. 954–965 (2009)
16. Das, S., Egecioglu, Ö., El Abbadi, A.: Anonymizing edge-weighted social network graphs. Computer Science, UC Santa Barbara, Tech. Rep. CS-2009-03 (2009)

Privacy Bubbles: User-Centered Privacy Control for Mobile Content Sharing Applications

Delphine Christin[1], Pablo Sánchez López[1], Andreas Reinhardt[2], Matthias Hollick[1], and Michaela Kauer[3]

[1] Secure Mobile Networking Lab, Technische Universität Darmstadt
Mornewegstr. 32, 64293 Darmstadt, Germany
`firstname.lastname@seemoo.tu-darmstadt.de`
[2] Multimedia Communications Lab, Technische Universität Darmstadt
Rundeturmstr. 10, 64283 Darmstadt, Germany
`andreas.reinhardt@kom.tu-darmstadt.de`
[3] Institute of Ergonomics, Technische Universität Darmstadt
Petersenstr. 30, 64287 Darmstadt, Germany
`kauer@iad.tu-darmstadt.de`

Abstract. A continually increasing number of pictures and videos is shared in online social networks. Current sharing platforms however only offer limited options to define who has access to the content. Users may either share it with individuals or groups from their social graph, or make it available to the general public. Sharing content with users to which no social ties exist, even if they were physically close to the places where content was created and witnessed the same event, is however not supported by most existing platforms. We thus propose a novel approach to share content with such users based on so-called *privacy bubbles*. Privacy bubbles metaphorically represent the private sphere of the users and automatically confine the access to the content generated by the bubble creator to people within the bubble. Bubbles extend in both time and space, centered around the collection time and place, and their size can be adapted to the user's preferences. We confirm the user acceptance of our concept through a user study with 175 participants, and a prototype implementation shows the technical feasibility of our scheme.

1 Introduction

In recent years, the public interest for online social media has continuously increased and led to an unprecedented amount of content generated and shared by users. Picture and video sharing has become particularly popular, as shown by the estimated 135,800 pictures uploaded every minute to Facebook [1] and the approximated 48 hours of video shared on YouTube every minute [4]. In existing sharing platforms, users protect their privacy by confining the access to the uploaded content based on social distance. For example, users can share pictures with individuals, friends, friends of friends, or everyone on Facebook. The assumption behind this relationship-based access control is that the stronger the social tie between users, the lower the expected threat to their privacy. As a

I. Askoxylakis, H.C. Pöhls, and J. Posegga (Eds.): WISTP 2012, LNCS 7322, pp. 71–86, 2012.
© IFIP International Federation for Information Processing 2012

result, sharing content with individuals or a group of persons to which no social ties exist is virtually impossible in existing platforms.

Let us however assume that two persons (Alice and Bob), who do not have any kind of social relationship to each other, attend the same event, e.g., a soccer match, a party, or a sightseeing tour. Using state-of-the-art solutions, Alice can only share the pictures she took with members of her social network or make them public. However, she cannot share them with Bob since they have no social ties. Sharing pictures with Bob may not pose a threat to Alice's privacy, though: both are likely to have observed the same scenes, because they have been to the same place concurrently. In this case, the perceived threat to Alice's privacy depends on the physical distance between Alice and Bob at the time the content was created as well as the time difference between Alice's and Bob's observations. If we further assume that Alice and Bob were situated close to each other, Alice might not feel that her privacy is endangered by sharing her pictures with Bob, while Bob can benefit from Alice's pictures.

We propose the use of *privacy bubbles* as a novel approach, which directly targets the aforementioned scenario, i.e., sharing content with strangers in a controlled manner. Note that our approach does not attempt to replace existing relationship-based access control mechanisms, but complements them by adopting a perspective which has received very little attention in the past. In order to share pictures with people in their physical vicinity, users create a privacy bubble by determining its radius and duration. The created privacy bubble is centered around the user and metaphorically represents his/her private sphere. The bubble sets spatiotemporal boundaries within which others users are granted access to the content created in the bubble. In particular, the radius of the bubble represents the maximal physical distance between the content creator and other users authorized to access the content. The duration of the bubble represents the maximal temporal difference between the time of capture and the presence of other users within the radius of the bubble. Users can customize both parameters depending on their privacy preferences. The smaller the radius and duration, the better the privacy protection. Note that users can still control which content is shared in the bubble. The access to content in the privacy bubbles of other users is transparently managed by the application. The applicability of the proposed concept is not confined to sharing pictures, and can easily be extended to additional user-generated contents such as video or audio recordings.

Our contributions can be summarized as follows:

1. We propose the concept of privacy bubbles, which enables sharing pictures between users having no social ties in a controlled manner.
2. We evaluate the viability of our concept by means of a user study involving 175 participants. Our evaluation focuses on: (1) the comprehensiveness of the concept, (2) the provided degree of user control, (3) the estimated management overhead, and (4) the user acceptance. We validate design drivers and design alternatives for the realization of privacy bubbles against the results of our user study.

3. We present our proof-of-concept implementation of the privacy bubble concept, which takes the findings of our user study into account.

The paper is organized as follows. We explain the operation of the privacy bubbles using an example in Section 2 and describe the underlying concept in Section 3. In Section 4, we present the modalities and findings of our user study. We
provide details about our prototype implementation in Section 5 and list possible future extensions to our concept in Section 6. After summarizing existing
work in Section 7, we make concluding remarks in Section 8.

2   Application Scenario

Let us examine the application of privacy bubbles in the realistic application
scenario illustrated in Figure 1. Three tourists (Alice, Bob, and Carlos) are
visiting London, where Alice and Bob join the same sightseeing tour, while Carlos
prefers to visit the city's sights by foot. Although the tourists do not personally
know each other, they are registered in the same photo sharing application which
supports the concept of privacy bubbles.

When boarding the sightseeing bus, Alice creates a new privacy bubble, which
has a validity duration of ± 5 minutes and encompasses a radius of 50 meters.
As a result, only persons located within 50 meters of Alice's location (the center
of the bubble) are allowed to access her captured photos, and only do so if they
have been at the location at most 5 minutes before or after the photo has been
taken. As the bubble follows Alice's moves, the persons authorized to access her
pictures are dynamically determined for each individual photo.

In contrast to Alice, Bob is more concerned about his privacy, and defines his
own bubble to only include people within 10 meters around him when he takes
a picture. In front of Westminster Abbey, Alice and Bob take a set of pictures,
while Carlos is walking by in a distance of 20 meters from the bus after having
taking photos of the sight. Back at home, Carlos is not fully satisfied with the
quality of his pictures and is looking for better pictures on the picture sharing
application that reflect the moment of his visit. As Carlos was located within
Alice's bubble while she took pictures, he is able to access her pictures of the
monument. However, he is not granted access to Bob's pictures since he was
outside Bob's bubble.

3   Privacy Bubbles: The Concept

In this section, we highlight the design drivers of the concept of privacy bubbles
and its principles. We detail their technical realization in Section 5.

3.1   Design Drivers

We aspire to develop an access control mechanism for sharing user-generated
mobile content with people who were located in physical proximity to the content

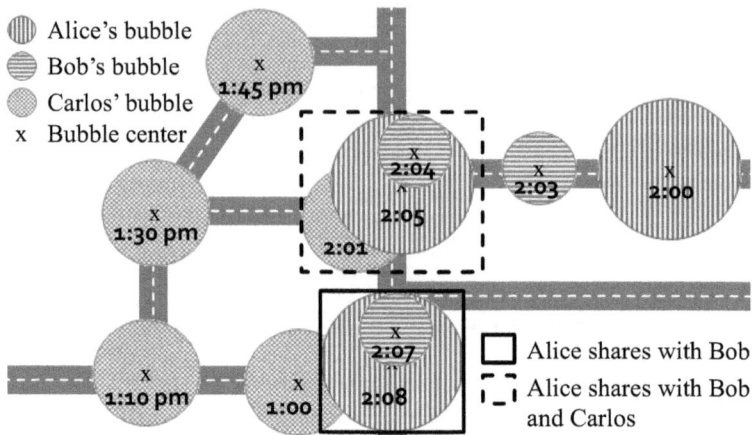

Fig. 1. Representation of Alice's, Bob's, and Carlos' bubbles for each taken picture

creator at the time of its creation. The designed access control mechanism should reflect the following design drivers:

1. **Comprehensiveness:** The mechanism should be intuitive and easy to comprehend, particularly for unexperienced users.
2. **User control:** Using this mechanism, the users should be able to control and customize the access to their generated content according to their personal preferences.
3. **Management overhead:** The required user interactions should however be kept to a minimum in order to limit the associated management overhead and foster its usage by potential users.
4. **User acceptance:** We believe that the users need to enjoy and feel comfortable with the proposed approach to adopt and accept it.
5. **Privacy protection:** Ultimately, the privacy of the users should be respected. This includes the control of the users over the pictures released to others and the selection of the bubble parameters according to their personal preferences. Furthermore, the collection of sensitive information by the sharing application should be kept to the minimum.

3.2   Concept and Principles

The concept of privacy bubbles serves as a metaphorical representation of the privacy spheres of the users. The user occupies the center of its bubble and can share information (we have chosen to design our prototype for the sharing of pictures) with other users located in his bubble in a protected manner. In contrast, users located outside his bubble are not allowed to access the shared pictures. Privacy bubbles can be dynamically created by the user that shares the content, who selects its radius and duration. The radius of the bubble determines the maximal distance at which other users should be from the bubble creator at the time of capture of the picture to be able to later access the picture. The duration of the bubble determines the maximal time range during which others users should be included in the bubble (i.e., at a distance inferior to the bubble radius) to access the picture. Let us assume that Alice has a bubble with a radius of 5 meters and a duration of 2 minutes and takes a picture at time t. Every user located at a distance of up to 5 meters from Alice in the time interval $[t-2\ \text{min},\ t+2\ \text{min}]$ will be able to access the picture taken by Alice if she decides to share it. Alice controls which pictures she shares in her bubble. She can therefore deselect pictures, which potentially compromise her privacy. These users are granted access to the picture until Alice decides not to share the picture anymore. The access authorization does not depend on the current location of the users when they search for shared pictures, but only on their location around the time of the capture of the picture. Moreover, the access authorization is not symmetric. This means that Alice can access the pictures of others if she was included in their bubbles, while they cannot access hers. In our solution, users do not share pictures according to a tit-for-tat mechanism, but the individual privacy preferences of each user (expressed by means of the bubble parameters) are respected. Note that the concept of privacy bubbles does not replace existing access control mechanisms but it complements these by a new sharing paradigm.

4   Evaluation of the Privacy Bubble Concept

We have conducted a user study in order to investigate how potential users perceive the concept of privacy bubbles. Since this study focuses on online picture sharing applications, we have specifically approached participants who could be potential users of such applications. We have recruited them by posting announcements on multiple forums and mailing lists at our university and partner universities. The study was conducted using an online questionnaire in order to collect responses from a broad spectrum of participants. The questions were written in English and their completion took approximately 15 minutes. In total, 175 participants anonymously answered our online questionnaire. In this section, we first present demographic information about our participants, before highlighting the findings of the study.

4.1   Demographic Information

The participants of our study were predominantly male ($n=118$) and aged between 21 and 55 ($m=28$, $SD=5$). Table 1 illustrates the distribution of the most represented nationalities, current jobs, and fields of occupation among the participants. Our sample of participants includes diverse profiles of potential users with various fields of occupation such as theology, law, or business. Among the participants, 81% indicated to have already shared pictures online ($n=142$). The estimated number of pictures shared by the participants is visualized in Figure 2,

Table 1. Demographics of the participants (n_{total}=175)

Nationality	n		Current job	n		Field of occupation	n
German	108		PhD student	72		Computer science	99
French	22		Undergraduate student	59		Electrical engineering	35
Spanish	9		Postdoctoral researcher	18		Psychology	5
Romanian	3		Professor	6		Biology	5
Indian	3		Administrative staff	5		Physics	4
Ukrainian	3		Technical staff	4		Mechanical engineering	4
Other	27		Other	11		Other	23

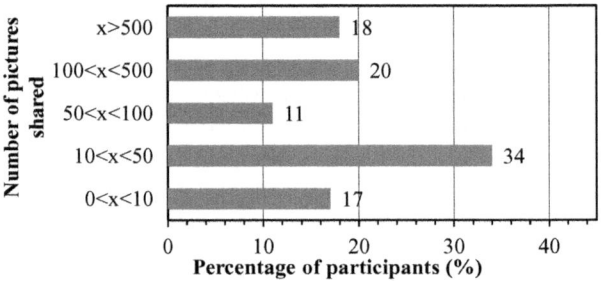

Fig. 2. Overall number of pictures shared

which shows that only 17% of the participants do not share pictures online. Furthermore, Figure 3 shows that more than 60% of the participants have shared photos that were taken with their mobile phones.

4.2 User Study Results

In this section, we present the findings of our user study classified by design drivers (cf. Section 3.1). We especially analyze whether the participants estimate that the design driver is reflected in the proposed concept of privacy bubbles. Moreover, we assess the suitability of different design alternatives for the implementation of our proof-of-concept presented in Section 5.

Comprehensiveness. The first design driver aims at providing for a solution which is easy to comprehend and intuitive for potential users. After a textual description of the privacy bubble concept, we first submitted the following statement to the participants: "The concept of privacy bubble is easy to comprehend". The participants indicated their degree of agreement with this statement on a seven point Likert scale. A score of 1 indicates a strong disagreement, 4 is neutral, and 7 indicates a strong agreement. Figure 4 illustrates the distribution of the resulting scores and shows that 72% of the participants agreed with the submitted statement, i.e., 72% of the participants found the privacy bubble concept easy to comprehend.

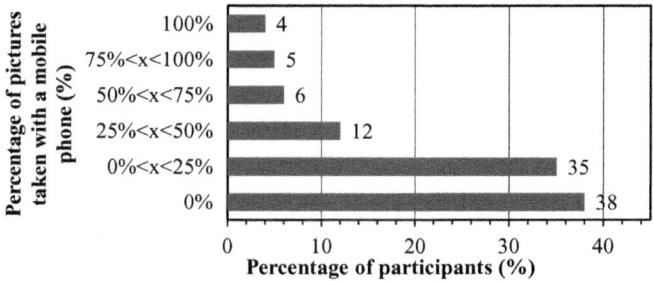

Fig. 3. Estimated percentage of shared pictures taken with a mobile phone

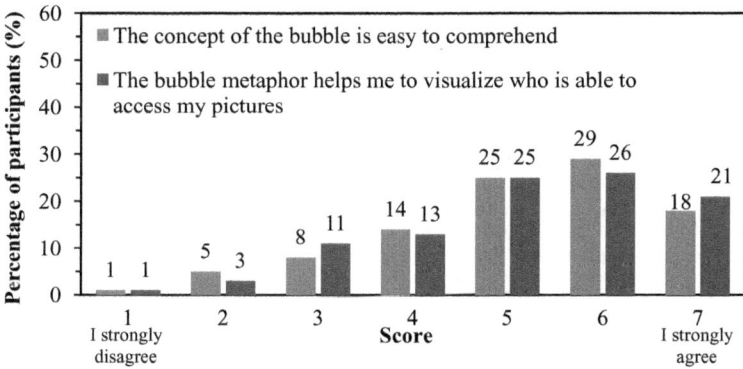

Fig. 4. Distribution of the answers about the comprehensiveness and intuitiveness of the privacy bubbles

User Control. The second design driver targets at allowing the users to tailor the access control to their individual preferences. In our solution, the users customize the radius and duration of their bubble to control the persons able to access their pictures. Figure 5 shows that 71% of the participants confirmed that "being able to determine the radius of the bubble is important for [them]", while 70% of the participants indicated that "being able to determine the duration of the bubble is important for [them]".

Furthermore, we have investigated different control options for the design of our prototype implementation in order to tailor its features to the feedback of the participants. Firstly, 88% of the participants wish to review their pictures before their release to other users (cf. Figure 6) — a feature easily integrable in our proof-of-concept implementation. Secondly, we examined if the participants wish reciprocal relationships with people authorized to access their pictures. Since 39% of the participants agreed that "it is important for [them] that people can access [their] pictures if [they] can access theirs", 18% remained neutral, and 43% disagreed, no trend can be clearly identified from the participants' answers (see Figure 6). We therefore have introduced this feature as an option in our prototype, which can be optionally activated by the users depending on their

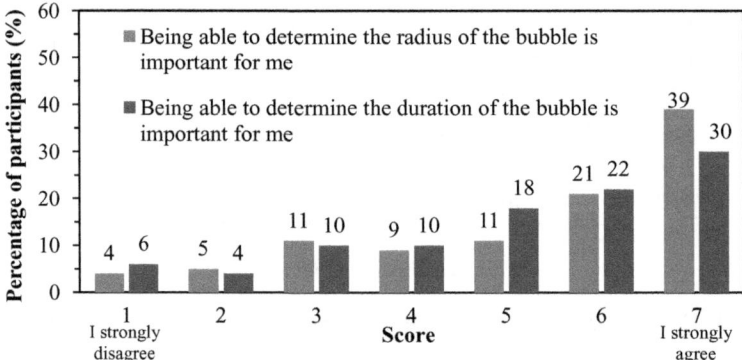

Fig. 5. Distribution of the answers about the importance of the control over the radius and the duration of the privacy bubbles

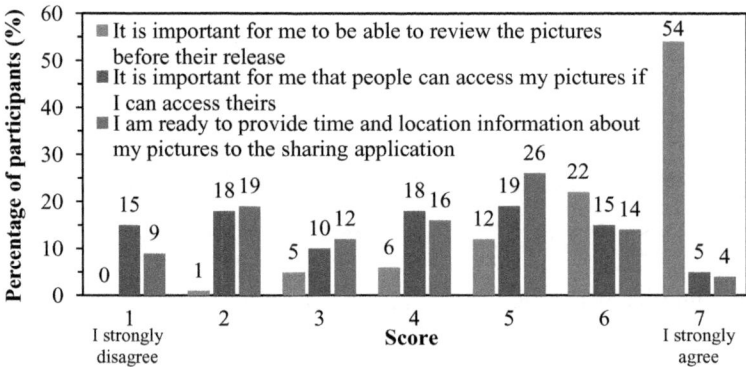

Fig. 6. Distribution of the answers about the importance of reviewing pictures before their release, the importance of reciprocal relationships, and the participants' readiness to provide spatiotemporal information

preferences. We finally asked the participants if "[they are] ready to provide time and location information about [their] pictures to the sharing application". As a result, 44% of the participants indicated to be ready to do it, 16% remained neutral, and 40% indicated not to be ready (see Figure 6). Again, no trend can be clearly identified from the given answers. Consequently, we have integrated two different mechanisms in our prototype, one is transmitting spatiotemporal information to the sharing applications, while the other one does not transmit any such data.

Management Overhead. The third design driver aims at limiting the management burden for the users to the minimum. In our solution, the users only have to select the duration and radius of their bubble and the access control is automatically and transparently managed by the application. The participants confirm the viability of this approach since 56% of the participants indicated

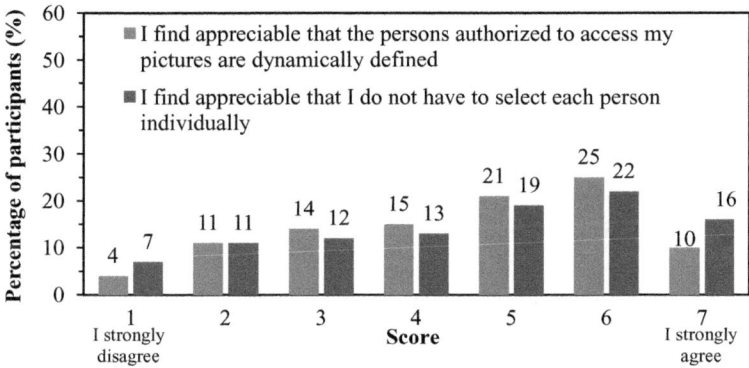

Fig. 7. Distribution of the answers about the appreciation of the dynamical and automatic nature of the privacy bubbles

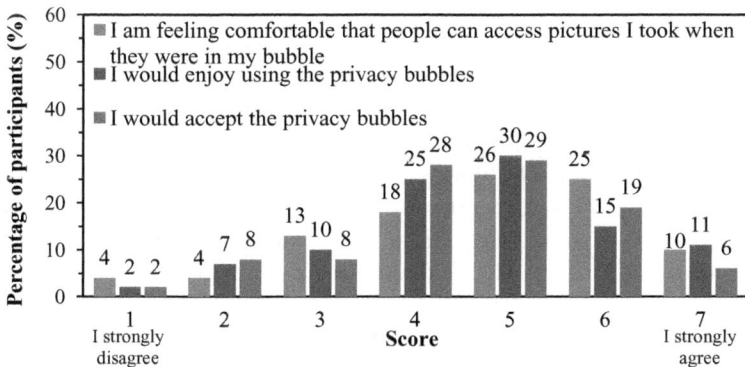

Fig. 8. Distribution of the answers related to the acceptance of the privacy bubbles by the participants

that "[they] find it appreciable that the persons authorized to access [their] pictures are dynamically defined", while 57% stated that "[they] find it appreciable that they do not have to select each person individually" as depicted in Figure 7.

In addition to the control over the radius and duration of the bubble, the participants wish additional features as shown in the above section, which complete the original concept described in Section 3.2. The integration of these features in the prototype implementation may introduce additional management overhead for the users. This overhead remains however limited and the additional features contribute to the acceptance of our approach by potential users.

User Acceptance. In addition to the analysis of three design drivers, we finally investigated whether the participants would accept this novel approach for controlling the access to their pictures. The results presented in Figure 8 show that 61% of the participants would "[...] feel comfortable that people can access pictures [they] took when they were in [their] bubble". Note that only 4%

strongly disagreed with this statement. Furthermore, Figure 8 shows that 56% of the participants "would enjoy using the privacy bubbles" (vs. 15% who would not) and 54% of the participants "would accept the privacy bubbles" (vs. 18% who would not). These results have been confirmed by the following comments left by the participants: "Privacy bubbles seem to be an easy process for sharing photos", "Interesting concept. I guess this would make things much easier", "It sounds like a great idea", "It sounds like an interesting new concept to share pictures with others based on their whereabouts when the picture was taken", or "Where could I access and test it?".

In summary, the participants have confirmed that the four design drivers are reflected in the proposed concept of privacy bubbles. Additionally, they have provided valuable insights about different design alternatives for the implementation of our prototype detailed in Section 5.

5   Proof-of-Concept Implementation

Based on the findings of the aforementioned user study, we have prototypically implemented the concept of privacy bubbles. Our proof-of-concept is based on Android Nexus S mobile phones and an application server, modeling an online sharing platform. Mobile phones are particularly adapted to the implementation of the concept of privacy bubbles, since 61% of the participants of our study have already adopted them to take the pictures they share (cf. Figure 3). Moreover, they enable an easy collection of contextual information about the users. In this section, we present the different steps conducted by the users and the corresponding mechanisms from the creation of a privacy bubble to the upload of the pictures and their access by other users. Note that the application server is secured against fraudulent access using well-established mechanisms and its different functions can be easily integrated into existing sharing applications.

5.1   Bubble Creation

Users start the creation of a new bubble via the main interface illustrated in Figure 9(a). They determine its radius using the second interface depicted Figure 9(b). Moreover, the proposed values for the radius can be customized by the users in order to reflect their personal preferences as good as possible. The creation of the bubble is completed by the selection of its duration.

5.2   Taking Pictures

The users then access the picture management interface shown in Figure 9(c) and can take pictures as usual with their mobile phone. While taking pictures, a mechanism transparent for the users captures information about the user's context in order to later determine which other users were included in the current privacy bubble.

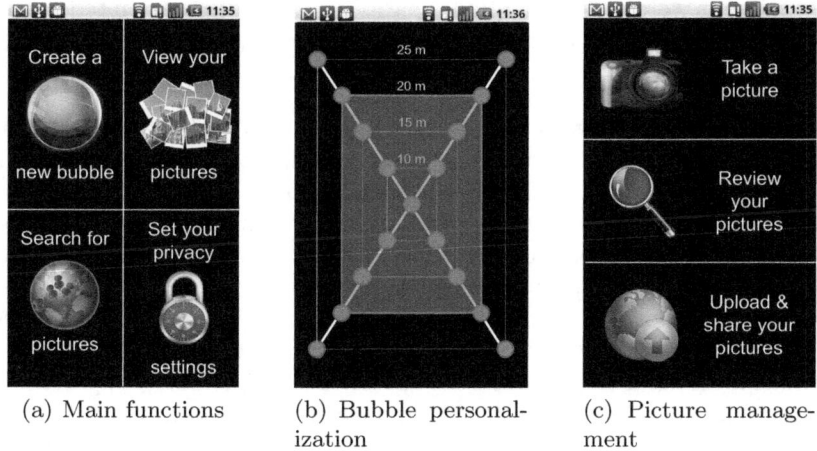

(a) Main functions   (b) Bubble personal-   (c) Picture manage-
                        ization   ment

Fig. 9. Screenshots of selected user interfaces

Indirect vs. Direct Localization Mechanism. We have first designed and implemented two mechanisms, which differ in the modality of the collected location information. In the first mechanism referred to as the *indirect* mechanism, the mobile phone collects spatiotemporal information about each taken picture. This includes the GPS coordinates, scanned Wi-Fi access points, and scanned Bluetooth devices. The collected information as well as the parameters (i.e., the duration and radius of the bubble) are then appended as metadata to the picture.

In comparison to the indirect mechanism, the *direct* mechanism does not collect absolute location information, but instead collects the IDs broadcasted by nearby users added to the picture's metadata. For the duration of the bubble, the mobile phone therefore periodically broadcasts messages advertising the ID of its user and listening for similar messages coming from other phones. In our implementation, we have used the AllJoyn technology [2], which supports Wi-Fi ad-hoc communication between Android phones. In the direct mechanism, the radius of the bubbles is determined by the range of the wireless technology. Users, who select to use this mechanism in the "Privacy settings" illustrated in Figure 9(a), may hence only configure the duration of their bubble and do not access the bubble personalization interface (shown in Figure 9(b)), which is exclusively used in the indirect mechanism.

In summary, the indirect mechanism allows the users to freely define the radius of their bubbles. This freedom however comes at the cost of reduced location privacy, since users need to provide spatiotemporal information to the sharing platform. On the other side, the direct mechanism does not reveal spatiotemporal information about the users to the application server, but restricts the bubble radius to the range of the employed wireless technology. We have included both indirect and direct mechanisms in our prototype implementation in order to foster the acceptance of our approach by potential users, since roughly half of the participants were ready to provide spatiotemporal information to the sharing platform, while the other users were reluctant to provide information about the location, in which their pictures were taken.

Picture-based vs. Periodic Location Detection Mechanism. In the above mechanisms, the spatiotemporal information and the collected user IDs are transmitted along with each uploaded picture. This implies that the pictures serve as grant for accessing further pictures, and that users thus need to take and share pictures in order to access pictures of other users. While this tit-for-tat aspect has been identified as important by 39% of the participants of our study, 43% judged it as unimportant (cf. Figure 6). We therefore propose extended versions of both the direct and indirect mechanisms with relaxed sharing conditions. In the extended indirect mechanism, the mobile phone periodically provides spatiotemporal information to the sharing application. Similarly, the mobile phones periodically broadcasts the identity of its user in the extended direct mechanism, even if no picture is taken. While these extended versions may increase the number of pictures accessible by each user, they come at the cost of providing additional information to the sharing platform, such as the locations visited by the user or the identities of the users encountered. The choice between the regular and the extended mechanisms is up to the user, as both mechanisms depend on their personal privacy conception and their willingness to access more content. An evaluation of the impact of both original and extended versions of the direct and indirect mechanisms on the sharing behavior of users as well as their respective acceptance by potential users is considered as future work.

5.3   Reviewing Pictures

The users can review the taken pictures and decide which pictures they are willing to share with the persons who were included in their bubbles. After having reviewed the pictures, the users upload the pictures to share to the application server, which stores and clusters them by user ID or spatiotemporal information to later facilitate the verification of the inclusion of potential retrievers in the bubbles.

5.4   Accessing Pictures from Other Users

In addition to sharing pictures, a user can also query the application server for pictures taken by other users. These pictures are however only accessible to a requesting user if he was included in the privacy bubble defined by the photographer at the time of capture of each picture. The verification of the potential inclusion in privacy bubbles happens at the server side in two steps. First, the server searches for pictures including the user ID of the requesting user in their metadata. Next, the server compares the spatiotemporal information provided by the requester and potential content providers by taking the corresponding bubble parameters into account. The spatiotemporal information of the requester can be included in his pictures or periodically delivered if he used the extended version of the indirect mechanism. Positive search results are then displayed on a map, which can be browsed by the users on their mobile phone.

6   Discussions and Future Work

Based on encouraging findings of our study and the proposed prototype implementation, we envision to improve both the concept and the realization of the privacy bubbles in the following dimensions:

6.1   Tampering with Spatiotemporal Information

In the current version of our prototype implementation, malicious users can tamper with the spatiotemporal information included in the uploaded pictures when using the indirect mechanism. For example, malicious users may upload the same fake picture with different metadata to fraudulently gain access to additional pictures. To be successful, attackers need to guess the combination of both the location and temporal information verifying the bubble parameters of a picture. The probability to guess a right combination increases with the number of fake uploaded pictures, but this simultaneously increases the risk to be detected by the application server, thus limiting the expected impact of this type of attack. In order to reduce the success probability of the attacker to zero, we however envision to examine different alternatives, such as the utilization of Trusted Platform Modules or Location Proofs [10] with regard to their applicability and acceptance in order to develop an adequate solution for our proof-of-concept implementation.

6.2   Falsification of User IDs

Malicious users using the direct mechanism may attempt to register the IDs of other users to the application server. This attack is however prevented by the authentication mechanisms at the application server. Next, an attacker can broadcast an user ID different from their own, granting the access to pictures taken in their proximity to another user. This attack is however useless, as an attacker needs to collude with the attacker having the broadcast ID to get access to pictures, which he could directly access by broadcasting his own user ID.

6.3   Location Privacy

Privacy bubbles require the disclosure of information about the users to the application server in order to match the persons included in the privacy bubbles and their creator. The more content users are willing to access, the more location information should be provided and hence, the more threats to location privacy arise. In our prototype implementation, we have proposed different mechanisms allowing users to choose both the type of information released to the application server and the corresponding frequency. The indirect mechanism leverages spatiotemporal annotations, while the direct mechanism monitors nearby user IDs (cf. Section 5.2). Both mechanisms can collect the information of interest either at the time of the capture of the picture or periodically. If users want to protect their location privacy, they can choose to use the direct mechanism, which only reveals the IDs of nearby mobile phones. Location privacy may however only be endangered if other users collude with the application server and reveal their location and thus the location of their victims. The likeliness of this attack is limited since it requires the physical proximity of the attackers to their victims. We envision to protect the location privacy of users using the indirect mechanisms by adding a trusted middleware to our current implementation and applying obfuscation mechanisms. For example, mechanisms based on the k-anonymity principle [11], such as tessellation [6] or microaggregation [5], can be applied. In the tessellation mechanism, the geographic area is divided into multiple tiles, each of them containing at least k users. The exact coordinates of the users are then replaced by either the geographical boundaries or the center of the current tile, which are then reported to the application server. Since k users are included in the same tile, they become indistinguishable. In comparison, the microaggregation scheme replaces the exact coordinates of the users by the average location of the k nearest users and similarly protects the location privacy of the k users. While both mechanisms increase the location privacy of the users, they simultaneously prevent the definition of fine-grained bubbles and lower the precision at which the inclusion of other users in bubbles can be verified. Consequently, further mechanisms should be examined to provide enhanced location privacy while still supporting the realization of the privacy bubbles.

6.4   Reliability of Location Information

We further plan to improve the precision of the location information provided by the mobile phones by completing the positioning information by additional sensing modalities (such as microphone and light sensor). Enhanced precision will refine the granularity of the bubbles and allow users to define even smaller bubbles, e.g., at room level. The reliability of the access control will also be improved since it currently only depends on precision of the GPS coordinates and the scanned Bluetooth and Wi-Fi access points.

6.5   Modular and Malleable Bubbles

The proposed bubbles are currently spheric and centered on the users. In the future, malleable bubbles could be used, which can dynamically adapt themselves to the form of a room where the users could freely move without modifying their bubbles in order to provide enhanced privacy protection.

6.6   Multimedia Contents

In this paper, the feasibility of privacy bubbles has been studied for picture sharing applications. Its applicability is however not confined to sharing pictures, and should be further investigated for additional user-generated contents such as videos or audio recordings.

6.7 Long-Term Evaluation

Once the above enhancements will be achieved, we will deploy our approach for a long-term user study. A set of users will evaluate the privacy bubbles under real-world conditions and provide additional feedback for their improvement.

7 Related Work

A wide range of existing work, such as [7,8], focuses on defining policies, rules, or semantics for access control mechanisms. They mainly contribute technical solutions, which remain invisible to the users and obscure for non-experts. Within the scope of this work, we however concentrate on existing mechanisms directly controlled by the users. Among the existing solutions, most of the mechanisms rely on individual authorizations managed by the users, who manually select individuals (or build groups of individuals) authorized to access their pictures. The way how groups are defined varies from an application to another, but the underlying principle remains the same. For example, Facebook utilizes scrolling lists, while Google+ proposes "circles" to visualize the groups of individuals formed. In contrast to these solutions, our concept differs in two dimensions: (1) the authorization to access pictures is delivered based on spatiotemporal conditions and (2) this authorization is dynamically and automatically managed by the system based on the radius and duration of the bubbles defined by the users. The "geofences" introduced in Flickr [9] allow users to define geographical zones on a map and select the persons able to access the pictures taken in theses zones. Even if the geofences includes a spatial component, the proposed solution remains static and the users need to set up each fence and select the authorized users individually. Moreover, our concept not only considers the location of the photographers at the time of capture of the pictures, but also the location of the persons able to access these pictures at the same time. The Color application [3,12] shares a number of similarities with our approach since people located in proximity of the photographers can directly access their pictures. Color does however not only limit their access to the nearby persons, but considers each picture as public, which endangers the privacy of the users.

8 Conclusions

In this paper, we have presented a complementary approach to the relationship-based access control mechanisms applied in most current online picture sharing platforms. We have defined design drivers for a novel concept called privacy bubbles, which allow users to share pictures with other users to which no social ties exist. Users control the bubbles, i.e., the sharing spatiotemporal boundaries, as well as the pictures shared within the bubbles. The privacy bubble paradigm is thus centered around the users and takes into account their individual privacy conception. We have hence thoroughly investigated the feasibility of our concept by submitting it to the 175 participants of our user study for evaluation. The results show that a majority of the participants would feel comfortable using our approach and would be ready to accept it. We have further implemented a proof-of-concept of our approach to examine its technical feasibility.

Acknowledgments. The authors would like to thank the participants of the user study and Stanislaus Stelle for their contributions to this paper. This work was supported by CASED (`www.cased.de`).

References

1. A Snapshot of Facebook in 2010, `http://www.facebook.com` (accessed in January 2012)
2. AllJoyn Peer-to-Peer, `http://developer.qualcomm.com` (accessed in January 2012)
3. Color Application, `http://www.color.com` (accessed in September 2011)
4. YouTube Statistics, `http://www.youtube.com/t/press_statistics` (accessed in January 2012)
5. Domingo-Ferrer, J., Mateo-Sanz, J.: Practical Data-oriented Microaggregation for Statistical Disclosure Control. IEEE Transactions on Knowledge and Data Engineering 14(1), 189–201 (2002)
6. Huang, K.L., Kanhere, S.S., Hu, W.: Preserving Privacy in Participatory Sensing Systems. Computer Communications 33(11), 1266–1280 (2010)
7. Joshi, J., Bertino, E., Latif, U., Ghafoor, A.: A Generalized Temporal Role-based Access Control Model. IEEE Transactions on Knowledge and Data Engineering, 4–23 (2005)
8. Kulkarni, D., Tripathi, A.: Context-aware Role-based Access Control in Pervasive Computing Systems. In: Proceedings of the 13th ACM Symposium on Access Control Models and Technologies (SACMAT), pp. 113–122 (2008)
9. Leung, D.: Introducing Geofences on Flickr! `http://blog.flickr.net` (accessed in January 2012)
10. Luo, W., Hengartner, U.: Proving Your Location Without Giving up Your Privacy. In: Proceedings of the 11th Workshop on Mobile Computing Systems and Applications (HotMobile), pp. 7–12 (2010)
11. Sweeney, L.: K-anonymity: A Model for Protecting Privacy. International Journal of Uncertainty, Fuzziness, and Knowledge-Based Systems 10(5), 557–570 (2002)
12. Upbin, B.: Color, a Twitter for Photo and Video, Launches with $41 Million, `http://www.forbes.com` (accessed in January 2012)

Privacy Preservation of User History Graph

Shinsaku Kiyomoto, Kazuhide Fukushima, and Yutaka Miyake

KDDI R & D Laboratories Inc.
2-1-15 Ohara, Fujimino, Saitama, 356-8502, Japan
kiyomoto@kddilabs.jp

Abstract. In this paper, we propose new ideas to protect user privacy while allowing the use of a user history graph. We define new privacy notions for user history graphs and consider algorithms to generate a privacy-preserving digraph from the original graph.

1 Introduction

Graph-structured data are useful for the analysis of relationships and trends of service use [6,4], and has been considered an analysis tool for a commercial services [10]. Graph-structured data sets are collections of user history data, which are anonymous, but contain sensitive information with implications for user privacy. A privacy concern for leakages of user history data has been reported [11]. Privacy-preserving analysis of such graphs remains a continuing concern as interest in the areas of privacy and data mining increases.

Current research focuses mainly on social network graphs without directed edges. In a social network graph, the anonymity of each node is important for privacy protection. How to obfuscate the relationships between users and nodes is the main issue for existing privacy protection mechanisms for graphs. A method [13] proposed by Yuan *et al.* constructs a k-degree anonymous graph by adding nodes and edges. In the k-degree anonymous graph, the probability that an attacker cannot identify a node of the target user is at most $\frac{1}{k}$. Several studies have examined [5,7,3] methods that use secret graph data and respond to queries with approximate results. Blaustein *et al.* formalized the problem of creating a protected account G' of a graph G and provided an algorithm [2] to create a maximally useful protected account of a sensitive social network graph. In the article [15], k-automorphism is proposed: k-automorphism requires that each node has at least $k-1$ other nodes with the same structure in a published graph. Some other techniques for protecting privacy in social networks have been proposed [12,14]. Privacy preserving data mining methods for link analysis of directed graphs was presented in [8,1].

In this paper, we propose new privacy notions for user history graphs and consider algorithms to generate a privacy-preserving digraph from the original graph. We assume that the user history graph is published and used for several analyses using non-interactive schemes. The notions are similar in approach to k-anonymity [9], and they are configured by two parameters k and v.

I. Askoxylakis, H.C. Pöhls, and J. Posegga (Eds.): WISTP 2012, LNCS 7322, pp. 87–96, 2012.
© IFIP International Federation for Information Processing 2012

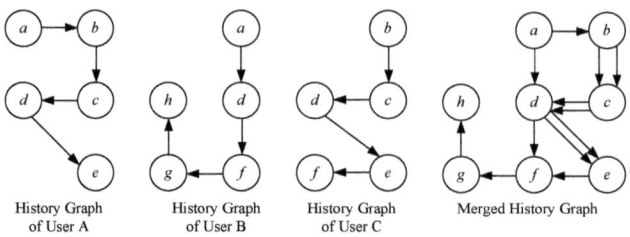

History Graph   History Graph   History Graph   Merged History Graph
of User A   of User B   of User C

Fig. 1. Example of Merged History Graph

The rest of the paper is organized as follows; user history graphs are explained in section 2. Section 3 provides privacy notions for user history graphs and section 4 presents algorithms for privacy-preserving graph data. Evaluation results of the algorithms are shown in section 5. We conclude this paper in section 6.

2   User History Graph

A history graph as shown in figure 1 is an efficient method to visualize the history of a user. We define a label for each edge to merge the history graphs of all users. A user history graph showing that users perform action a and then b is transformed into a labeled digraph $(a \rightarrow b)$: the label $L(a \rightarrow b)$ denotes the number of users who perform the action from a to b. For simplicity in the definition, we assume that the user does not repeat his previous actions, even though our discussion in this paper can be applied to that case. First, a history for each user is transformed into a labeled digraph such that the label is $L(a \rightarrow b) = 1$. Then, digraphs of all users are merged as follows;

- all nodes that denote the same action are merged into one node.
- The labels are updated to $L(a \rightarrow b) = n$, where digraphs of n users have the same label $L(a \rightarrow b) = 1$.

Note that the digraph $(a \rightarrow b)$ is different from the digraph $(b \rightarrow a)$, so the label is defined for each digraph.

Let $start$ be a group of nodes that the number of outgoing edges for a node is larger than the number of incoming edges for the node and end be a group of nodes the number of incoming edges for a node is larger than the number of outgoing edges for the node. The symbol $start \rightarrow x$ denotes the routes from the nodes $start$ to x, and the symbol $x \rightarrow end$ denotes the routes from x to the end nodes. The symbols $\mathcal{N}_{start \rightarrow t}$ and $\mathcal{N}_{t \rightarrow end}$ respectively denote all nodes on all possible routes from $start \rightarrow t$ and all nodes on all possible routes from $t \rightarrow end$, where the symbol $\mathcal{N}_x$ denotes a group of nodes that satisfy the condition x. If $start = \emptyset$, $\mathcal{N}_{start \rightarrow t}$ consists of all nodes that can be reached from node t to trace the digraph backwards. For $end = \emptyset$, $\mathcal{N}_{t \rightarrow end}$ consists of all nodes that can be reached from node t to trace the digraph forwards. The symbol $\emptyset$ denotes an empty set. For the merged history graph in figure 1, $\mathcal{N}_{start \rightarrow d}$ is the set of nodes $\{a, b\}$, and $\mathcal{N}_{d \rightarrow end}$ is the set of nodes $\{e, f, h\}$.

3 Privacy Notion

3.1 Adversary Model

Privacy leakage from a merged history graph is the disclosure of the actions of a particular person from the graph. Attacks against user history graphs are intended to obtain private information on a particular user from the graph. We assume that the merge process is executed on a trusted domain and only the merged history graph is published. We summarize an adversary model as follows:

Adversary against a Merged History Graph. It is assumed that an adversary knows a victim A executed an action t. The objective of the adversary is to obtain actions that A executed before or after the action t. Thus, the adversary searches the merged history graph that includes actions of other people and finds actions of A using the knowledge that action t was executed.

3.2 Notions for Untraceability of Graph

We consider two levels of privacy notions: partial k-untraceability, and complete k-untraceability. Partial k-traceability accepts leakage of some partial actions of a user, but prevents all actions of the user from being revealed. The definition of complete k-untraceability involves meeting the reqirement that no action of the user is leaked. The symbol $Act^A_{N_{x \to y}}$ for user A denotes the sequence of all actions of user A from action x to action y. For example, the sequence of actions from the first action to action x and the sequence of actions from action x to the final action are denoted $Act^A_{N_{start \to x}}$ and $Act^A_{N_{x \to end}}$, respectively.

Generally, there are many trivial actions, performed by many users. It is not important for privacy purposes where we keep the information about such actions. Thus, we relax the above definitions to produce an anonymized graph that includes a lot of information for analyses of user history. Let v be the threshold value for the number of performing users that establishes that an action is trivial, that is, we judge the actions $x \to y$ to be trivial if the label $L(x \to y) \geq v$. Both definitions are denoted as follows:

Definition 1. *Partial (k, v)-untraceability.* We assume that an adversary knows an action t of a user A, and we consider all possible adversaries defined for any t in the merged graph. If at least k sequences of actions that are potentially associated with the user A and $k - 1$ other users exist as candidates respectively for all actions $Act^A_{N_{start \to t}}$ and $Act^A_{N_{t \to end}}$ except trivial actions $x \to y$ that have a label $L(x \to y) \geq v$, it is said that the digraph satisfies partial (k, v)-untraceability for A. If the digraph satisfies the above condition for all users, the digraph is said to satisfy partial (k, v)-untraceability.

Definition 2. *Complete (k, v)-untraceability.* We assume that an adversary knows an action t of a user A, and we consider all possible adversaries defined for any t in the merged graph. If at least k actions that are potentially associated with the user A and $k - 1$ other users exist as candidates for each action in $Act^A_{\mathcal{N}_{start \to t}}$ and $Act^A_{\mathcal{N}_{t \to end}}$ except trivial actions $x \to y$ that have a label $L(x \to y) \geq v$, it is said that the digraph satisfies complete (k, v)-untraceability for A. If the digraph satisfies the above condition for all users, the digraph is said to satisfy complete (k, v)-untraceability.

In a complete (k, v)-untraceable graph, each action t except trivial actions has k outgoing edges and incoming edges; thus, an action of the user A which connects to the action t cannot be identified from k candidates. Thus, the graph satisfies untraceability for the adversary who knows the action t of the user. It is trivial that a complete (k, v)-untraceable graph satisfies partial (k, v)-untraceability; all actions except trivial actions are connected to k potential actions in a complete (k, v)-untraceable graph. A graph that satisfies partial (k, v)-untraceability generally produces much information than a complete (k, v)-untraceable graph, where the partial (k, v)-untraceable graph and the complete (k, v)-untraceable graph are generated from a user history graph. However, the (k, v)-untraceable graph may reveal partial actions of users due to the relaxed definition of the privacy notion; an attack is successful where an adversary obtains all actions of a user. To trace all actions of the user, the adversary has to select a sequence of actions from k sequences of actions; thus, all actions of the user is untreaceable, even though some actions are treaceable for the adversary. The parameter k means that an action (or a sequence of actions) is potentially associated with a user and $k - 1$ other users in the untraceable graph, and the parameter v means that v users do the same action in the graph. Generally, we should select the parameter $v = k$ with regards to a privacy requirement for a merged graph. Actions of a user are hidden in actions of a group that consists of k members including the user. A privacy notion for the graph should be selected from the above two notions according to a use case of the graph and its privacy requirements. Tradeoffs between privacy and the amount of information that is provided by the untraceable graph will be evaluated in section 6.

4   Algorithm

4.1   Algorithm Generating Partial (k, v)-Untraceable History Graph

Details of the algorithm are denoted as **Algorithm 1**, where oe_t and ie_t are respectively defined as the number of outgoing edges and incoming edges of a node t. The algorithm to generate a partial (k, v)-untraceable history graph is as follows.

1. This step consists of a part of the detailed algorithm, from line 1 to line 3. For input of a user history graph **G**, the algorithm adds a virtual incoming edge $(s_r \to r)$ to each node $r \in start$ until the number of the incoming edges is the same as the number of outgoing edges. Then, the the algorithm adds a virtual outgoing edge $(q \to u_q)$ to each node $q \in end$ until the number of the outgoing edges is the same as the number of incoming edges. A label of a virtual incoming edge $L(s_x \to x)$ denotes the number of users who first do the action, and a label of a virtual outgoing edge $L(y \to u_y)$ denotes the number of users who do the action at the end.

2. This step consists of a part of the detailed algorithm, from line 4 to line 12. The algorithm searches for a node t that has fewer outgoing edges than k and for which all lower nodes $\mathcal{N}_{t \rightarrow end \backslash t}$ have fewer outgoing edges than k. Then, the algorithm removes all outgoing edges $(t \rightarrow *)$ that satisfy $L(t \rightarrow *) < v$. Next, the algorithm searches for a node t' that receives incoming edges numbering less than k and all upper nodes $\mathcal{N}_{start \rightarrow t' \backslash t'}$ that receive fewer incoming edges than k. Then the algorithm removes all incoming edges $(* \rightarrow t')$ that satisfy $L(* \rightarrow t') < v$. The algorithm repeats this step until no node that meets the conditions has found.

3. This step is the same as line 13, line 14 and line 15 in the detailed algorithm. The algorithm removes virtual incoming and outgoing edges, removes nodes that has no edges, and outputs the modified graph.

Algorithm 1. Generation of a Partial (k, v)-Untraceable History Graph

---

Input: User History Graph G, parameters k and v
Output: Anonymized Graph $G^\alpha(G, k, v)$
1: $G^\alpha(G, k, v) \leftarrow G$
2: Add virtual incoming edges to *start* nodes
3: Add virtual outgoing edges to *end* nodes.
4: $T \leftarrow$ all nodes t, where $oe_{\mathcal{N}_{t \rightarrow end}} < k$ and its all edges are not $L(t_i \rightarrow *) \geq v$
5: $T' \leftarrow$ all nodes t', where $ie_{\mathcal{N}_{start \rightarrow t'}} < k$ and its all edges are not $L(* \rightarrow t'_j) \geq v$
6: **while** $T \neq \emptyset$ or $T' \neq \emptyset$ **do**
7:      Choose t_i from T
8:      Remove all outgoing edges of t_i, where $L(t_i \rightarrow *) < v$ from $G^\alpha(G, k, v)$
9:      Choose t'_j from T'
10:     Remove all incoming edges of t'_j, where $L(* \rightarrow t'_j) < v$ from $G^\alpha(G, k, v)$
11:     Update T and T'
12: **end while**
13: Remove virtual edges
14: Remove all node t'' where $oe_{t''} = 0$ and $ie_{t''} = 0$ from $G^\alpha(G, k, v)$
15: **return** $G^\alpha(G, k, v)$

Example. We show an example of the execution for the merged history graph in figure 2, where we set $k = v = 2$. The algorithm checks whether each node satisfies the condition for outgoing edges which is described in the step 2, and find that the nodes h and g satisfy the condition. Because, the nodes $\{a, d, e, f\}$ have two outgoing edges, and the nodes b and c have edges $L(b \rightarrow c) = 2$, $L(c \rightarrow d) = 2$, respectively. Then, the outgoing edges $(g \rightarrow h)$ and $(h \rightarrow u_h)$ are removed. The algorithm has no node that satisfy the condition for incoming edges which is described in the step 2. Note that the incoming edge $(s_a \rightarrow a)$ satisfies $L(s_a \rightarrow a) \geq 2$. The algorithm removes virtual edges from the graph, and then the algorithm removes the node h that has no connection with other nodes. Thus, the output of the algorithms for the example graph is the graph including seven nodes as described in figure 2.

Any adversary who knows an action of a user cannot find sequences of all actions of the user from the output of **Algorithm 1**. For example, if an adversary knows that a user do the action g, there exist at least two possible sequences of the actions, $(a \rightarrow d \rightarrow f \rightarrow g)$ and $(a \rightarrow d \rightarrow e \rightarrow f \rightarrow g)$.

Computational Cost. We estimate the computational cost of the algorithm 1. Let E and N be the total number of edges in the graph and the total number of nodes in the graph. The cost of line 1 is $O(1)$. The computational cost from line 2 to line 5 is $O(N + E)$. Lines 6 to 12 require $O(N^2 + NE)$ computation and lines 13 and 14 require $O(N)$ computation, respectively; thus the total cost from line 1 to line 14 can be estimated as $O(N^2 + NE)$. Where the graph is a dense graph ($E = O(N^2)$), the computational cost is $O(N^3)$.

4.2 Algorithm Generating Complete (k, v)-Untraceable History Graph

Details of the algorithm are denoted as **Algorithm 2**. The algorithm to generate a complete (k, v)-untraceable history graph is as follows;

1. The algorithm first executes **Algorithm 1** except line 13 and line 15.
2. This step consists of a part of the detailed algorithm, from line 3 to line 11. The algorithm searches for a node t that has fewer outgoing edges than k and removes all outgoing edges $(t \rightarrow *)$ that satisfy $L(t \rightarrow *) < v$, until no node is found. Then, the algorithm searches for a node t' that receives fewer incoming edges than k and removes all edges $(* \rightarrow t')$ that satisfy $L(* \rightarrow t') < v$. The algorithm repeats this step until no node that meets the conditions has found.
3. This step consists of line 12, line 13, and line 14 in the detailed program. The algorithm removes virtual edges, removes nodes to which no edge is connected, and outputs the modified graph.

Example. An example of the output by **Algorithm 2** is shown in figure 2. We set $k = v = 2$. After the step 1, the algorithm checks whether each node satisfies the conditions described in the step 2, and find that the node g satisfies the condition for incoming edges, because the node g has a incoming edge of $L(f \rightarrow g) = 1$. Then, the incoming edge $(f \rightarrow g)$ is removed. Next, the algorithm finds the node f satisfies the condition for outgoing edges, and removes the virtual edge $(f \rightarrow u_f)$. In the final step, the virtual edges are removed from the graph, and then the node f that has no edge is removed.

Any adversary who knows an action of a user cannot find any action of the user from the output of **Algorithm 2**. For example, if an adversary knows that a user do the action e, the adversary knows a trivial action d, and possible actions $\{a, b, c\}$ that are potentially associated with other users.

Computational Cost. We can calculate the total computational cost of **Algorithm 2** in the same manner. The total computational cost is estimated as $O(N^3)$.

5   Evaluation

We implemented a prototype module for **Algorithm 1** and **Algorithm 2**, and evaluated the transaction time for generating an anonymized history graph on a

Algorithm 2. Generation of a Complete (k, v)-Untraceable History Graph

Input: User History Graph G, parameters k and v
Output: Anonymized Graph $G^\alpha(G, k, v)$
1: $G^\alpha(G, k, v) \leftarrow G$
2: Execute **Algorithm 1** except line 13 and 15
3: $T \leftarrow$ all nodes t, where $oe_t < k$ and its all edges are not $L(t_i \rightarrow *) \geq v$
4: $T' \leftarrow$ all nodes t', where $ie_{t'} < k$ and its all edges are not $L(* \rightarrow t'_j) \geq v$
5: **while** $T \neq \emptyset$, or $T' \neq \emptyset$ **do**
6:      Choose t_i from T
7:      Remove all outgoing edges of t_i, where $L(t_i \rightarrow *) < v$ from $G^\alpha(G, k, v)$
8:      Choose t'_i from T'
9:      Remove all incoming edges of t'_j, where $L(* \rightarrow t'_j) < v$ from $G^\alpha(G, k, v)$
10:     Update T and T'
11: **end while**
12: Remove vertual edges
13: Remove all node t'' where $oe_{t''} = 0$ and $ie_{t''} = 0$ from $G^\alpha(G, k, v)$
14: **return** $G^\alpha(G, k, v)$

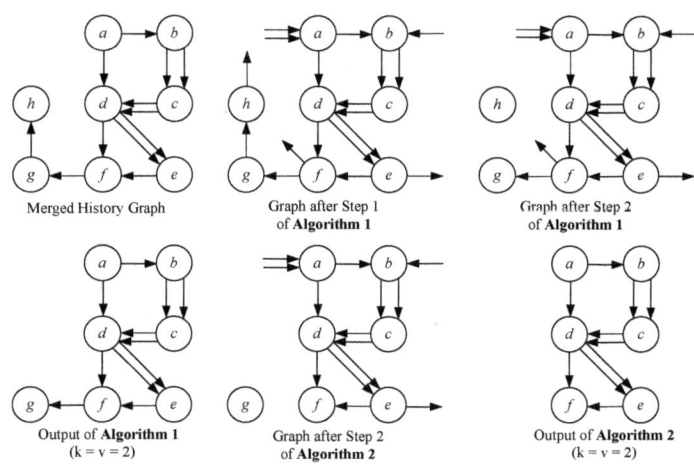

Fig. 2. Outputs of Algorithms

PC (Core i7 2.93GHz, 4.00GB Memory). We randomly generated merged user history graphs in two steps. In the first step, we generated a merged user history graph of n nodes under the condition that the probability of node connection $L(a, b) = 1$ was p; we first obtained an n-node merged graph where all labels are $L(a, b) = 1$. Then, we randomly assigned $n^{\frac{1}{2}}$ actions of $10 \times n^{\frac{1}{2}}$ users to digraphs and updated the labels in the graph. The data format described a user history graph $a \xrightarrow{L(a,b)} b$ as a tuple of three data $\{a, b, L(a, b)\}$.

Performance. The evaluation results of the average transaction time for 20 graphs are summarized in table 1 and table 2. The tables show the transaction time of **Algorithm 1** and **Algorithm 2**, respectively. We examined two different probabilities of node connections with five patterns of k. We set $v = k$ for all experiments. The transaction time depends on the number of processed nodes that are input into T and T', and the number of processed nodes is configured

Table 1. Transaction Time of Partial (k, v)-Untraceable History Graph Generation

(second)	100 nodes	150 nodes	200 nodes	300 nodes	400 nodes	500 nodes	700 nodes	1000 nodes	1500 nodes	2000 nodes
p=0.01, k=2	0.01	0.01	0.03	0.07	0.08	0.14	0.21	0.27	0.67	1.04
p=0.01, k=5	0.01	0.04	0.21	0.52	1.03	1.67	2.98	4.32	10.80	19.22
p=0.01, k=10	0.01	0.07	0.36	2.33	6.51	17.85	24.45	30.99	62.06	138.72
p=0.01, k=20	0.01	0.07	0.38	2.34	6.82	14.27	42.79	128.22	425.58	834.59
p=0.01, k=30	0.01	0.07	0.39	2.39	6.37	14.66	41.41	127.87	424.65	931.05
p=0.1, k=2	0.01	0.01	0.01	0.02	0.03	0.06	0.11	0.23	0.55	0.97
p=0.1, k=5	0.01	0.02	0.03	0.06	0.13	0.21	0.52	1.08	3.31	7.53
p=0.1, k=10	0.06	0.12	0.19	0.52	1.16	2.12	5.42	14.27	46.89	109.14
p=0.1, k=20	0.18	0.55	1.41	4.35	9.41	18.11	43.58	113.71	305.10	622.19
p=0.1, k=30	0.18	0.55	1.32	4.32	10.32	19.46	51.31	146.82	472.82	1039.43

Table 2. Transaction Time of Complete (k, v)-Untraceable History Graph Generation

(second)	100 nodes	150 nodes	200 nodes	300 nodes	400 nodes	500 nodes	700 nodes	1000 nodes	1500 nodes	2000 nodes
p=0.01, k=2	0.01	0.02	0.04	0.09	0.14	0.18	0.27	0.50	1.14	1.80
p=0.01, k=5	0.01	0.06	0.22	0.61	1.10	1.98	4.19	6.25	13.26	23.81
p=0.01, k=10	0.01	0.07	0.43	2.40	6.35	17.27	26.19	32.87	68.87	138.77
p=0.01, k=20	0.01	0.08	0.43	2.43	6.98	14.75	42.81	128.02	427.77	885.70
p=0.01, k=30	0.01	0.08	0.42	2.38	6.48	14.27	41.89	128.13	425.65	936.94
p=0.1, k=2	0.01	0.01	0.02	0.04	0.07	0.11	0.22	0.41	0.97	1.61
p=0.1, k=5	0.02	0.03	0.05	0.10	0.18	0.32	0.67	1.37	4.17	8.32
p=0.1, k=10	0.07	0.13	0.21	0.57	1.18	2.19	5.54	14.56	51.84	109.92
p=0.1, k=20	0.18	0.56	1.39	4.32	9.42	18.01	45.52	114.35	305.09	787.99
p=0.1, k=30	0.17	0.54	1.31	4.31	10.07	19.49	51.21	148.97	473.55	1040.19

by values of k, v and the number of nodes in the merged user history graph; thus, the transaction time was increased according to increases of $k(= v)$ and the number of nodes of the original graphs. A dominant part of the transaction time of **Algorithm 2** is the transaction time of **Algorithm 1**, where k is large; it is expected that many nodes are removed by **Algorithm 1**, and edges of almost all nodes are removed at the first iteration of the *do-while-loop* in the **Algorithm 2**. Example cases of $k = v = 10$ for **Algorithm 1** (denoted P) and **Algorithm 2** (denoted C) are shown in figure 3. The transaction time is approximately proportional to N^3.

Tradeoff. We evaluated the number of nodes that were outputs of algorithms, where we changed parameters k and v. Evaluation results are shown in figure 4. The evaluation results denote reductions of information that is provided by (k, v)-untraceable history graph, where a privacy requirement is tightened. We used random graphs of $n = 1000$ and $p = 0.01$, and evaluated three cases: k was fixed ($k = 10$) and v was changed, k and v were changed ($k = v$), and k was changed and v was fixed ($v = 10$). For both partial (k, v)-untraceable history graphs and complete (k, v)-untraceable history graphs, a result in the case $v = 10$ was almost same as that in the case $k = v$. Changes of the parameter v did not affect partial (k, v)-untraceable history graphs, but strongly affected complete (k, v)-untraceable history graphs. In any of the cases, there are threshold values for parameters k and v; the number of nodes is dramatically reduced, where k and v is increased over the threshold values. Thus, we should choose appropriate values for parameter sets, k and v in an operation of each history graph, even though there is a tradeoff between privacy and the amount of

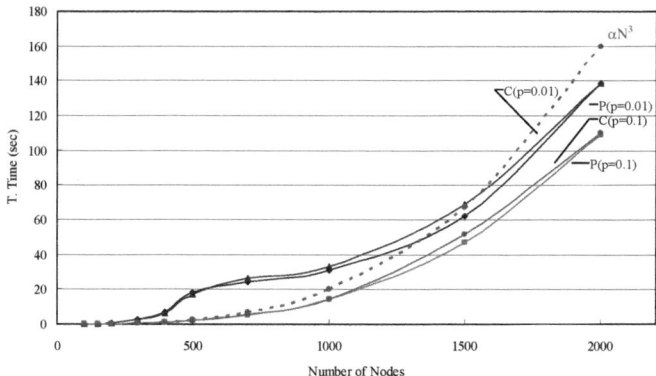

Fig. 3. Transaction Time of Algorithms ($k = 10$)

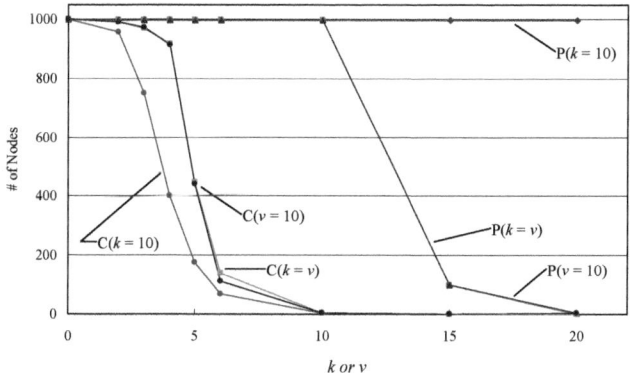

Fig. 4. Number of Nodes for Each Parameters k and v

information. Especially, the partial (k, v)-untraceable history graph is useful since it holds almost nodes and the graph is close to the original random graph, where k and v are small.

6 Conclusion

In this paper, we have presented concrete algorithms for generating graph data that satisfies the notions. Furthermore, experimental results for performance and tradeoff analyses of the algorithms have been presented.

The extension of the adversary model remains an open issue for our future work. We will consider an adversary who knows an action for a fraction of users in the merged history graph and an adversary who knows some continuous actions of a user in the graph, and effects of the extended adversary models will be analyzed. We will also evaluate the feasibility of graphs using real data.

Acknowledgement. The authors would like to thank anonymous reviewers and program committee members for useful comments on an earlier version of this manuscript.

References

1. Arai, H., Sakuma, J.: Privacy Preserving Semi-supervised Learning for Labeled Graphs. In: Gunopulos, D., Hofmann, T., Malerba, D., Vazirgiannis, M. (eds.) ECML PKDD 2011, Part I. LNCS, vol. 6911, pp. 124–139. Springer, Heidelberg (2011)
2. Blaustein, B., Chapman, A., Seligman, L., Allen, M.D., Rosenthal, A.: Surrogate parenthood: Protected and informative graphs. In: Proc. of the 37th International Conference on Very Large Data Bases, VLDB 2011, pp. 518–527 (2011)
3. Hay, M., Li, C., Miklau, G., Jensen, D.: Accurate estimation of the degree distribution of private networks. In: Proc. of the 2009 9th IEEE International Conference on Data Mining, ICDM 2009, pp. 169–178 (2009)
4. Heer, J., Mackinlay, J., Stolte, C., Agrawala, M.: Graphical histories for visualization: Supporting analysis, communication, and evaluation. IEEE Transactions on Visualization and Computer Graphics 14(6), 1189–1196 (2008)
5. Karwa, V., Raskhodnikova, S., Smith, A., Yaroslavtsev, G.: Private analysis of graph structure. In: Proc. of the 37th International Conference on Very Large Data Bases, VLDB 2011, pp. 1146–1157 (2011)
6. Kurashima, T., Bessho, K., Toda, H., Uchiyama, T., Kataoka, R.: Ranking Entities Using Comparative Relations. In: Bhowmick, S.S., Küng, J., Wagner, R. (eds.) DEXA 2008. LNCS, vol. 5181, pp. 124–133. Springer, Heidelberg (2008)
7. Rastogi, V., Hay, M., Miklau, G., Suciu, D.: Relationship privacy: output perturbation for queries with joins. In: Proc. of the 28th ACM SIGMOD-SIGACT-SIGART Symposium on Principles of Database Systems, PODS 2009, pp. 107–116 (2009)
8. Sakuma, J., Kobayashi, S.: Link analysis for private weighted graphs. In: Proc. of the 32nd International ACM SIGIR Conference on Research and Development in Information Retrieval, pp. 235–242 (2009)
9. Samarati, P., Sweeney, L.: Generalizing data to provide anonymity when disclosing information. In: Proc. of the 17th ACM SIGACT-SIGMOD-SIGART Symposium on Principles of Database Systems (PODS 1998), p. 188 (1998)
10. TWIMPACT UG. TWIMPACT (2011), `http://twimpact.com/`
11. Weinberg, Z., Chen, E.Y., Jayaraman, P.R., Jackson, C.: I still know what you visited last summer: Leaking browsing history via user interaction and side channel attacks. In: 2011 IEEE Symposium on Security and Privacy, pp. 147–161 (2011)
12. Ying, X., Wu, X.: Randomizing social networks: a spectrum preserving approach. In: Proc. of the 8th SIAM Conference on Data Mining, SDM 2008, pp. 739–750 (2008)
13. Yuan, M., Chen, L., Yu, P.S.: Personalized privacy protection in social network. In: Proc. of the 37th International Conference on Very Large Data Bases, VLDB 2011, pp. 141–150 (2011)
14. Zhou, B., Pei, J.: Preserving privacy in social networks against neighborhood attacks. In: Proc. of the 24th International Conference on Data Engineering, ICDE 2008, pp. 506–515 (2008)
15. Zou, L., CHen, L., Özsu, M.T.: k-automorphism: a general framework for privacy preserving network publication. In: Proc. of the 35th International Conference on Very Large Data Bases, VLDB 2009, pp. 946–957 (2009)

HiPoLDS: A Security Policy Language for Distributed Systems

Matteo Dell'Amico[1], Gabriel Serme[2], Muhammad Sabir Idrees[1],
Anderson Santana de Oliveira[2], and Yves Roudier[1]

[1] Eurecom, Sophia-Antipolis, France
[2] SAP Research, Sophia-Antipolis, France

Abstract. Expressing security policies to govern distributed systems is a complex and error-prone task. Policies are hard to understand, often expressed with unfriendly syntax, making it difficult to security administrators and to business analysts to create intelligible specifications. We introduce the Hierarchical Policy Language for Distributed Systems (HiPoLDS). HiPoLDS has been designed to enable the specification of security policies in distributed systems in a concise, readable, and extensible way. HiPoLDS's design focuses on decentralized execution environments under the control of multiple stakeholders. Policy enforcement employs distributed reference monitors who control the flow of information between services. HiPoLDS allows the definition of both *abstract* and *concrete* policies, expressing respectively high-level properties required and concrete implementation details to be ultimately introduced into the service implementation.

1 Introduction

Service-oriented architectures (SOAs) are a major software development pattern that builds applications based on loosely coupled services which can be run by different entities. Because of their complexity and of the varying degrees of trust between locations in which code is deployed and executed, it is challenging to make these systems secure. In particular, security is a *crosscutting* requirement: security-related code is generally scattered over several pieces of code and locations. What is worse, a local vulnerability or a mismatch between the security mechanisms adopted at different location can have dire consequences, potentially putting large systems at stake.

The CESSA project[1] focuses on the daunting task of making large SOAs secure by using aspect-oriented structuring and modularizing security across administrative and technological domains. It is with this goal in mind that we introduce the HiPoLDS security policy language. This language aims at being an efficient tool to express policies in diverse and complex distributed systems, where several entities interact in complex scenarios. SOAs are our motivating use case and they have driven our design, but HiPoLDS has been designed to be applicable to any kind of distributed system.

---

[1] http://cessa.gforge.inria.fr

I. Askoxylakis, H.C. Pöhls, and J. Posegga (Eds.): WISTP 2012, LNCS 7322, pp. 97–112, 2012.
© IFIP International Federation for Information Processing 2012

HiPoLDS provides the following features which are not present together in existing security policy languages:

- Allowing to describe the security policy also by way of *abstract* requirements: this should allow the writer of the policy to mention *which* security properties they want (*e.g.*, confidentiality, authentication, *etc.*) along with how they are implemented (*e.g.*, encryption, signatures. *etc.*).
- Expressing the security policy of a service-oriented architecture centrally despite its decentralized enforcement. A single abstract requirement (*e.g.*, confidentiality or authentication) often needs to be implemented distributedly with several pieces of code at different locations (*e.g.* encrypt somewhere and decrypt in another place, or analogously for signature and verification). HiPoLDS aims to make the relationship between the abstract requirement and its distributed implementation clear.
- Keeping specifications clear and understandable, minimizing the need for code duplication and helping maintainability – even when policies are drafted cooperatively by several entities.

After discussing the state of the art on distributed policy languages in Section 2, we introduce the main constructs of HiPoLDS (Section 3), which is based on a hierarchy of *policy domains*, each of them being a set of locations at which security policies apply. HiPoLDS security rules are handled exclusively by reference monitors (RMs) running at each policy domain and controlling the flow of information crossing their borders. We show various use cases highlighting how HiPoLDS makes it easier to express complex security requirements, and relate security mechanisms with them (Section 4).

HiPoLDS has been designed with a top-down approach, by taking into account concrete practical use cases and deriving the features that were needed in such situations [9,10]. We discuss our plans towards a complete HiPoLDS implementation (Section 5), also discussing automated and semi-automated strategies to relate requirements with mechanisms that implement them. We conclude (Section 6) by highlighting open research issues related to HiPoLDS and discussing our agenda for future research.

2   Related Work

The expression of a security policy is central when it comes to describing how to secure a system. We review in this section a few of these approaches and in particular how appropriate they are for the distributed deployment of a service-oriented architecture. A large number of security policy specifications aim at mediating and restricting access to a central database. Those approaches cannot qualify for SOAs due to their distributed nature. In addition, the security policy of a SOA has to capture responsibilities about the enforcement of the security policy and the fact that not all execution environments where services are running can be controlled.

Even in decentralized settings, access control policies have generally been well covered. The SecPal language [2] is one such proposal for describing decentralized access control which formalizes the use of SPKI certificates. It is interesting in that, similarly to the underlying PKI infrastructure, it captures rather well the notion of trusted authorities and their respective competences for authentication. However, SecPal expressions are restricted to the access control model to be enforced and cannot describe any manipulation of messages required for more complex security policies. This means it also would not be very appropriate for analyzing complex and extensible protocols like those encountered in service-oriented architectures. Contrary to SecPal, some policy languages aim at extensibility rather than formal verifiability; this is the case of Li et al.'s approach [14]. The policy model is captured through facts and inference rules, which may be interesting for introducing additional concerns.

Information centric approaches like the Decentralized Label Model [16] or its variants aim at specifying formally the security properties of the information flow in a system. This description is implemented through the typing of information flows with labels, in particular confidentiality labels in the case of Myers and Liskov's label model. One advantage of this approach is that it is also very declarative and may describe many different properties beyond access control. Implementing policy enforcement may however be rather difficult to implement: some automation is required when moving to low-level operations, in particular with respect to the selection of the cryptographic mechanisms used and to the key distribution operations. All of those are left outside the security policy specification, thus likely preventing the customized combination of multiple encryption techniques; it is also implicitly assumed that this implementation will be "correctly" deployed, whatever that may mean to the security expert. Furthermore, while they are simple because of their high-level of abstraction, information flow security models require handling the declassification of information, which more or less breaks the regularity of the policy. Still, the DLM is at an advantage here compared with similar models by making this declassification operation explicitly described in the language.

It is worth noting that the security policy specifications described above approach the expression of the policy as a high level statement of security objectives or properties for the sake of separating the policy model from its implementation. However, by not considering low-level concerns related to policy enforcement they also fail to capture network boundaries, network domains, and the protocols between them, all which are however extremely important for the specification of relevant policies.

In contrast, the SPL language [21,20] is quite inspirational in that it expresses the distributed enforcement of obligation policies at different levels of abstraction. Those policies easily map to reference monitors for enforcement. SPL also aims at providing a unifying framework for policies expressed at multiple places in a company. Still, SPL assumes that the enforcement is performed by a trusted entity which is not adapted for addressing SOA security in general. Furthermore, the policies expressed in SPL are simply access control related in that some information is authorized or forbidden, the expression of that requirement being essentially focused on the description of the reference monitor operation.

Ponder [7] is another language based on obligation and filtering whose expressivity is more extended. It too fails to express the existence of multiple entities for enforcement.

The Law Governed Interactions approach [23] (LGI) also constitutes a very interesting attempt at specifying policies over multiple domains, like network domains. LGI aims at rather diverse types of policies, even beyond security ones, encompassing for instance quality of service concerns. Policy enforcement in LGI is based on the realization of a policy based middleware in which communication is mediated by reference monitors between domains. In this approach, domains can be considered as governed by a mandatory policy, their law. However, the approach fails short to account for multiple stakeholders by not considering that the enforcement might not always be possible - or at least not by an authority that is trusted enough to ensure the application of the law. Unlike LGI, in HiPoLDS reference monitor do not need to be trusted by all participating entities, and need to be as trusted as the applications running in their domains.

All three approaches above feature the idea that the concept of domains is not only central to enforcement by an associated reference monitor but also central to the very specification of security policies. Our work builds on the idea that a domain does not only mean a consistent policy is enforced, but that the enforcement is under the control of a single authority. Given that authority model, this architecture may to some extent also help solve policy composition issues [1], even though we do not address this issue in this paper.

Using AOP for policy enforcement is not an original idea in itself. Several works apply AOP for building inline reference monitors for access control, such as [19,25,8] or to specify other requirements such as availability [6]. The particularity in our approach is its application to the information flow in a distributed systems, which requires the use of specific aspect mechanisms [13].

Hierarchical policies also require another approach to policy composition and conflict resolution. In previous work, conflicts are mostly solved by disambiguating among diverging policy decisions [3,15,11]. We advocate that the hierarchical organization of HiPoLDS policies essentially impacts the enabled information flows between domains controlled by different authorities. Handling such issues rather requires advanced negotiation techniques when policies cross domains.

3   Language Overview

In service oriented architectures, complex processes are carried out by several interacting entities. It is essential to support a concise way of specifying high-level policies that need to be applied in the whole architecture or in large parts of it, as well as fine-grained requirements that need to be applied in smaller domains. In HiPoLDS, we do this by defining the whole system architecture as a hierarchical structure of *policy domains*, and using *reference monitors* that enforce security policies at the border of policy domains.

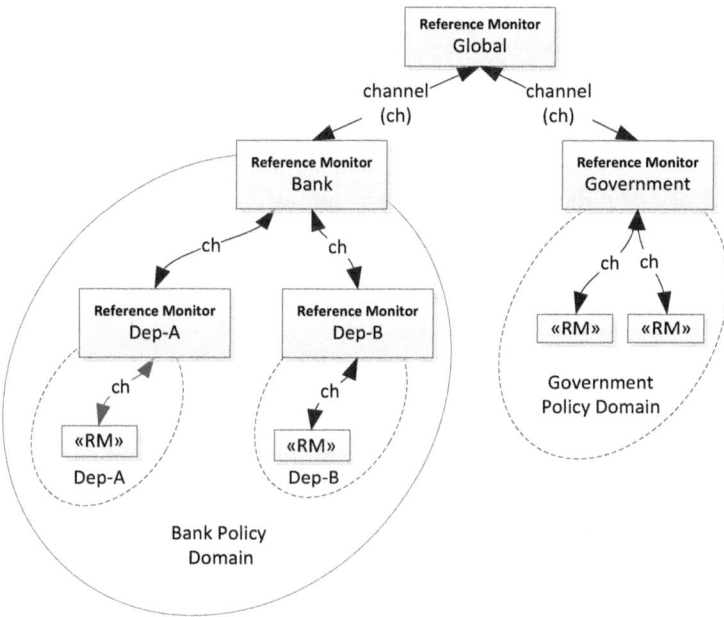

Fig. 1. Domain Hierarchy Example

A HiPoLDS document is composed of two parts: a declaration of the domain hierarchy, and a set of rules. The domain hierarchy, complemented by domain attributes, describes the global system architecture, while rules describe security policies that will take place. In this Section, we will introduce them along with the syntax, by means of simple examples.

3.1   Policy Domains

Policy domains can represent very different entities, such as corporations, individuals, down to the level of real or virtual machines, or even applications running on those machines. They are the scope for HiPoLDS rules, and they correspond to sets of entities that have particular properties that can be relevant to security (for example, a security domain can correspond to an organization, an individual, a place, a real machine, a virtual machine, and even a single application). Leaves of a policy domain hierarchy should be small enough that no security enforcement is needed for communications within a single policy domain. This is illustrated in Figure 1, which shows an example hierarchy for a loan negotiation scenario, where a bank communicates with a governmental information system in order to evaluate the eligibility of its customers to loan aids. We will use this scenario as a running example throughout this paper.[2]

---

[2] A complete HiPoLDS specification for this scenario is available in [9].

Policies regulate the exchange of information between different domains. They are enforced and monitored *at the borders* of policy domains. In this way it is possible to make sure that, for example, particular information sets remain confined within a domain (*e.g.*, to fulfill a privacy requirement) or get annotated with additional security metadata (*e.g.*, a Message Authentication Code or a cryptographic signature). The hierarchical structuring of policy domains allows the coexistence of policies that cover a wide set of locations (such as an organization) and of very specific ones (for example, access to a particular service).

Any domain can contain any number of subdomains, up to an arbitrary level of nesting. For a domain included within a parent domain, policies both in the enclosing and the inner domains will apply. This allows us to naturally define rules both at large (*e.g.*, organizations) and small (*e.g.*, services) scales. The hierarchy of policy domains also allows drafting a security policy cooperatively: the language supports the definition of rules that only apply within one, or more, policy domains. In our framework, administrators from involved entities should agree on "top-level" security policies applying to all domains, but they can be free to define additional security policies applying only to a domain of their competence. Data fields can be attached to policy domains, for example to contain encryption keys used by a principal.

In very complex scenarios, the number of policy domains might become very large, making the policy domain hierarchy unwieldy to handle manually. Currently, HiPoLDS does not handle this problem, which can be however managed by resorting to an external macro language such as, for example, GNU M4.[3]

In a deployed implementation, the definition of the domain hierarchy should also include a way to match the addressing scheme used for communication between services with the policy domains, in order to allow reference monitors to evaluate the origin and destination policy domain for a message.

Domain Attributes. We allow specifying an arbitrary number of additional *attributes* for each policy domain, when defining the policy domain hierarchy. Domain attributes are text labels allowing to attach additional information to the containment relationships implied by the hierarchical domain policy structure.

Domain attributes allow to specify policies that apply to several policy domains without the need to list them explicitly, allowing them to "cross" the policy domain hierarchy. For example, all policy domains corresponding to mobile devices can be labeled as "mobile"; afterwards, it will be easy to define policies that apply to all mobile devices in the policy domain hierarchy, or some sub-hierarchy of it, by writing policies that apply only to domains with a "mobile" attribute. Such a feature is essential for avoiding repetitions and keeping rules as terse as possible.

Domain attributes can be used for several purposes, such as describing what a policy domain corresponds to (*e.g.*, an organization, an individual or a device) or some technical architecture details (*e.g.*, the kind of operating system running on a machine).

---

[3] http://www.gnu.org/s/m4/

All such information are potentially relevant with respect to the security policies, and domain attributes can be used to specify policies that apply to domains with common characteristics, even in different parts of the domain hierarchy. Using policy domain attributes increases maintainability: when a new policy domain is created, it will be sufficient to label it with the appropriate attributes and the relevant security policies will be applied to it as well.

Example. We show the HiPoLDS declaration of part of the domain hierarchy for the loan negotiation scenario. The nesting of policy domains is expressed by enclosing inner domains in curly braces, and for each domain the list of domain attributes is written as comma-separated between parentheses. Here, domain attributes make it possible to differentiate the clerks from the manager. For brevity, we omit data items attached to domains, such as for example the encryption key IDs used by the bank employees.

```
Bank (organization) {
    Dept-A (department, organization)
    {
        employee (manager),
        Sub-department (subdomain, department),
        {...},
    }

    Dept-B (department, organization)
    {
        employee (clerk),
        ...
    }
}
```

3.2   Reference Monitors

In our model, security is at stake if proper measures are not taken when information traverses policy domains. For example, due to a confidentiality requirement, one or more pieces of information should not be readable outside a given set of policy domains, and this requirement is not fulfilled when the information is sent unencrypted outside of the allowed domains, or the encryption keys are divulged. In our system model, a *reference monitor* per domain monitors all the information entering or exiting the domain and alters it as needed. A reference monitor communicates exclusively with the services in its own domain and with the reference monitors of the neighbors in the domain hierarchy (*i.e.*, parent and child domains).

Reference monitors are as trusted as anything in their policy domain: rather than being a trusted infrastructure (as, for example, in LGI), they are simply used to enforce and/or monitor the security mechanisms, separating them when possible from the business logic of the application. Reference monitors intercept, and take action, on communications across trust domain boundaries. They work similarly to "customs control", enforcing restrictions about what gets in and out of a domain. Some actions that reference monitors can apply are:

- filtering: reference monitors can implement access control to resources outside of their original policy domain[4] by filtering unauthorized messages; +
- cryptography: information can be encrypted, decrypted or signed when leaving or entering policy domains;
- managing security metadata: in our system, information is augmented with metadata that we label as *information tags* (see Section 3.4).

In other cases, reference monitors can enforce security policies by triggering actions that will take place in their policy domain.

3.3   HiPoLDS Rules

Rules are the way in which security requirements are specified in HiPoLDS. The form of a rule is SCOPE {LEFTPART → RIGHTPART}.

- The **scope** identifies the part(s) of the policy domain hierarchy in which the rule needs to be enforced. If omitted, the default scope for a rule is the whole domain hierarchy.
- The **left part** is a set of comma-separated clauses that describe the conditions that trigger rule enforcement. The rule is enforced when all the clauses on the left part are true.
- The **right part** describes the properties that are required to hold. The rule is satisfied when all the clauses on the right part are true.

A first example of a rule is the following one:

$$\text{x} \rightarrow \text{x} \; is \; \texttt{confidential}(Bank, Government)$$

The scope here is omitted, meaning that the rule applies to the whole policy domain hierarchy. The left part of the rule, in this case, matches the only variable x. In HiPoLDS, variables match pieces of information; if they appear on the left side, they are implicitly quantified universally. In this case, the variable x therefore matches any piece of information exchanged in the whole domain hierarchy. If a variable appears only on the right side of the rule, it is instead implicitly quantified existentially, meaning that security enforcement mechanism must ensure that such an assignment to the variable exists such that the right part of the rule is satisfied.

   On the right side, *confidential* is a security property – specified by a list of domains – that must be ensured. Security properties in HiPoLDS are preceded by the **is** keyword. The *confidential* property requires that pieces of information will

---

[4] Policy domains can be made as small as required; for example, to enforce access control to a service from any other location, a policy domain can enclose only the original service.

not be readable outside of the specified policy domains – Bank and Government, in this case.

This particular rule requires that the *confidential* property is ensured, but it is underspecified, in the sense that it can be implemented in different ways. For example, all messages that leave Bank or Government can be encrypted with keys only available in those domains, or messages can just be filtered when they leave any of those domains. We refer to rules that can be implemented in several possible ways as *abstract* rules, as opposed to *concrete* rules that give a complete specification that can be executed by reference monitors. Since abstract rules are less verbose and more focused on the security properties that are needed, we consider the ability to express them as very beneficial towards having clear and maintainable security policies. The development of inference techniques that would help writers of security policies derive concrete rules starting from high-level, abstract ones is currently an open issue on which we are still working.

Rules are *not monotonic*. For example, consider a sub-domain B of domain A. If we consider requirements on data confidentiality, a piece of information can be allowed to be readable only within B and not in the rest of A, but also the opposite can apply: if B for some reason is considered "less trusted" than the rest of A (*e.g.*, a mobile device that can fall more easily in the hands of an attacker), then restrictive rules can be applied whenever some data is sent to B.

It is possible that rules will require actions that are impossible to satisfy or in conflict with other rules. We plan to investigate how to detect conflicting rules, both statically (*i.e.*, when drafting the security policy) and at runtime, and on determining ways to manage them. Conflicts within a policy domain are the easiest to solve as they only correspond to local policies as defined by the same authority. In the current proposal, we limit ourselves to an order-based prioritization of rules within a policy domain, in the style of most firewall policies; other approaches for solving conflicts have been vastly explored in the literature and might be applied as well. In contrast, conflicts between policies defined in different domains are harder to solve as they are defined by potentially different authorities and thus require some negotiation. Due to the style of HiPoLDS policies which only adds further security constraints to the diffusion of information flows between policy domains, those conflicts cannot increase the rights granted to principals; instead they may impede communication between two policy domains, especially if an intermediate domain prohibits information to flow across. In this current proposal, we will limit ourselves to a simple priority rule, by choosing the more specific rules (*i.e.*, those defined for inner policy domains) and, to discriminate between rules defined at the same hierarchy level, we will give priority to the one defined first.

3.4   Information Tags

Information tags are free-form text labels representing some security metadata that is attached to information and categorizes it. It is possible to define HiPoLDS rules that apply to information that has particular tags; when combined with domain attributes this allows us to naturally define policies that apply to large sets of information and span different policy domains. Reference monitors manage information tags and use information tags to decide which actions to take. For example, based on the tags it has, information can be filtered, transformed (*e.g.*, through encryption, stripping of confidential information, sanitization against injection attacks) and/or rerouted. Information tags are stripped before sending information to the original services, which will behave as if no security mechanisms were put in place. The following example shows how an information tag can be used in HiPoLDS.

$$\begin{aligned} &\mathtt{m} : message, \ \mathtt{x} : customer\text{-}info \ \epsilon \ \mathtt{m}.contents, \\ &\mathtt{m}.from == \mathtt{y} :: employee, \ \mathtt{y}.key == P_k \qquad \rightarrow \mathtt{x} \ is \ \mathtt{signed}(P_k) \end{aligned} \tag{1}$$

In this case, the scope of the rule is the `Bank` domain. In its place, a domain attribute could have been there (for example, `bank`) to specify that the rule applies to all banks in the domain hierarchy. In this rule, we see for the first time the ':' and '::' constructs, which are used respectively to match variables representing data with information tags and those representing domains with domain attributes. In addition, data fields on information and on policy domains are accessed via the dot notation seen in `m.contents` and `m.from`.

In this case, the left side of the rule uses information tags and domain attributes to match any message m sent from an employee y in the Bank. Since variables appearing on the left side of the rule are quantified universally, the contents of the message m are bound to x. Then y's key is bound to the variable P_k; finally, the right side of the rule requires that the message is signed with the key P_k. When the message is sent, reference monitors will verify the state of the message; if the left side matches and the right side does not (*i.e.*, the message is not signed) the appropriate reference monitor can add the signature – if it has access to the private key P_k – or drop the message. In summary, the rule above can be read as follows in plain English: *"The following rule applies only to the policy domain of bank. For each message m sent by an employee y with a public key P_k, P_k must be used to sign the contents of the message."*

4   Examples

After introducing the basic structure of HiPoLDS, we now show how its features can be adopted in a realistic case. We illustrate the relationship between concrete and abstract rules, discuss the role of reference monitors, and show how domain attributes can be used to describe role-based security rules. We will continue our discussion using the loan negotiation example from the previous section.

4.1   Abstract and Concrete Rules

Let us consider a security requirement of the following form: *"Customers' private information should only be disclosed to the Bank and the Government, and its integrity has to be guaranteed"*. Such a requirement would translate to the following HiPoLDS *abstract* rule:

$$m : message, \; x : customer\text{-}info \; \epsilon \; m.contents$$
$$\rightarrow x \; is \; \texttt{confidential}(Bank, Government), \; m \; is \; \texttt{integrity\_verified} \quad (2)$$

In this case, we use the `customer-info` information tag to denote messages that contain the kind of information that is affected by the rule, and limit the disclosure of data to the Bank and Government domains, and to their subdomains. In this case, the abstract properties we require are `confidential` and `integrity_verified`. We discuss the mechanisms with which we recognize information characteristics and add information tags in Section 5.3.

Since this is an abstract rule, it can be implemented in several ways. A first option is adopting asymmetric cryptography: for example, when a message is sent from the Bank to the Government, the following rule might be applied in the reference monitors in the Bank domain:

Bank {
$$m : message, \; x : customer\text{-}info, \; m.to == t \; in \; Government$$
$$\rightarrow x \; is \; \texttt{asym\_encrypted}(t.P_k) \quad (3)$$
}

In this case, `asym_encrypted` is a *concrete* rule applying to all the messages that are sent to any recipient in the Government domain (*i.e.*, whose `to` field is within a policy domain contained in `Government`). This is a concrete rule because it dictates the specific mechanism to use in order to obtain the required property, which is confidentiality.

Such a rule has to be accompanied by other rules: the companion rule enforcing decryption when messages are received in the Government, and a set of analogous rules for messages sent from the Government to the Bank which are tagged with `customer-info` as well.

Other concrete implementations of the same abstract requirement are possible. For example, this can be done with a symmetric cryptography implementation using a shared key:

Bank {
$$m : message, \; x : customer\text{-}info, \; m.to == t \; in \; Government$$
$$\rightarrow x \; is \; \texttt{sym\_encrypted}(Bank.shared\_key) \quad (4)$$
}

The above concrete policy rule can implement the required abstract property; however, there are cases for which such a solution would not be acceptable: for example, if the abstract property of non-repudiability were requested, it would not be achievable with only this mechanism.

More elaborate scenarios are conceivable: for example, if a reference monitor (say, on a mobile device representing a subdomain of Bank) is considered not trusted enough to hold a system-wide shared key - like in the example before - and not powerful enough to process asymmetric encryption, multi-step protocols can be envisaged. In this case, for example, the reference monitor on the mobile device can use a shared key to use symmetric encryption with the **Bank** reference monitor, which can then re-encrypt the messages towards the intended recipient with asymmetric encryption. Such a policy is within the expressive capabilities of HiPoLDS, and can be expressed as follows.

```
MobileDevice {
```
$\quad$ m : $message$, x : $customer\text{-}info$, m.$to ==$ t $in\ Government$

$\quad \rightarrow$ x is **sym_encrypted**($MobileDevice.shared\_key$), m : $step1\_applied$
```
}
```
```
Bank {
```
$\qquad\qquad\qquad\qquad\qquad\qquad\qquad\qquad\qquad\qquad\qquad\qquad\quad$ (5)

$\quad$ m : $step1\_applied\ \rightarrow$ m is **sym_decrypted**($MobileDevice.shared\_key$),

$\quad$ m is **asym_encrypted**($m.to.P_k$),
```
}
```

In this case, the **step1_applied** information tag is used to mark the first processing step where it is applied; processing will further continue at the **Bank** reference monitor. As before, further matching rules will decrypt messages at the recipient, and deal with sending messages in the opposite direction.

We consider the ability of expressing both abstract and concrete rules as a key feature of HiPoLDS; in Section 5.1 we discuss our plans for deriving or verifying concrete policies based on abstract ones.

4.2   Roles and Policy Domains

It is worth noting that rules based on roles can be expressed via HiPoLDS. Indeed, roles can be expressed by assigning policy domain attributes to policy domains that represent individuals. The following (abstract) rule states that all messages tagged as **classified** should remain confidential between managers:

$\quad$ m : $classified \rightarrow$ m is **confidential**($manager$)

In this case, we remind that **manager** is a domain attribute, and this rule would be equivalent to enumerating all policy domains with the **manager** attribute. Using domain attributes in this way helps maintainability and avoids repeating the same rule for different domains. The rule can be implemented using concrete rules similar to what we have seen in Section 4.1.

Let us furthermore suppose that we want to avoid sending classified messages to mobile devices, even if they are owned by a manager (*i.e.*, they are subdomains of a domain with **manager** attribute). Such a rule writes as

$\quad$ m : $classified \rightarrow$ m is **filtered**($mobile$)

In this case, **filtered** is a new property requiring that messages should not arrive to the listed domains. Again, **mobile** is a domain attribute and using it is equivalent to listing all domains tagged as **mobile**.

To enforce this rule, reference monitors in a `manager` domain with `mobile` subdomains should enforce the filtering. This kind of rule is applicable because correctly-behaving reference monitors communicate with each other only through the hierarchical channels as shown in Figure 1 on page 101, so the parent node is the only point from which information can reach a domain. It is exactly because, in this case, `mobile` domains are feared to not behave correctly (*e.g.*, have side communication channels) that confidential information is filtered before reaching them.

Here, we reinforce the fact that each reference monitor is as trusted as the domain it is in, and such trust is non-monotonic. In fact, the only reference monitors that handle confidential information unencrypted are those in the domains that have access to it. We point out that this might mean that reference monitors at high levels in the hierarchy might not have any concrete rule to apply – this means that they can effectively be removed. In particular, the top-level global reference monitor could be complex to deploy and to implement, and concrete rules that do not need it could be advisable.

5   From Specification to Enforcement

We focused on describing the design design of the HiPoLDS language; we now turn our attention towards the implementation of an enforcement architecture. We outline the policy refinement process, presenting the main alternatives that will guide the next steps in this research, and then discuss the requirements for the correct implementation of reference monitors.

5.1   From Abstract to Concrete Policies

We describe below the three main approaches for deriving concrete policies from abstract ones.

Fully automated refinement. Addressing the semantic gap from abstract to concrete policies: it is necessary to create a translation framework linking the abstract concepts of HiPoLDS policies to lower level system concepts. Assuming that the mapping is correct and reliable, the automated concrete policy generation would produce possible overhead such as for instance, encrypting a communication channel more than once, as soon as the policies governing a domain hierarchy may require confidentiality under overlapping conditions. Nevertheless the major difficulty in such an approach is to create the refinement process itself, by identifying decidable classes of HiPoLDS policies and establishing the correctness of the generated concrete policies considering the formal semantics at the abstract and concrete levels.

Partially automated refinement. Since processing abstract policies in HiPoLDS would involve a high number of assumptions about the domain in question with a large number of semantic relationships among the tags, attributes, roles and the domain hierarchy, one can imagine an automated tool would be able to produce a partial concrete policy as an output that would need to be manually edited or corrected by a security expert. As soon as basic considerations about enforcement could be reasonably handled by the automated refinement process, the effort of the security expert could be reduced. However, significant research and development effort would be necessary, probably as much as for the fully automated refinement alternative.

Manual refinement with tool support. A more realistic approach would be to rely on the expertise of the security administrator to manually refine abstract policies into concrete ones, using their knowledge of the domain topology and its components. The process can be supported by tools to check the abstract and concrete policies, such as model checkers, which can work without needing much intervention. For instance, the ASLAN++ language and system [18] allows to model distributed systems communication protocols for the verification of security goals.

5.2   Firewall-Based Realization

A common solution to enforce security policies in relying on firewall or network filters. The term *firewall* is commonly associated to packet filter devices operating up to the layer 4 of the ISO/OSI model. The task of analyzing and filtering higher layer protocols (such as HTTP) is instead entrusted to the so-called Application-Level Gateways (ALG). ALGs can, for example, protect against malformed requests or they can be used to limit the access to certain resources.

The same concepts have also been extended to the SOAP protocol. Web-Server firewalling has been studied by academia [12], [4], industry [22], and standard bodies [24]. In fact, most of the vendor in the network security area already propose solutions tailored for the protection of web-services environment (e.g., Citrix Netscaler [17] or CISCO XML Gateway [5]). These firewalls are essentially application gateways that inspect the payload. This approach is less appropriate when payloads are encrypted as the encrypted content necessarily escapes the firewall analysis.

5.3   Introducing Information Tags

The information tags introduced in Section 3.4 are central to our approach to describe security metadata and categorize information. Reference monitors need these tags to correctly enforce HiPoLDS policies.

Information tags can be created in two possible ways: first, as metadata that annotate the processing done on messages by reference monitors; second, by examining and annotating the content of exchanged messages, leading to tags such as `customer-info` in the examples of Section 4.1. The first case is supported in the language by requiring the presence of a tag in the right hand of a rule, as done for `step1_applied` in rule 5 on page 108; the second depends on the particular implementation of monitored services, and requires inspecting the data which is present in messages and potentially also obtained through cross-layer analysis. The details of how such an inspection should work would depend on a choice of the particular message exchange protocol taken into consideration.

6   Conclusion

In this paper, we introduced the design of and main implementation directions of a new security policy language, HiPoLDS, intended for specifying security in complex distributed systems typically encountered in service-oriented architectures. We believe that, on the one hand, HiPoLDS is expressive enough to describe tersely several real-world policies; at the same time, the complexity of implementing HiPoLDS is manageable.

In future work, we plan to expand on this work with a more formal and concrete definition of the language. Other problems would require further work:

- Reasoning on the relationships between abstract and concrete policies. We can think of inference mechanisms to verify whether concrete policies implement the abstract required policies. Such mechanisms should report inconsistencies between two representation levels or detect non-enforceable rules.
- Weaving concrete policies in the domain hierarchy. Monitors have to be consistently distributed along the hierarchy in order to reliably support the HiPoLDS metaphor of watching the system borders. It is also necessary to provide correct information about the environment, originated from heterogeneous sources and from different architectural layers. We believe that distributed aspect-oriented languages can support the extraction and interception of sensible information that need to be provided to the reference monitors, through the implementation of inlined reference monitors.

References

1. Bauer, L., Ligatti, J., Walker, D.: A language and system for composing security policies. Tech. Rep. TR-699-04. Princeton University (2004)
2. Becker, M.Y., Fournet, C., Gordon, A.D.: SecPAL: Design and semantics of a decentralized authorization language. J. of Computer Security 18(4), 619–665 (2010)
3. Bonatti, P.A., di Vimercati, S.D.C., Samarati, P.: An algebra for composing access control policies. ACM Trans. Inf. Syst. Secur. 5(1), 1–35 (2002)
4. Bunge, R., Chung, S., Endicott-Popovsky, B., McLane, D.: An operational framework for service oriented architecture network security. In: Proc. HICCS, p. 312 (2008)
5. CISCO ACE XML Gateway (2010),
   http://www.cisco.com/en/US/products/ps7314/index.html
6. Cuppens, F., Cuppens-Boulahia, N., Ramard, T.: Availability enforcement by obligations and aspects identification. In: Proc. ARES, pp. 229–239 (2006)
7. Damianou, N., Dulay, N., Lupu, E.C., Sloman, M.: The Ponder Policy Specification Language. In: Sloman, M., Lobo, J., Lupu, E.C. (eds.) POLICY 2001. LNCS, vol. 1995, pp. 18–38. Springer, Heidelberg (2001)
8. Dantas, D.S., Walker, D.: Harmless advice. In: Morrisett, J.G., Jones, S.L.P. (eds.) POPL, pp. 383–396. ACM (2006)
9. Dell'Amico, M., Idrees, M.S., Roudier, Y., de Oliveira, A.S., Serme, G., Harel, G.: Language definition for security specifications. Deliverable D2.2, The CESSA project (May 2011), http://cessa.gforge.inria.fr/lib/exe/
   fetch.php?media=publications:d2-2.pdf

10. Douence, R., Grall, H., Mejía, I., Royer, J.C., Südhold, M., Idrees, M.S., Roudier, Y., Leroux, J., Rivard, F., Pazzaglia, J., Serme, G.: Survey and requirements analysis. Deliverable D1.1, The CESSA project (June 2010), `http://cessa.gforge.inria.fr/lib/exe/fetch.php?media=publications:d1-1.pdf`

11. Dougherty, D.J., Kirchner, C., Kirchner, H., de Oliveira, A.S.: Modular Access Control Via Strategic Rewriting. In: Biskup, J., López, J. (eds.) ESORICS 2007. LNCS, vol. 4734, pp. 578–593. Springer, Heidelberg (2007)

12. Gruschka, N., Luttenberger, N.: Protecting web services from DOS attacks by SOAP message validation. Security and Privacy in Dynamic Environments (2006)

13. Sabir Idrees, M., Serme, G., Roudier, Y., de Oliveira, A.S., Grall, H., Südholt, M.: Evolving Security Requirements in Multi-layered Service-Oriented-Architectures. In: Garcia-Alfaro, J., Navarro-Arribas, G., Cuppens-Boulahia, N., de Capitani di Vimercati, S. (eds.) DPM 2011 and SETOP 2011. LNCS, vol. 7122, pp. 190–205. Springer, Heidelberg (2012)

14. Li, J.X., Li, B., Li, L., Che, T.S.: A policy language for adaptive web services security framework. In: ACIS International Conference on Software Engineering, Artificial Intelligence, Networking, and Parallel/Distributed Computing, vol. 1, pp. 261–266 (2007)

15. Moses, T. (ed.): Extensible access control markup language (xacml) version 2.0. Tech. rep. OASIS Standard (2005)

16. Myers, A.C., Liskov, B.: Protecting privacy using the decentralized label model. ACM Transactions on Software Engineering and Methodology 9(4), 410–442 (2000)

17. CITRIX NetScaler (2010), `http://www.citrix.com/english/ps2/products/product.asp?contentid=21679`

18. von Oheimb, D., Mödersheim, S.: ASLan++ — A Formal Security Specification Language for Distributed Systems. In: Aichernig, B.K., de Boer, F.S., Bonsangue, M.M. (eds.) FMCO 2011. LNCS, vol. 6957, pp. 1–22. Springer, Heidelberg (2011)

19. de Oliveira, A.S., Wang, E.K., Kirchner, C., Kirchner, H.: Weaving rewrite-based access control policies. In: Ning, P., Atluri, V., Gligor, V.D., Mantel, H. (eds.) FMSE, pp. 71–80. ACM (2007)

20. Ribeiro, C., Ferreira, P.: A policy-oriented language for expressing security specifications. International Journal of Network Security 5(3), 299–316 (2007)

21. Ribeiro, C., Zuquete, A., Ferreira, P., Guedes, P.: SPL: An access control language for security policies with complex constraints. In: Proc. of NDSS (2001)

22. Room, S.I.I.R.: XML Firewall Architecture and Best Practices for Configuration and Auditing (2007), `http://www.sans.org/reading_room/whitepapers/firewalls/xml-firewall-architecture-practices-configuration-auditing_1766`

23. Serban, C., Zhang, W., Minsky, N.: A decentralized mechanism for application level monitoring of distributed systems. In: 5th International Conference on Collaborative Computing: Networking, Applications and Worksharing, CollaborateCom 2009, pp. 1–10. IEEE (2009)

24. Singhal, A., Winograd, T., Scarfone, K.: Guide to Secure Web Services. NIST Publication

25. Song, E., Reddy, R., France, R.B., Ray, I., Georg, G., Alexander, R.: Verifiable composition of access control and application features. In: Ferrari, E., Ahn, G.J. (eds.) SACMAT, pp. 120–129. ACM (2005)

ROAC: A Role-Oriented Access Control Model

Nezar Nassr and Eric Steegmans

Katholieke Universiteit Leuven,
Dept. of Computer Science and Engineering,
Leuven, Belgium
{nezar.nassr,eric.steegmans}@cs.Kuleuven.be

Abstract. Role-Based Access Control (RBAC) has become the de facto standard for realizing authorization requirements in a wide range of organizations. Existing RBAC models suffer from two main shortcomings; lack of expressiveness of roles/permissions and ambiguities of their hierarchies. Roles/permissions expressiveness is limited since roles do not have the ability to express behaviour and state, while hierarchical RBAC cannot reflect real organizational hierarchies. In this paper, we propose a novel access control model: The Role-Oriented Access Control Model (ROAC), which is based on the concepts of RBAC but inspired by the object-oriented paradigm. ROAC greatly enhances expressiveness of roles and permissions by introducing parameters and methods as members. The hierarchical ROAC model supports selective inheritance of permissions.

Keywords: Access Control, RBAC, Authorization, Role Hierarchies.

1 Introduction

The deployment of software applications on distributed networks and on the web has exposed them to many new security threats. One major risk is that an application can be accessed by unauthorized users in an easier way than in the past. Governments and commercial organizations are continuously seeking strong access control models that can help them prevent unauthorized access to their systems. Therefore, they maintain their reputation as safe institutions where confidential information is safeguarded. For example, WikiLeaks could have been prevented should better access controls have been in place [1]. Role based Access Control (RBAC) [2] has been used by organizations to protect resources in their software systems against unauthorized access. RBAC has become the dominant access control model that is widely accepted in enterprise, health, and governments systems.

RBAC is based on four principles: abstract privileges, separation of administrative functions, least privilege and separation of duties [3]. RBAC is expressed in terms of users, roles, permissions, objects and operations [4]. Permissions are assigned to roles and roles are assigned to users. Permissions are privileges to access objects or to execute operations. RBAC models often support role hierarchies. This feature is known as *hierarchical* RBAC. Role hierarchies define

I. Askoxylakis, H.C. Pöhls, and J. Posegga (Eds.): WISTP 2012, LNCS 7322, pp. 113–127, 2012.
© IFIP International Federation for Information Processing 2012

partial orders on roles; this is analogous to inheritance in the object-oriented paradigm. The central advantage of RBAC is that it simplifies the management of access rights and offers a high level view on security in organizations by bridging the gap between functional requirements of organizations and the technical authorization aspects of their security policies [3], [5].

Despite robustness of RBAC, it has received a great academic attention from researchers. The literature shows many notable contributions that address limitations and suggest improvements to RBAC. However, in its current form, RBAC does not seem to have enough power to express a wide range of security requirements and capture fine access control granularity when put into practice [5]. Two main shortcomings of standard RBAC are its lack of expressiveness when defining roles [5], [6] and ambiguities that may arise in hierarchical role models [7]. Hierarchies in standard RBAC only support the *is-a* hierarchy which does not reflect real organizational hierarchies as we will see later. On the other hand, parametrized RBAC [5], [6],[8] has been proposed to address the lack of expressiveness by associating parameters to roles. Shortcomings related to role hierarchies were addressed by many initiatives. More discussions regarding this are contained in the next section.

Existing RBAC models consider roles as entities of a simple type that cannot have member attributes and operations, except parameters as suggested by parametrized RBAC. This provides a relatively simple and straightforward type for roles, but it lacks flexibility when defining roles. Roles in RBAC are blind in the sense that they are not aware of the application environment. They cannot access data in the system or perform any actions. Roles cannot hold variables, status, methods, etc. More so, the generalization concept in existing RBAC models does not reflect real organizational hierarchies. In most organizations, superiors do not need full access on permissions of their inferiors, and hence application of the *is-a* inheritance in these situations results in assignment of undesired privileges to superiors. This conflicts with the least privilege concept of RBAC. In many situations, senior users have supervision relations to junior users. Organizations are seeking flexibility when defining hierarchies in the access control model that can reflect the nuances above.

In this paper, we propose the Role Oriented Access Control model (ROAC) as a novel access control model. ROAC addresses limitations of existing RBAC models through benefiting from object-oriented concepts. ROAC makes analogies between roles and classes in object-oriented programming languages, then utilizes their concepts for constructing a new robust and extendible access control model. The main contributions of ROAC are:

1. To the best of our knowledge, ROAC is the most expressive access control model yet defined. ROAC greatly enhances the expressiveness of access control through associating variables and methods to permissions and roles. This architecture provides a means to defining one role and then defining multiple instances from the role with different levels of granularity. More so, application code is able to invoke methods to validate role parameters that are defined as part of roles permissions. This helps separating the access

control management from the application logic. This all results in stronger security and minimizes the risk of different interpretations of parameters among developers of the application.

2. ROAC greatly enhances RBAC hierarchies by adopting standard object-oriented inheritance concepts. At the same time, it extends hierarchical facilities with supervision relationships among roles. It also offers means for selective inheritance of permissions of junior roles by senior roles. In this way, ROAC better reflects organizational hierarchies. In other words, ROAC supports both the *is-a* and selective inheritance.

3. ROAC addresses scalability issues of existing RBAC models. In addition to the points mentioned above, ROAC provides a new kind of parameters, referred to as static parameters. Static parameters have common values for all instances of the role. Static parameters help updating all instances of the role at once. For example, if an organization often switches between two roles, it must be able to disable one type of role and enable the other type. A static parameter can then be introduced to specify whether or not all instances of the role are enabled. Moreover, by using validators, organizations can also provide assertions over the parameters and static parameters. Validators can also implement authorization policies that can be checked before authorizing operations. In ROAC, roles and permissions can hold state. Roles can connect to databases and can have data structures to hold data. This can be of great usage for auditing and tracking authorizations.

The remainder of this paper is organized as follows: In the next section we review related work, then in the third section we overview the ROAC model. In section four, we provide the data model of ROAC. In the fifth section we explain the generalization model of ROAC. Section six provides a discussion about how ROAC can implement next generation RBAC concepts and the trade-off between complexity and fine granularity. Finally, section five concludes our work and highlights future tracks.

2 Background and Motivation

RBAC has received a lot of attention from academic researchers and from commercial organizations. This has lead to many improvements to the standard RBAC model [4]. RBAC research can be broadly classified into two main categories: improvements to features existing in standard RBAC and extensions to standard RBAC. Improvements to standard RBAC have been mainly focusing on improving role hierarchies of the standard RBAC model and on improving expressiveness of roles by parametrization. Extensions to standard RBAC have been focusing on adding new features to RBAC such as supporting cross domain roles, role delegation models, etc. In this paper, we focus on improvements to RBAC.

In standard RBAC, role hierarchies support multiple inheritance; meaning that a role can inherit permissions from multiple roles. The general roles hierarchies concept in standard RBAC has two main properties; firstly, the possibility to derive roles from multiple roles, and secondly, the role hierarchies concept provides a uniform treatment of user/role and role/role relations. Users can be included in the role hierarchy, using the same relation to denote the user assignment to roles. More so, standard RBAC supports the limited role hierarchy concept, in which hierarchies are limited to the single immediate descendent [4]. The roles hierarchies concept in standard RBAC suggests that when a senior role inherits from a junior role, all permissions of the junior role are transferred to the senior role.

The most familiar form of collaborative working is hierarchical in nature. In organizational hierarchies, the superior may not take part in the details of a task, but rather acts as the instigator of the task [9]. In other words, the most typical form of hierarchy in organizations is the supervision hierarchy [11]. More so, in some situations it is required to keep a role private and inhibit others from extending it. Sandhu [3], [10] has introduced the concept of the private role, which is a role that cannot be further extended. In situations where users have private documents that they need to protect from their superiors, a new private role has to be introduced for each user. This results in an increased number of roles in the system. This counter-balances the advantage gained by using hierarchies which is reducing number of roles in the system [11]. Xuexiong et al [12] have proposed an approach to tackle excessive inheritance that occurs when users get more permissions than they should have by permission inheritance. They resolve the issue by segregating role permissions into private permissions and public permissions. Then only public permissions are transferred through inheritance to superiors. If a role r has a set of permissions P, then P is divided into two sets P_{prv} for private roles, and P_{pub} for public roles. When a senior role r_s inherits from r, only P_{pub} are transferred to r_s. The drawbacks of this approach are that the private permissions of a role won't be inherited by any other role. In organizations, it might be the case that private permissions are different between two superiors of a junior role. In this situation, it won't be possible to define the inheritance for the two roles.

Lack of expressiveness in role definition has received attention from researchers as well. In many organizations, different users may require different granularity levels of the same role. For example, two tellers in a bank might have the same role that enables them to perform transactions. But the maximum amount of the transactions both of them can perform might be different depending on their seniority. Standard RBAC can be adapted to capture such fine grained authorizations by dramatically increasing the number of distinct roles. Parametrized roles [5], [6], [8] have been proposed to address the lack of expressiveness of roles. One of the good attempts to address lack of expressiveness of RBAC by using parametrized roles was defined by Jaeger et al. [8]. The formal definition of parametrized RBAC was introduced by Abdallah et al. [5]. Parametrized RBAC provides finer granularity by creating instances of RBAC components according to the contexts of their use [5]. This is achieved by associating parameters with roles. Parameters are used to define the granularity level of the role. In the example of the bank tellers presented previously, the teller role can be parametrized by an amount limit parameter. Then each teller can be assigned a maximum amount limit when assigned to the role.

Fischer et al. [6] have proposed the object-sensitive RBAC (ORBAC), which is a generalized RBAC model for object-oriented languages. ORBAC addresses the lack of expressiveness of RBAC by using parametrized roles. In ORBAC, privileged operations are parametrized by a set of index values, which are used to distinguish the granularity level of the roles between users. A privileged operation can only be invoked if both the required role is assigned to the user who invokes the operation and the role's index values matches the operation's index values.

Parametrized RBAC was the first initiative to address the lack of expressiveness in role definitions, but parametrized RBAC is still not sufficient to express many authorization requirements. In the example discussed above, it is not possible to check the amount against currencies and to find the amount value against the home currency of the bank. Expressiveness of RBAC can be further improved should we introduce possibilities to make validations on parameters. In addition, we provide a new type of parameters that can have values common to all instances of roles. In our proposed access control model (ROAC), we address these limitations and further improve the concept of roles and permissions.

3   The Role-Oriented Access Control Model Overview

In the previous section, we have shown that parametrized RBAC was proposed to address standard RBAC's lack of expressiveness when defining roles. The proposed approach adds some flexibility when defining roles. In parametrized RBAC, computations involving parameters of roles must be performed at the application side. This is similar to plain old record types of *structs* in procedural programming languages. Object oriented programming languages have introduced the notion of encapsulation that is wrapping data and methods within classes in combination with implementation hiding [13]. The idea here is to transplant those ideas to the definition of roles. With parametrized RBAC it is possible, for example, to specify an amount limit and a currency as parameters to the teller role. But it cannot provide further possibilities to compute the amount against the home currency. As an example, if we pass to the teller role 1000 as an amount and *EUR* as a currency, the amount is not equivalent to 1000 with *USD* currency. Moreover, it provides no way of adding static parameters to roles, i.e. when the static parameter is changed it takes effect on all instances of the role. If an organization requires to disable a role from the access control system, but the organization cannot delete it, since it is associated with records in their audit trail. Deleting the role causes inconsistencies within the system. A better way to cope with this issue is to flag the role as deleted.

In ROAC, we address limitations of existing RBAC models by adjusting and transplanting concepts of object oriented programming languages to the context of roles and permissions. Roles and permissions in ROAC are analogous to objects in object oriented programming languages. Like objects, roles and permissions can hold data (variables) and operations (methods). Similarly, objects can inherit from other objects typically expressing an *is-a* relation, roles can be organized into hierarchies with different relationships between superior nodes and their subnodes.

The core ROAC model consists of three main elements, users, roles and permissions. Users are principals requiring access to a software system. Roles project job functions within organizations. Roles can be further fine grained to represent sub-functions e.g. a job function can be a *teller* and a sub-function can be *AccountHolder*. Permissions are privileges to execute operations or access objects in the system. Users are assigned to role instances and permissions instances are assigned to roles. Since permissions usually correspond to operations and/or objects in a software system, parameters and validators should be included in permissions and propagated back to roles when permissions are assigned to roles. This means that roles combine all parameters of their assigned permissions. The values of parameters are set during users to roles assignment. The structure of the ROAC model is shown in Fig. 1.

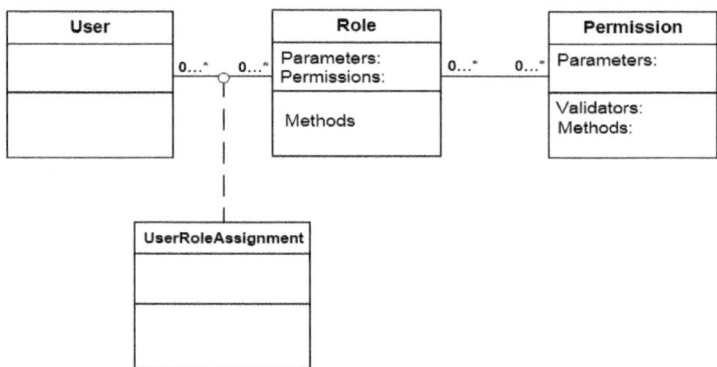

Fig. 1. UML diagram of the ROAC model

ROAC hierarchical model supports two hierarchies; the *is-a* hierarchy and the supervision hierarchy. In the *is-a* hierarchy, senior roles inherit all permissions and definitions of junior roles. The *is-a* hierarchy in ROAC does not necessarily reflect roles hierarchies defined in the standard RBAC model, it could be also used for deriving new roles and re-using definitions of existing roles. The other kind of hierarchy supported by ROAC is the supervision hierarchy. The supervision hierarchy reflects organizational hierarchies. Hierarchical ROAC model is explained in more detail in the fifth section.

4   ROAC Reference Data Model

The central notion of ROAC is that instances of roles and permissions are considered as objects, and hence, they are able to encapsulate data and perform operations. In this section, we summarize the main features of ROAC in a reference data model.

In the ROAC model, we extend the principle of roles and permissions to become analogous to object oriented classes. Both roles and permissions are equipped with variables and methods. Parameters are firstly defined in permissions and then propagated back to roles. Parameters are attributes (also called fields or data members) as in object-oriented languages. Once permissions and roles are defined, instances of both roles and permissions can be created. Roles are assigned in a many-to-many relation with permissions instances. Roles can also have extra parameters defined that are not in permissions instances assigned to the roles instances. These parameters are of type static. Static parameters can be defined in permissions and in roles. Once a value is set for a static parameter, it takes effect for all instances of the role or permission. Static parameters are similar to static variables in object oriented languages. Static variables in object oriented languages store values for the variables in a common memory location, all objects of the same class are affected if one object changes the value of a static variable [14]. Static parameter values can be initialized when static parameters are defined and their values can be changed by static *setter* methods. Roles and permissions can also have private parameters which are variables defined to be used in methods or validators internally.

Definition 1: Role and Permission Parameters. Role and permission parameters are attributes of roles and permissions. Parameters are declared by specifying the parameter name, data type and modifiers.

Methods are either used as validators or administrative functions such as setters and getters. Validators are methods defined in permissions for computing the authorization decision. The simplest form of a validator, is an empty validator. An empty validator grants authorization on an operation in a software system to any user that possesses a role that is assigned the permission that contains the validator definition. Extended form of validators takes inputs from the environment, and may connect to external systems to compute the authorization decision. Validators always return a *Boolean* value, true if it grants authorization and false otherwise. The convenient operations that validators most often perform are to check parameters values extracted from user/role assignment against parameters passed to operations in software systems protected with the ROAC model. Validators can also implement authorization policies. The choice of parameters, static parameters and validators often depends on the organization and the type of operations and objects they need to protect. Static parameters can hold temporal information about the roles. These temporal properties can be validated by validators. It could be useful in an organization when they, for example, add a new role in their access control system and they decide to start using the role on a specific date. The organization can define the role with a static parameter *StartDate* and assign the role to users. Then they can validate the *StartDate* before granting access on an operation. There are many scenarios where static parameters can help organizations maintain dynamic properties of their access control system.

Methods in ROAC are of great importance. Methods can be defined in roles and in permissions. The purpose of methods in ROAC is to provide administrative functions over roles and permissions and to handle operations on role and permission parameters.

Definition 2: Permissions Validators. A validator is a permission member operation that provides an authorization decision. Validators definitions consist of a signature and a body. The signature specifies the validator name and input parameters. Validators always return Boolean values. True if authorization is granted and false if denied. The body of the validator is the implementation of validator that consists of a sequence of programming statements implementing the authorization conditions.

Definition 3: Permissions and Roles methods. Methods in permissions and roles are member operations. Methods definitions consist of a signature and a body. The signature specifies method name, input parameters and a return value. The body of the method represents the method's business logic implementation by a sequence of programming statements.

Definition 4: ROAC Permissions. A Permission is a data type characterized by operations and attributes. Operations and attribute definitions are the same for all instances of a given permission. Permission non-static attributes values are specific to instances derived from a given permission. A permission determines an access authorization on one or more objects or one or more operations in a software system. Permissions in ROAC consist of: parameters, validators and methods. Parameters are attributes, while validators and methods are operations.

Definition 5: ROAC Roles. A Role is a data type characterized by operations and attributes. Attributes in roles correspond to role parameters propagated from permissions assigned to the role, and to static attributes of the role. Role operations correspond to role methods that provide administrative operations.

Definition 6: ROAC Data Types. Data types in ROAC correspond to the type of parameters in permissions and roles. Data types supported by ROAC depend on the programming language at stake, which usually are primitive data types and reference data types (objects).

Definition 7: User-Role Assignment. Let U be a set of user instances from user, R be a set of role instances created from different roles. Let M be a set of parameters of roles and V be a set of possible values for parameters. The user-role assignment is a many-to-many relation, given by the following mapping:

$$UA = ([u,r] (m_1{=}v_1, ., m_n{=}v_n)) , u \in U , r \in R, m_1..m_n \in M, v_1..v_2 \in V$$

Definition 8: Role-Permission association. Let R be a set of different roles, let P a set of permissions instances, let M be a set of permissions parameters and let R be a role instance created from R. The role-permission association is given by the following mapping:

RA = (r,p(m_1..m_n)) r ∈ R ,m_1..m_n∈M , r = r(p_{pre},p) r∈R, p_{pre} is the existing role permissions

We have until now defined the different elements of the role-oriented access control model. We now discuss how interactions between the different elements are established. Afterwards we use an example to explain these interactions.

In ROAC, users are assigned to roles and permissions are assigned to roles. Actually, one of the major advantages of RBAC is simplification of permissions management. Users can be easily reassigned from one role to another. Roles can be granted new permissions as new applications and systems are incorporated, and permissions can be revoked from roles as needed [3]. This is a great advantage that can be provided if user-role associations and role-permission assignments can be achieved dynamically. We have designed relations between ROAC elements to be implemented dynamically. In user-role association, users are associated to roles instances by role administrative methods. The role definition is not changed during this process. Parameter values of roles are set also during user-role assignment. This enables organizations to define different parameter values for different users, and hence provide different granularity levels of roles. The roles-permissions associations are also achieved similarly. If a new permission is to be added to the access control system, it does not need redefinition of roles that need to be assigned the new permission. Roles have an enumeration that contains all permissions assigned to roles. The enumeration can be dynamically updated by administrative roles methods for associating new permissions instances to roles. Roles also have enumerations that contain the parameters of permissions. Parameters of a role are the set of parameters of all permissions associated to the role. The parameters enumeration is updated each time a new permission instance is associated to the role. As well, since multiple permissions may share similar parameters, such as an *amount* value of a bank teller role permissions; all similar permissions parameters are considered as one parameter. The only condition is that those parameters must share the same name and data type. It might happen that a new permission is added to a role in a live environment where the role is already assigned to users, so an administrative function is also provided to set and update particular parameter values for particular users. More so, depending on authorization requirements, more administrative methods can be added to roles. When permissions are assigned to roles, static parameters are not propagated back to roles. Since static parameters are corresponding to the permission and their values are common to all instances of permissions.

Fig. 2. shows an example of a role definition and a permission definition. The role reflects a junior *teller* role in a bank. The permission is a privilege for withdrawing money from a bank account. The *Withdraw* permission has two parameters; *AmountLimit* represents the maximum amount of a transaction the teller can perform. *ListOfCurrencies* represents the allowed currencies for the teller. The static parameters of the role are: *StartDate*: determines when the role is activated. *ExpiryDate* determines when the role expires and is retired. The *Disabled* flag determines if the role is enabled or disabled, the *withdraw* permission has also a *disabled* flag. The *Withdraw* permission has one validator to validate the *Amount* specified in the transaction against the *AmountLimit* of the role and to check if the currency of the transaction is in *ListOfCurrencies* of the role. The *ValidateHomeAmount()* validator converts the currency of the transaction to the home currency of the bank, and then it compares the transaction amount with the *AmountLimit*. This computation is required as the home amount value depends on the currency of the transaction. For example; if the user has an *AmountLimit=10000*, and the home amount is *EUR*, and the amount of the transaction is 20000 with the *YEN* currency. Then the transaction should be authorized. The static methods defined in the role are used for setting and getting values of static parameters and for modifying and querying permissions. The *ValidateHomeAmount* validator may check if the permission is enabled or not before deciding to authorize.

5   Generalization in Role Oriented Access Control Model

In the object-oriented paradigm, inheritance is a mechanism that implements *is-a* relationships between classes. Inheritance allows hierarchically related classes to reuse and absorb features by inheriting class members (variables and methods). Most existing RBAC models support role hierarchies based on a similar inheritance mechanism found in object-oriented languages.

The advantages most commonly associated with inheritance in the object oriented paradigm are: malleability and reusability, malleability facilitates program construction, maintenance, and extension through factoring the definitions common to a set of classes into a single class called the superclass and then any change required in the common behavior can be done only once in the superclass. Reusability facilitates the reuse of code and data by defining abstractions in terms of existing abstractions. This greatly reduces development efforts by reusing existing software components [15].

Hierarchical ROAC supports multiple inheritance by allowing a role to have more than one parent. Despite advantages of multiple inheritance, it introduces a new complexity: two or more parents may define identifiers with the same name [15]. Roles have multiple members such as parameters, static parameters and validators. The definition of roles in ROAC might introduce some challenges as encountered when defining inheritance in object-oriented languages. One challenge is name conflicts. When two junior roles are to be inherited by a third senior role, where the two junior roles have two parameters (or static parameters) that have identical names. This problem has been exposed in object-oriented languages and there have been some approaches put together to address this problem. In object oriented languages, strategies for resolving conflicts in multiple inheritance are divided into two main categories, depending on whether resolving the

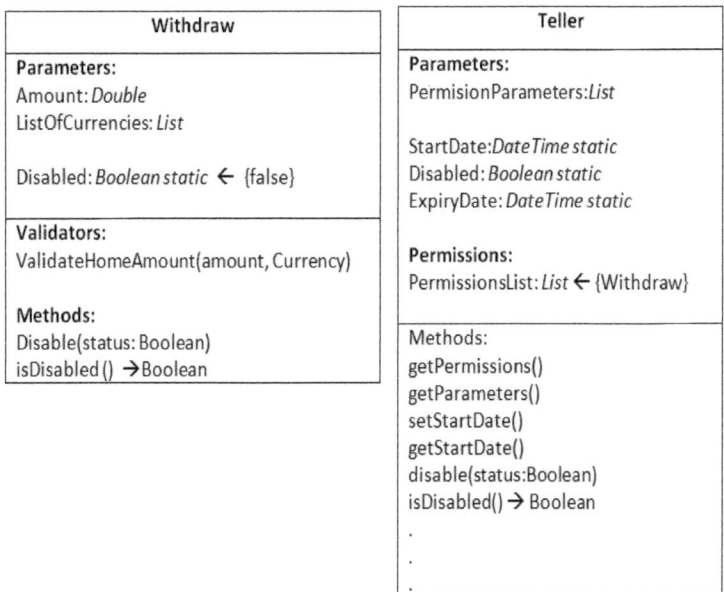

Fig. 2. An example role and permission

conflict requires interaction with the user or not [16]. In the category where no interactions are required from the users, object-oriented languages automatically resolve the conflict. They rank the objects parent and take the property with highest rank. They use linearization to construct a total ordering of all classes. Linearization solves runtime conflicts without human interventions, but it has two drawbacks: it masks ambiguities between otherwise unordered ancestors, and it fails with inheritance graphs that it deems inconsistent [15]. The other technique used to solve name conflicts requires interventions from users, such as explicit designation as in C++, exclusion as in *CommonObjects* and renaming as in Eiffel [16]. Renaming gives the developer the power to decide on properties names and to choose appropriate names. It also avoids complexity and inefficiency of linearization. In our approach to role inheritance, we adopt the renaming approach. If a role is inheriting from two roles that have the same parameter or static parameter names, then we rename the parameter if the two parameters are different and we retain parameter names if they are identical and hence combined into one parameter, in this case the two parameters must have identical data types. Fig. 3 shows an example of how conflicts are solved in ROAC by renaming. In part one of the figure, role R_3 is inheriting roles R_1 and R_2. R_1 has two parameters P_1 and P_2. R_2 has two parameters P_2 and P_3. If P_2 of R_1 is identical to P_2 of R_2, then R_3 inherits only three parameters P_1, P_2 and P_3. In part two of the figure, P_2 of R_1 is different from P_2 of R_2. Then R_3 inherits four parameters, and P_2 of R_1 and P_2 of R_2 must be renamed as shown in Fig. 3.

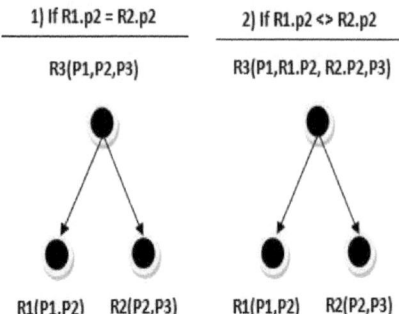

Fig. 3. Name conflict resolution in ROAC

Generalization in ROAC has two sides: roles and permissions definition inheritance and permissions inheritance. In the roles and permissions definition inheritance, the objective is re-usability by factoring the definitions common to a set of roles or permissions into a single role or permission. Permissions instances associated to roles are not considered in roles definitions inheritance. In permissions inheritance, senior roles can inherit subsets of permissions from the junior roles. In many organizations, the actual hierarchies are supervision hierarchies rather than *is-a* hierarchies. As an example, in a bank, the branch manager could inherit the *teller* role, but he might not need to inherit the permission of initiating payments of the *teller* role. While it might be required those other senior users inherit the teller role, and require the permission of initiating payments, but they do not need the permission of initiating transfers. So, the inheritance model must enable selective inheritance of roles, to enable selecting permissions from junior roles.

In the object-oriented paradigm, encapsulation is a technique used for hiding data within classes and preventing outsiders from manipulating class members directly. Some object-oriented languages such as Java define access control rules that restrict the members of a class from being used outside the class. This is achieved by access control modifiers. The encapsulation model in object-oriented languages is not satisfactory for access control. As in access control, it is required to be more selective regarding permissions when performing inheritance hierarchies. As a consequence, we have designed ROAC with two sides inheritance. Firstly, the inheritance for roles and permissions, in which only the definition of the role or permission is transferred to subnodes. This is useful for re-using already defined roles and permissions. Another advantage is that a basic role and a basic permission can be defined and equipped by all administrative methods needed to manipulate administrative functions over roles and permissions. Then all other roles and permissions in the system can inherit from the basic role and the basic permission. Secondly, the permission inheritance has to be defined which applicable only for roles. In permission inheritance, permissions of super roles are transferred to sub-roles. Permission inheritance supports selective inheritance, where a set of role permissions can be excluded from being transferred by inheritance. Permissions can be excluded by providing the permissions exclude list when de"fining permissions inheritance. For example, let X be a role defined with a set of permissions $(p_1,p_2,p_3,..)$ and let Y be a descendent of X, the exclusion list is (p_1, p_2).

Our target is to provide a mechanism for specifying which permissions can be inherited from a junior role by a senior role. In ROAC, permissions list is defined as a enumeration in the role. We can now specify what permissions can be inherited by what senior roles. This enables us to implement supervision as well as the *is-a* hierarchies.

6 Discussion

RBAC supports three well-known security principles: least privilege, separation of duties, and data abstraction [3]. RBAC suggests that users are assigned to roles, roles are assigned to permissions and recommends that roles are assigned only the minimum set of permissions required for tasks needed by members of the roles.

The advances in software systems and the high dependability of organizations on software systems have demanded more requirements on access control. Sandhu and Bhamidipati [17] have offered five founding principles for next-generation access control including next-generation RBAC, summarized as ASCAA for Abstraction, Separation, Containment, Automation and Accountability. The first two are included in RBAC96 [3]. Containment includes three principles; least privilege, separation of duty from RBAC96 and incorporates usage limits. Usage limits are constraints on how users can use roles. ROAC directly supports the user limits concept. Conditions on role usage can be easily implemented in roles by specifying them in permissions validators, and using static parameters to set values for global parameters. As an example, if it is required to restrict the number of times a role can be exercised in a time frame, we can define two static parameters; one for the time frame and the other for number of exercises, then in the validators we can assert this condition. Similarly we can define a time frame where the role can be exercised and the role becomes inactive outside the time frame. Similarly, the automation principle can be implemented in ROAC. Constraints can be defined in administrative methods for user-role assignment. For example expiry of assignment can be defined by using parameters to hold the expiry dates and then implementing the condition in the administrative method that is used to assign users to the role. Different conditions can be implemented for each role. Accountability can be implemented in a combination of three ways. Firstly, sensitive operations require enhanced audit trail, secondly, by notification that requires sensitive operations to trigger a message to an appropriate user, and finally, by escalating the authentication required for sensitive operations [17]. The first and second ways can be incorporated in ROAC. Developers are can add any required definitions for roles in validators. Audit information can be supplied to validators in applications and then validators can store them in data bases or send them to audit trail systems.

ROAC is an expressive access control model that helps large organizations to provide fine granularity of roles while reducing the number of roles. However, this is applicable when multiple roles can be reduced to single role by using parameters. There is a trade-off between simplifying the management of access rights and providing fine granularity [5]. So, organizations should pay attention to the design of roles in a way that provides more granularity but reducing the number of roles. The hierarchical form of ROAC can be used to reflect organizational hierarchies which also simplify the management and the view of roles.

We have validated the ROAC model by simulating an implementation using the Java programming language. We have tested the implementation on a security service that was implemented by the authors of the paper.

7   Conclusion and Future Work

The contribution of this paper is proposing a new access control model, the role-oriented access control model (ROAC). In ROAC roles and permissions are defined as object-oriented classes, where they can have member attributes and operations. ROAC has many advantages compared to existing access control models. One of the main advantages is expressiveness and the possibility to reflect precise organizational hierarchies by ROAC. Another advantage is that organizations can implement any specific requirements for granting authorizations on operations by using validators. The permissions and roles implementation can contain access to external systems like databases and audit log systems to either extract or provide information.

We have discussed some related work on existing RBAC models. We have explained how existing models attempted to tackle shortcomings of access control models that are encountered when they are put into practice. We have focused on two points which are expressiveness of RBAC models and on hierarchical RBAC models.

ROAC concepts were validated by an implementation using the Java programming language. In the implementation we have created an API that can be used for creating roles and permissions, as well as defining relations between the different elements of ROAC such as user/role assignment, role/permissions assignments, and the administrative functions of ROAC. Moreover, the implementation has simulated the hierarchical ROAC model. Our future direction from this point is to provide a full feature access control system based on ROAC. Our ideas are to encapsulate separation of duty, role delegation, as well as other features. The target is to make an API that can used by organizations and researchers, which they can use for constructing their customized access control systems.

References

1. eWeek, http://www.eweek.com/c/a/Security/
   Rethinking-Access-Controls-How-WikiLeaks-Could-Have-Been-Prevented/1/
2. Ferraiolo, D., Kuhn, D.: Role-based access control. In: Proceedings of the 15th National Computer Security Conference (1992)

3. Sandhu, R., Coyne, E., Feinstein, H., Youman, C.: Role-based access control models. IEEE Computer, 38–47 (1996)
4. ANSI INCITS 359, Standard for Role Based Access Control (2004)
5. Abdallah, A., Khayat, E.: A Formal Model for Parameterized Role-Based Access Control. In: Dimitrakos, T., Martinelli, F. (eds.) FAST 2004. IFIP, vol. 173, pp. 233–246. Springer, Boston (2005)
6. Fischer, J., Marino, D., Majumdar, R., Millstein, T.: Fine-Grained Access Control with Object-Sensitive Roles. In: Drossopoulou, S. (ed.) ECOOP 2009. LNCS, vol. 5653, pp. 173–194. Springer, Heidelberg (2009)
7. Kalam, A., Benferhat, S., Miege, A., Baida, R., Cuppens, F., Saurel, C., Balbiani, P., Deswarte, Y., Trouessin, G.: Organization based access control. In: Proceedings of the 4th IEEE International Workshop on Policies for Distributed Systems and Networks (POLICY 2003). IEEE Computer Society, Washington, DC (2003)
8. Jaeger, T., Michailidis, T., Rada, R.: Access Control in a Virtual University. In: Proc. of the 8th International IEEE Workshops on Enabling Technologies: Infrastructure for Collaborative Enterprises, California, USA, pp. 135–140 (1999)
9. Barka, E.: Framework for Role-Based Delegation Models. PhD Thesis, George Mason University (2002)
10. Sandhu, R.: Role activation hierarchies. In: Proceedings of the Third ACM Workshop on Role-Based Access Control (RBAC 1998), pp. 33–40. ACM, New York (1998)
11. Moffett, J., Lupu, E.: The uses of role hierarchies in access control. In: Proceedings of the Fourth ACM Workshop on Role-Based Access Control (RBAC 1999), pp. 153–160. ACM, New York (1999)
12. Xuexiong, Y., Qinxian, W., Changzheng, X.: A Multiple Hierarchies RBAC Model. In: International Conference on Communications and Mobile Computing (2010)
13. Eckel, B.: Thinking in Java, 2nd edn., p. 261. Prentice-Hall (2000)
14. Liang, D.: Introduction to Java Programming, Comprehensive Version, 5th edn. Prentice Hall (2006)
15. Chambers, C., Ungar, D., Chang, B., Holzle, U.: Parents are shared parts of objects: inheritance and encapsulation in SELF. Lisp Symb. Comput., pp. 207–222 (1991)
16. Ducournau, R., Habib, M., Huchard, M., Mugnier, M.L.: Monotonic conflict resolution mechanisms for inheritance. In: Conference Proceedings on Object-Oriented Programming Systems, Languages, and Applications (OOPSLA 1992). ACM, New York (1992)
17. Sandhu, R., Bhamidipati, V.: The ASCAA Principles for Next-Generation Role-Based Access Control. In: Proc. 3rd International Conference on Availability, Reliability and Security (ARES), Barcelona, Spain (2008)

Optimal Parameters for Efficient Two-Party Computation Protocols

Chaya Ganesh[1] and C. Pandu Rangan[2]

[1] Indian Institute of Technology, Madras, India
chaya.ganesh@gmail.com
[2] Indian Institute of Technology, Madras, India
prangan@iitm.ac.in

Abstract. We study the optimal parameters to minimize the cheating probability and communication complexity in protocols for two party computation secure against malicious adversaries. In cut-and-choose protocols for two party computation, we analyze the optimal parameters to keep the probability of undetected cheating minimum. We first study this for a constant number of circuits, and then generalize it to the case of constant bandwidth. More generally, the communication cost of opening a circuit is different from retaining the circuit for evaluation and we analyze the optimal parameters in this case, by fixing the total bits of communication. In the second part of our analysis, we minimize the communication complexity for a given probability of undetected cheating. We study, what should be the parameters to achieve a given cheating probability in minimum amount of communication in a given cut-and-choose protocol. While still keeping the security guarantees, that is, the cheating probability negligible, we achieve a concrete improvement in communication complexity by using optimal parameters in existing cut-and-choose protocols.

Keywords: secure computation, malicious adversaries, cheating probability, communication complexity.

1 Introduction

Secure two party computation. Secure two-party computation allows two parties with respective private inputs x and y to jointly compute a functionality $f(x, y) = (f_1(x, y), f_2(x, y))$, such that the first party receives $f_1(x, y)$ and the second party receives $f_2(x, y)$. The security requirements are privacy and correctness, that is, nothing should be learned from the protocol other than the output, and that the output should be distributed according to the prescribed functionality. The formal definition blends both the requirements and follows the simulation paradigm [2]. Security must be guaranteed even when one of the parties is adversarial. An adversary may be semi-honest, in which case it follows the specification of the protocol, but attempts to learn additional information by analyzing the transcript of messages of the protocol execution. In contrast, the

I. Askoxylakis, H.C. Pöhls, and J. Posegga (Eds.): WISTP 2012, LNCS 7322, pp. 128–143, 2012.
© IFIP International Federation for Information Processing 2012

adversary may even be malicious, in which case it can arbitrarily deviate from the specifications of the protocol. Yao [11] presented the first general solutions for the problem of secure computation, with security against semi-honest adversaries for the two-party case, and Goldreich, Micali and Wigderson [1] gave the solution for the multi-party case with security even against malicious adversaries.

Yao's Protocol. Yao gave a constant-round protocol for the secure computation of any functionality in the presence of semi-honest adversaries. Let f be the functionality that the two parties agree to compute, and let x,y be their respective inputs. (for simplicity, assume that both parties wish to receive $f(x,y)$). In Yao's protocol, party P_1 first generates an encrypted (called "garbled") circuit computing $f(x,\cdot)$ and then sends it to P_2. The circuit is such that it reveals nothing in its garbled form and therefore reveals nothing to P_2. P_2 can, however, obtain the intended output $f(x,y)$ by "decrypting" the circuit. This decryption must ensure that it reveals nothing more than $f(x,y)$ to P_2. That is, P_2 should learn the value on the circuit output wire without learning the values on any of the internal wires. This is accomplished by P_2 obtaining a series of keys corresponding to its input y, such that given the garbled circuit and these keys, the output value $f(x,y)$, and only this value, may be obtained. Now, P_2 must somehow receive these keys from P_1 while making sure not to reveal anything about y to P_1. This is accomplished by running secure 1-out-of-2 Oblivious Transfer (OT) protocol [8]. A detailed description of Yao's protocol, and a proof of security can be found in [5]. Yao's generic protocol is known to be efficient, and even practical, for functionalities that have relatively small circuits.

Malicious behavior and cut-and-choose. Yao's protocol is secure only in the presence of relatively weak semi-honest adversaries. Goldreich, Micali and Wigderson gave the first positive results for general secure computation against malicious adversaries. The compiler of GMW [1] converts any protocol that is secure for semi-honest adversaries into one that is secure for malicious adversaries. The compiler, however, is based on reducing the statement that needs to be proved (the honesty of the parties' behavior in this case) to an NP-complete problem, and using generic zero-knowledge proofs to prove the statement. The secure protocol resulting from the compiler runs in polynomial time but is rather inefficient.

Lindell and Pinkas gave an efficient protocol secure against malicious adversaries, based on cut-and-choose methodology in [4]. Let us consider what happens when P_1 is malicious. It can construct a garbled circuit that computes a function which is different than the one P_1 and P_2 jointly agreed to compute. The "cut-and-choose" technique is a solution to this problem. P_1 first constructs many garbled circuits and sends them to P_2. Then, P_2 randomly chooses half of them and asks P_1 to "open" the chosen half, that is, reveal the decryption keys corresponding to the chosen circuits. P_1 opens the chosen half, and P_2 checks that they were constructed correctly. If they were indeed correct, then P_2 evaluates the remaining circuits and computes the output. The opened and checked circuits are called check circuits, and the rest are evaluation circuits. The idea behind the cut-and-choose methodology is that if a malicious P_1 constructs the circuits incorrectly, then it will be caught by P_2 with high probability. This solution solves the problem of P_1 constructing the circuit incorrectly. Now, since the parties evaluate a number of circuits, some mechanism must be employed to force the parties to use the same input when evaluating each circuit; otherwise, an adversarial party could learn more information than allowed. This, and other requirements that are not met by just applying the cut-and-choose technique are handled by the protocol implementation given in [4], where the authors give a cut-and-choose based solution, and a simulation based proof of security.

Motivation. In a cut-and-choose protocol for two party computation, half of the total number of garbled circuits are check circuits in all protocols in literature. We ask, *what should be the number of check circuits, so as to minimize the probability of undetected cheating* by P_1? We study this question in two settings: same cost circuits, and cheaper check circuits. Then, we ask, *what should be the number of check circuits to achieve a given cheating probability in minimum amount of communication?* With increasing interest from both within and outside the cryptographic community in secure protocols that are efficient enough to be implemented in practice, efficiency issues are an important consideration. Communication complexity of interactive protocols is one of their most important complexity measures. Bandwidth optimization is interesting in settings where communication is expensive, e.g, for a mobile roaming user. This is the motivation of our work in this paper.

Our Results. We study the optimal parameters for cut-and-choose protocols for general secure computation. Consider a cut-and-choose protocol: the total number of garbled circuits constructed by P_1, the number of circuits opened out of the total (these are called check circuits and the rest are evaluation circuits) are the parameters of the protocol, and the protocol achieves some (negligible) probability of undetected cheating incurring a certain communication complexity. Each garbled circuit has a communication cost associated, which is the number of bits that needs to be communicated in order to send the circuit to the other party. In general, the communication cost of a check circuit need not be the same as the cost of an evaluation circuit. In this paper, we analyze the optimal parameters to achieve minimum probability of undetected cheating and minimum communication complexity. We first study the optimal fraction of the total number of circuits that should be check circuits, so as to minimize the probability of undetected cheating by P_1. We then generalize this to the case when the communication cost of a check circuit is cheaper than the cost of an evaluation circuit (as in [3]). We show the optimal number of check circuits to minimize the cheating probability in this setting.

Further, we minimize the communication complexity of a cut-and-choose protocol, while still keeping the probability of undetected cheating by P_1 negligible. We study the optimal number of check circuits to minimize the communication complexity while achieving a given cheating probability. Our analysis yields parameters which can be used in any of the existing cut-and-choose protocols and get a concrete improvement in the communication complexity.

Related work. Efficient protocols for secure two party computation based on the cut-and-choose technique have been studied in [7], [4], [10] and [6]. The optimization of parameters for secure computation protocols has been done earlier only in [9]. Our results are more general, we use a different technique to arrive at optimal parameters for minimum probability of undetected cheating, and our techniques further extend to a more general case of cheaper check circuits. Furthermore, we study the optimal parameters for minimum communication complexity, while achieving a given cheating probability.

2   Background

2.1   Cut-and-Choose Protocol

Lindell and Pinkas gave an efficient two party protocol secure against malicious adversaries [4]. Their construction is based on applying cut-and-choose techniques to the original Yao's circuit and inputs. Security is proved in the ideal/real simulation paradigm.

A malicious P_1 is forced to construct the garbled circuit correctly so that it indeed computes the desired function. P_1 constructs many independent copies of the garbled circuit and sends them to P_2. Party P_2 randomly chooses half of them, and asks P_1 to open the chosen circuits. Now, P_2 checks that the opened circuits are constructed correctly. If they are, then P_2 is convinced that most of the remaining garbled circuits are also constructed correctly. If there are many circuits that are incorrectly constructed, then with high probability, one of those circuits will be in the set that P_2 challenges P_1 to open. The parties then evaluate the remaining circuits as in the original Yao's protocol for semi-honest adversaries, and take the majority output. The protocol also has to force both P_1 and P_2 to use the same inputs in each circuit. Such consistency checks are necessary, because if the parties were allowed to use different inputs to different copies of the circuit, then they can learn information that is more than just the desired output of the function. P_2 can do so, since it observes the outputs of all circuits, but in fact even P_1, who only gets to see the majority output, can learn additional information: For example, if the protocol computes n invocations of a circuit computing the inner-product between n bit inputs. A malicious P_2 could provide the inputs $\langle 10\cdots 0\rangle, \langle 010\cdots 0\rangle, \cdots, \langle 0\cdots 01\rangle$ to the n different garbled circuits, and learn P_1's input completely. If P_1 is malicious, it could also provide the inputs $\langle 10\cdots 0\rangle, \langle 010\cdots 0\rangle, \cdots, \langle 0\cdots 01\rangle$. P_2 now sends P_1 the majority output value, which is equal to the majority value of P_2's input bits. A malicious P_1 could thus get additional information about P_2's input. The protocol enforces consistency checks by having P_1 commit to the garbled circuits and also to the garbled values corresponding to the input wires of the circuits. We give a high-level overview of the protocol here.

Parties P_1 and P_2 have respective inputs x and y, and wish to compute the agreed function $f(x, y)$.

1. The parties first decide on a circuit C that computes f. This circuit is then changed by replacing each input wire of P_2 by a gate whose input consists of

s new input wires of P_2 and whose output is the exclusive-or of these wires. The number of input wires of P_2 increases by a factor of s.

P_2's input is encoded in this way to prevent the following attack by P_1: A malicious P_1 may provide corrupt input to one of possible inputs of P_2 in an OT protocol. In case P_2 chooses to learn this input it will not be able to decrypt the garbled tables which use this value, and will have to abort. If on the other hand, P_2 chooses to learn the other input associated with this wire then it will never know that the first input is corrupt. P_1 can thus learn P_2's input by observing whether or not P_2 aborts. Checking that the circuit is correctly constructed will not help in preventing this attack, since the attack is based on changing P_1's input to the OT protocol. The attack is prevented by replacing the input bits of P_2 with s new input bits whose exclusive-or is used instead of the original input. P_2 can now encode a 0 input in 2^{s-1} ways, and encode a 1 in 2^{s-1} way. Given its input, P_2 chooses an encoding with uniform probability. The protocol is then executed with the new circuit, and P_2 uses oblivious transfer to learn the garbled values of its new inputs. As is shown in [4], if P_1 supplies incorrect values as garbled values that are associated with P_2's input, the probability of P_2 detecting this cheating is almost independent of P_2's actual input.

2. P_1 commits to s different garbled circuits, all of them computing f, where s is a statistical security parameter. Additionally, P_1 also commits to the garbled values corresponding to the input wires of the circuits.

   P_1 can prove consistency of its inputs the following way. The proof is based on a cut-and-choose test for the consistency of the commitment sets combined with the cut-and-choose test for the correctness of the construction of circuits. P_1 constructs s pairs of sets of commitments, for each of its input wires. One set in every pair contains commitments to the 0 values of this wire in all circuits, and the other set is the same with respect to value 1. The protocol now randomly chooses a subset of these pairs, and a subset of the circuits, and checks that these sets give consistent inputs for these circuits. The protocol then evaluates the remaining circuits, and asks P_1 to open, in each of the remaining pairs, and only in one set in each pair, its garbled values for all evaluated circuits. This way, nothing is revealed to P_2 about whether these garbled values correspond to a 0 or to a 1. For the committed sets and circuits to pass P_2's checks, there must be large subsets C and S, of the circuits and commitment sets, respectively, such that every choice of a circuit from C and a commitment set from S results in a circuit and garbled values which correctly compute f. P_2 accepts the verification stage only if all the circuits and sets it chooses to check are from the subsets C and S, respectively. If P_2 does not abort, then circuits which are not from C are in a minority of the evaluated circuits with high probability, and similarly for S. Therefore the majority result of the evaluation stage is correct.

3. Parties P_1 and P_2 run a 1-out-of-2 oblivious transfer protocol for every input bit of P_2 in which P_2 learns the garbled values of input wires corresponding to its input.

4. P_1 sends to P_2 the garbled circuits, as well as all the commitments that it prepared above.

5. P_1 and P_2 run a coin-tossing protocol to choose a random string. The resulting string defines which garbled circuits and commitments will be opened.

6. P_1 opens the garbled circuits and commitments which are chosen in the previous step. P_2 verifies that the opened circuits are correct and runs the consistency checks on the input values.

   P_2 checks the correctness of the check circuits. It verifies that each check circuit is a garbled version of the circuit C. The input tables are constructed by checking that the decommitments in the above step are valid, and associating the first value with the garbled value for 0 and the second value with 1. P_2 next checks the decommitments to P_1's inputs. Finally, given all the garbled values to the input wires and their associated binary values, P_2 now decrypts the garbled circuit and compares it to the circuit C. If any of the checks fail, P_2 aborts.

7. P_1 sends the garbled values corresponding to P_1's input wires in the unopened garbled circuits (evaluation circuits), P_2 runs consistency checks on these values, that is, for every evaluation circuit, all of the commitments that P_1 opened in evaluation sets commit to the same garbled value.

8. If all the checks pass, P_2 evaluates the unopened circuits, and takes the majority value as output.

2.2   Efficient Two Party Computation Protocols - Cheaper Check Circuits

In [3], the authors design an efficient multi party computation protocol in the covert adversary model. The techniques used in the two party case generalize to the case of two party computation protocols secure against standard malicious adversaries. To achieve an improvement in communication complexity, they take a different approach to constructing the garbled circuit. To construct a garbled circuit and commitments for the input keys, P_1 first generates a short random seed and feeds it to a pseudorandom generator. This generates the necessary randomness. P_1 then uses this randomness to construct the garbled circuit and the commitments. When the protocol begins, P_1 sends only a hash of each garbled circuit using a collision-resistant hash function to P_2. P_2 chooses half of the circuits at random. In order to expose the secrets of each of the chosen circuit later, P_1 sends the seeds corresponding to the circuit, and not the whole opened circuit. P_2 uses the pseudorandom generator to generate the randomness from the sent seed and constructs the check circuits, and checks that they are indeed garbled versions of the agreed circuit. Once the checks go through, P_1 sends the remaining circuits, called the evaluation circuits to P_2. The communication cost of a check circuit is therefore, not the whole circuit but only a hash as opposed to the cost of an evaluation circuit.

We briefly give the garbling procedure of [3]. Let G be the description of a pseudorandom generator, *seed* a seed of suitable length, C be the description of the circuit that computes the agreed function, which is to be garbled.

$Garble(G, seed, C, 1^s)$ denotes the garbling procedure where s is the security parameter. The randomness required for constructing the garbled circuits includes, the random keys corresponding to the circuit wires, the random permutation chosen for the garbled entries of each gate table, and the random string chosen for each encryption. A random string of length $O(s|C|)$ is sufficient for garbling. A pseudorandom generator $G : \{0,1\}^{n_1} \to \{0,1\}^{n_2}$, where n_1 is polynomial in s and $n_2 = O(s|C|)$ is used. The algorithm $Garble$ runs G on $seed$ to generate the randomness required for the circuit, and then computes the garbled circuit for C as described in [5].

3   Optimal Number of Check Circuits

In the cut-and-choose protocol described in Section 2.1, we have the flexibility of choosing the number of check circuits. This is the subject of this section; we study what is the optimal number of circuits that should be check circuits to minimize the probability of undetected cheating by Party P_1. In Section 3.1, we keep the total number of garbled circuits a constant, and minimize the cheating probability. In the next subsection, we generalize this to the case where a constant amount of communication bits is allowed (but the total number of circuits is not fixed). We minimize the cheating probability in these settings by choosing the optimal number of check circuits, c. In [9], the authors show the optimal number of check circuits, but our techniques to get an approximation for the expression of cheating probability makes the analysis extendible to the more general case of cheaper check circuits. We discuss both the cases, of same cost circuits and cheaper check circuits as the latter is an extension of the computations done for the former case.

3.1   Same-Cost Circuits

We consider the case where both check circuits and evaluation circuits have the same communication cost. Let n be the number of garbled circuits constructed by P_1, and let c be the number of circuits checked.

Assume that i out of n circuits are constructed incorrectly by a cheating P_1. P_1's cheating is not caught if all the check circuits are constructed correctly, and P_2 does not abort after evaluation of the remaining circuits.

Now, the probability of P_1's cheating not caught is given by

$$\frac{\binom{n-i}{c}}{\binom{n}{c}}$$

If $i < \dfrac{n-c}{2}$, then the majority output is correct, and if $i > n - c$, corrupt P_1 is caught in one of the check circuits.

Therefore, the cheating probability is,

$$P = \max_i \frac{\binom{n-i}{c}}{\binom{n}{c}}$$

$$= \frac{1}{\binom{n}{c}} \max_i \binom{n-i}{c}$$

The above is maximum for $i = \dfrac{n-c}{2}$. Thus,

$$P = \frac{\binom{\frac{n+c}{2}}{c}}{\binom{n}{c}}$$

$$= \frac{\left(\frac{n+c}{2}\right)!}{c!\left(\frac{n-c}{2}\right)!} \frac{(n-c)!\,c!}{n!}$$

$$= \frac{\left(\frac{n+c}{2}\right)!}{\left(\frac{n-c}{2}\right)!} \frac{(n-c)!}{n!}$$

By Stirling's approximation,

$$n! \approx \sqrt{2\pi n} \left(\frac{n}{e}\right)^n$$

$$P \approx \frac{(n+c)^{\frac{n+c+1}{2}} (n-c)^{\frac{n-c}{2}}}{2^c \, n^{n+\frac{1}{2}}} \tag{1}$$

To minimize P for a given n, we differentiate partially with respect to c and set the resulting expression to 0.

Taking logarithm of (1), we get,

$$\log P = \left(\frac{n+c+1}{2}\right)\log(n+c) + \frac{n-c}{2}\log(n-c) - c\log 2 - \left(n+\frac{1}{2}\right)\log n$$

Now differentiating,

$$\frac{dP}{dc} = \frac{P}{2}\left(\log\frac{n+c}{4(n-c)} - \frac{n-c}{n-c} + \frac{n+c+1}{n+c}\right)$$

We now have,

$$\frac{dP}{dc} = 0$$

$$\log\frac{n+c}{4(n-c)} - \frac{n-c}{n-c} + \frac{n+c+1}{n+c} = 0$$

$\frac{n+c+1}{n+c} \approx 1$, Therefore, we have,

$$\log\frac{n+c}{4(n-c)} = 0$$

$$\frac{n+c}{4(n-c)} = 1$$

This yields,

$$c = \frac{3n}{5}$$

Therefore, for a given number of total circuits, n, minimum cheating probability is achieved when the number of check circuits is $3/5$th of n.

Theorem 1. *For a given total number of garbled circuits n, constructed and sent by P_1 in the cut-and-choose protocol, P_2 should ask $\frac{3}{5}$th of them to be opened, to minimize the probability of undetected cheating by P_1.*

Thus, challenging P_1 to open $3/5$ of the circuits is better for P_2 than challenging half as is done in existing cut-and-choose strategies. Independent of us, the above result is also obtained in [9], by counting the number of bad circuits that optimizes the cheating probability. They do not derive an explicit expression for the cheating probability as we do above, which we use in the generalization to cheaper check circuits which is the subject of the next section.

3.2   Cheaper Check Circuits

In this section, we consider the more general case of cheaper check circuits. A given number of communication bits does not fix the total number of circuits when the costs of a check circuit and an evaluation circuit are different. Consider the protocol of [3], i.e applying the ideas of [3] to the protocol of the previous section. In this protocol, P_1 uses a short seed and a pseudorandom generator to generate the required randomness for construction of the garbled circuits. A hash of the n garbled circuits are sent to P_2. P_2 asks for a random half of them to be opened, and P_1 sends only the short seeds of the selected half. P_2 verifies that they are constructed correctly. The evaluation circuits are now sent by P_1. The cost of a check circuit is therefore, less than the cost of an evaluation circuit; once the hashes of all n circuits are sent, only a short seed is communicated in case of a check circuit, whereas the whole garbled circuit is the communication cost for an evaluation circuit. In this case, we analyze the optimal number of check circuits for minimum cheating probability. In the previous case when the costs of a check circuit and an evaluation circuit are the same, fixing the communication bits k, also fixes the total number of circuits n. We now study the general case when a check circuit is cheaper than an evaluation circuit. Given a constant amount of communication bits, we minimize the cheating probability. Our analysis yields the total number of circuits to be constructed and the number of circuits to be challenged so as to achieve minimum probability of undetected cheating in a given amount of communication bandwidth.

Let k be the number of bits of communication allowed. Let c be the number of check circuits, e the number of evaluation circuits and n the total number of circuits.

Then,

$$c \cdot Cost_{check} + e \cdot Cost_{eval} = k$$

Let q be the ratio of the cost of check circuits to the cost of evaluation circuits.

$$cq + e = s$$

where,

$$q = \frac{Cost_{check}}{Cost_{eval}}, s = \frac{k}{Cost_{eval}}$$

Using $n = c + e$ and $e = s - cq$ in the cheating probability, we have,

$$
\begin{aligned}
P &\approx \frac{(n+c)^{\frac{n+c+1}{2}} (n-c)^{\frac{n-c}{2}}}{2^c \, n^{n+\frac{1}{2}}} \\
&= \frac{(2c+e)^{\frac{2c+e+1}{2}} e^{\frac{e}{2}}}{2^c \, (e+c)^{e+c+\frac{1}{2}}} \\
&= \frac{(2c+s-cq)^{\frac{2c+s-cq+1}{2}} (s-cq)^{\frac{s-cq}{2}}}{2^c \, (s-cq+c)^{s-cq+c+\frac{1}{2}}}
\end{aligned}
\tag{2}
$$

We now differentiate with respect to c and equate the resulting expression to zero.

Taking logarithm of (2) we get,

$$\log P = \frac{(2-q)c + s + 1}{2} \log\left((2-q)c + s\right) + \frac{s - cq}{2} \log\left(s - cq\right)$$

$$- c \log 2 - \left(c(1-q) + s + \frac{1}{2}\right) \log\left(c(1-q) + s\right)$$

Differentiating with respect to c we have,

$$\frac{1}{P}\frac{dP}{dc} = \frac{2-q}{2} \log\left((2-q)c + s\right) - \frac{q}{2} \log(s - qc) - \log 2 - (1-q) \log\left((1-q)c + s\right)$$

Now setting the derivative to zero,

$$\frac{dP}{dc} = 0$$

$$\log\left(\frac{((2-q)c+s)^{\frac{2-q}{2}}}{2(s-qc)^{\frac{q}{2}}((1-q)c+s)^{1-q}}\right) = 0$$

$$\frac{((2-q)c+s)^{\frac{2-q}{2}}}{2(s-qc)^{\frac{q}{2}}((1-q)c+s)^{1-q}} = 1$$

This implies,

$$((2-q)c+s)^{\frac{2-q}{2}} = 2(s-qc)^{\frac{q}{2}}((1-q)c+s)^{1-q} \tag{3}$$
$$(2c+e)^{1-\frac{q}{2}} = 2\,e^{\frac{q}{2}}\,(c+e)^{1-q}$$
$$(n+c)^{1-\frac{q}{2}} = 2\,(n-c)^{\frac{q}{2}}\,n^{1-q}$$
$$\left(1+\frac{c}{n}\right)^{2-q} = 4\left(1-\frac{c}{n}\right)^{q} \tag{4}$$

Let r be the fraction of the circuits which are check circuits. i.e

$$r = \frac{c}{n}$$

Using this in (4) yields,

$$(1+r)^{2-q} = 4\,(1-r)^{q}$$
$$(1+r)^{2} = 4\,(1-r^{2})^{q} \tag{5}$$

Given q, the ratio of costs, we can solve the above equation for r.

The total number of circuits to be sent n is then given by,

$$n = \frac{k}{(1-r)\,Cost_{eval} + r\,Cost_{check}}$$

Given that we are allowed a constant k bits of communication, the total number of circuits, and the number of check circuits can be set as in the above analysis to minimize the cheating probability by P_1. If the cost of check circuit is the same as the cost of the evaluation circuit,
i.e when,

$$Cost_{check} = Cost_{eval}, q = 1$$

Setting $q = 1$ in equation (5) yields,

$$r = \frac{3}{5}$$

and this agrees with our earlier conclusion when the costs are same.

Theorem 2. *Let q be the ratio of the communication cost of a check circuit to the cost of an evaluation circuit in a two party cut-and-choose protocol, and k, a constant amount of communication bits allowed. Then, probability of cheating by P_1 is minimized if the ratio of the number of check circuits to the number of evaluation circuits, r is as given by, $(1+r)^2 = 4\left(1-r^2\right)^q$, and the total number of circuits, $n = \dfrac{k}{(1-r)\,Cost_{eval} + r\,Cost_{check}}$.*

4   Communication Complexity

In this section, we minimize the number of communication bits for a given cheating probability. We show how to achieve a given negligible probability of undetected cheating in minimum communication. We show that, for our choice of parameters, the communication complexity of existing cut-and-choose protocols can be improved. The communication complexity of existing protocols are stated in the following theorems.

Theorem 3. *([10]) Let n be the number of circuits, and g the number of gates in the circuit. The protocol of [10] is secure in the malicious model with inverse exponential (in n) probability of undetected cheating. The communication complexity is $O(ng)$.*

Theorem 4. *([7]) The equality-checker protocol of [7] is secure in the malicious model with probability of undetected cheating ϵ. If g is the number of gates the circuit, and I the number of input bits, the communication complexity of the scheme is $O(ln\left(\frac{1}{\epsilon}\right)g + ln\left(\frac{1}{\epsilon}\right)^2 I)$.*

4.1   Minimize Communication Complexity

We now formulate the problem as minimizing the communication complexity which is a function of two variables, given a cheating probability. Given a cheating probability p, for what relation between the check circuits and the total number of circuits, is p achieved in minimum number of communication bits? Minimize the function,

$$f(c,n) = c \cdot Cost_{check} + (n-c) \cdot Cost_{eval}$$

That is, minimize,

$$k = c + (n-c)Q$$

subject to the constraint that,

$$p = \frac{1}{2^c} \frac{(n+c)^{\frac{n+c+1}{2}} (n-c)^{\frac{n-c}{2}}}{n^{n+\frac{1}{2}}}$$

where,

$$Q = \frac{Cost_{eval}}{Cost_{check}}$$

Since the constraint equation is exponential, we go back to the expression of cheating probability and try to get a more friendly approximation.

$$p \approx \frac{\binom{\frac{n+c}{2}}{c}}{\binom{n}{c}}$$

We know that,

$$\binom{x}{y} \geq \left(\frac{x}{y}\right)^{y}$$

$$\binom{x}{y} \leq \frac{x^{y}}{y!} \leq \frac{x^{y}}{2^{y-1}}$$

Therefore,

$$p \geq \frac{\left(\frac{n+c}{2c}\right)^{c}}{\frac{n^{c}}{2^{c-1}}} = \left(\frac{n+c}{cn}\right)^{c} \frac{2^{c-1}}{2^{c}}$$

$$p \geq \frac{1}{2}\left(\frac{1}{c} + \frac{1}{n}\right)^{c}$$

$$(2p)^{\frac{1}{c}} \geq \frac{1}{c} + \frac{1}{n}$$

$$\frac{1}{n} \leq (2p)^{\frac{1}{c}} - \frac{1}{c}$$

$$n \geq \frac{c}{c(2p)^{\frac{1}{c}} - 1}$$

Since we do not get a closed form for c in terms of n and p, we investigate, of what order c should be in, so that k is minimized while keeping p negligible.

Let $n - c = n^{\epsilon}$, and, $\epsilon = \dfrac{\log \log n}{\log n}$
For this value of ϵ, $n^{\epsilon} = \log n$, and $n - n^{\epsilon} = c = n - \log n$.

For the case when check circuits are cheap as opposed to evaluation circuits, the total communication is dominated by the number of evaluation circuits. For the above value of c, p is still negligible. We now show that the cheating probability p is negligible when $c = n - \log n$.

$$p = \frac{1}{2^{c}} \frac{(n+c)^{\frac{n+c+1}{2}} (n-c)^{\frac{n-c}{2}}}{n^{n+\frac{1}{2}}}$$

For $c = n - \log n$,

$$p = \frac{1}{2^{n-\log n}} \frac{(2n - \log n)^{\frac{2n - \log n + 1}{2}} (\log n)^{\frac{\log n}{2}}}{n^{n+\frac{1}{2}}}$$

For large n, and $c = n - n^\epsilon$, p is still negligible. That is, $p \approx \dfrac{1}{n^{\frac{1}{2} + \frac{\log n}{2}}}$.

We observe that, the cheating probability p remains negligible, for $\epsilon = \dfrac{\log \log n}{\log n}$, giving communication cost dominated by the cost of evaluation circuits. Therefore, we get constant factor improvement on the communication complexity by the new choice of parameters; by choosing the number of check circuits to be, $c = n - \log n$. Thus, the communication cost of existing cut-and-choose protocols can be improved, while still retaining the security guarantees, i.e. keeping the cheating probability negligible. The communication complexity and the cheating probability achieved by the above optimal parameters in a cut-and-choose protocol are stated in the following theorem.

Theorem 5. *The number of check circuits to achieve near optimal communication cost is given by $c = n - \log n$, where n is the total number of circuits. The communication complexity is dominated by $O(C \log n)$, and the probability of undetected cheating is $p \approx \dfrac{1}{n^{\frac{1}{2} + \frac{\log n}{2}}}$, where C is the communication cost of an evaluation circuit.*

The improvement by using the above parameters in the setting of cheaper check circuits [3], is discussed in the following section. Using the above choice of parameters for ϵ, the number of check circuits c and the technique of [3] as applied to cut-and-choose protocol for general secure two party computation, we get an improvement in the communication complexity in concrete terms compared to the protocols of [7], [10], [6].

4.2   Comparison of Communication Cost

In the previous section, we analyzed in detail the parameter values such as the number of circuits to be challenged and arrived at optimal values to achieve minimum communication complexity. We now show how the use of these optimal parameters in existing protocols significantly improve the communication complexity. In particular, we sketch how our optimal parameters along with the technique of [3], improve the efficiency of existing cut-and-choose constructions. Informally, in the setting of [3], P_1 sends only a hash of the check circuits, and the entire garbled circuit is sent only for an evaluation circuit. Check circuits are therefore cheaper than evaluation circuits. Let the total number of circuits be n. From the analysis of Section 4.1, we choose the number of evaluation circuits to be optimal for minimum communication cost which is $\log n$. We summarize our results below.

Let the size of a garbled circuit be, $|GC| = 4g|E|$, where $|E|$ is the size of the ciphertext of the encryption scheme, g the number of gates in the circuit and I the input size. Let $|E|$ also be the output size of the commitment scheme. If t is the number of garbled circuits in [7], the number of bits communicated is $t|GC| + t^2 I|E| = 4tg|E| + t^2 I|E|$ (Theorem 4). The same protocol, by using the parameters of our analysis communicates, roughly, $4g|E| \log n + (\log n)^2 I|E|$

bits, where n is the total number of circuits (Theorem 5). Consider a circuit with 32 gates and input wires, $g = I = 32$. The cheating probability and the communication complexity achieved by [7] and by incorporating the optimal choice from our analysis in [7] is shown in the table below.

Table 1.

Scheme	Communication Complexity	Cheating Probability
[7]	$128t|E| + 32t^2|E|$	$2 \cdot (1/2)^{t/4}$
This paper	$128|E|\log n + 32(\log n)^2|E|$	$1/n^{\frac{1}{2}+\frac{\log n}{2}}$

For the purpose of our comparison, we fix the cheating probability. Setting the number of circuits t and n, in the two variants such that, the cheating probability is the same, say, 2^{-50}, we get $t = 196$ and $\log n = 10$. Substituting the values of t and n in the number of communication bits shown above, we see that the communication bits using our optimal parameters is around 20 times less than the communication bits of [7]. It is also important to note that this factor of improvement increases as the number of gates and input wires in the circuit increase.

We now consider the protocol of [10]. If t is the number of garbled circuits in [10], the number of bits communicated is roughly $4tg|E|+2tI|E|+tg+tI|E|$. The number of bits communicated by using our techniques is, roughly, $4g|E|\log n + 3\log nI|E|$ (Theorem 5), where n is the total number of circuits. If we consider a circuit with 32 gates and input wires, $g = I = 32$, and set the parameters t and n such that the cheating probability is the same, then, $t = \dfrac{\log n}{2} + \dfrac{(\log n)^2}{2}$. Now, for a cheating probability of 2^{-50}, we get $t = 50$ and $\log n = 10$. Substituting the values of t and n in the number of communication bits shown above, we see that the communication bits using our optimal parameters is a factor of 9 less than the scheme of [10].

More recently, in [6], Lindell and Pinkas presented a protocol using the cut-and-choose methodology relying on DDH assumption, and significantly improved the efficiency. We give the improvement in communication cost by using optimal parameters in [6]. The communication complexity of [6] is the exchange of $5tI + 14I + 7t + 5$ group elements and t copies of the garbled circuit. The cheating probability is $1/2^{t/4}$. The communication cost is dominated by the garbled circuits. Using the techniques in this paper, the communication cost of sending the garbled circuits is $4\log ng|E|$, for a cheating probability of $\dfrac{1}{n^{\frac{1}{2}+\frac{\log n}{2}}}$. To achieve the same cheating probability, say 2^{-50} we set $1/2^{t/4} = 2^{-50}$ and compute the number of GC's required as $t = 200$. We now set $\dfrac{1}{n^{\frac{1}{2}+\frac{\log n}{2}}} = 2^{-50}$, and solve the quadratic equation to get $\log n = 10$. This gives a factor of 20 improvement in the communication cost. Thus, for the same cheating probability, our techniques lead to a factor of 20 less communication between the parties in the protocol of [6]. We also remark that the increase in computational complexity is feasible. $\log n = 10 \Rightarrow n = 2^{10}$ implies that the total number of GC's the parties need is 1024.

Table 2.

Scheme	Cheating Probability
[6]	$1/2^{t/4}$
This paper	$1/n^{\frac{1}{2}+\frac{\log n}{2}}$

5   Conclusion

In this paper we gave an analysis for optimal parameters in cut-and-choose protocols to achieve: (a) minimum probability of undetected cheating for same-cost circuits and cheaper check circuits, and (b) minimum communication bits in which a given cheating probability can be achieved. It would be interesting from a practical point of view, to carry out such optimization as part of an actual implementation of a specific protocol.

References

1. Goldreich, O., Micali, S., Wigderson, A.: How to play any mental game or a completeness theorem for protocols with honest majority. In: Proceedings of 19th Annual ACM Symposium on Theory of Computing, pp. 218–229 (1987)
2. Goldreich, O.: Foundations of Cryptography. Basic Applications, vol. II. Cambridge University Press (2004)
3. Goyal, V., Mohassel, P., Smith, A.: Efficient Two Party and Multi Party Computation Against Covert Adversaries. In: Smart, N.P. (ed.) EUROCRYPT 2008. LNCS, vol. 4965, pp. 289–306. Springer, Heidelberg (2008)
4. Lindell, Y., Pinkas, B.: An Efficient Protocol for Secure Two-Party Computation in the Presence of Malicious Adversaries. In: Naor, M. (ed.) EUROCRYPT 2007. LNCS, vol. 4515, pp. 52–78. Springer, Heidelberg (2007)
5. Lindell, Y., Pinkas, B.: A proof of yao's protocol for secure two-party computation. Journal of Cryptology 22(2), 161–188 (2009)
6. Lindell, Y., Pinkas, B.: Secure Two-Party Computation via Cut-and-Choose Oblivious Transfer. In: Ishai, Y. (ed.) TCC 2011. LNCS, vol. 6597, pp. 329–346. Springer, Heidelberg (2011)
7. Mohassel, P., Franklin, M.: Efficiency Tradeoffs for Malicious Two-Party Computation. In: Yung, M., Dodis, Y., Kiayias, A., Malkin, T. (eds.) PKC 2006. LNCS, vol. 3958, pp. 458–473. Springer, Heidelberg (2006)
8. Rabin, M.: How to exchange secrets by oblivious transfer. Technical Memo, TR-81, Aiken computation laboratory, Harvard U (1981)
9. Shelat, A., Shen, C.-H.: Two-Output Secure Computation with Malicious Adversaries. In: Paterson, K.G. (ed.) EUROCRYPT 2011. LNCS, vol. 6632, pp. 386–405. Springer, Heidelberg (2011)
10. Woodruff, D.P.: Revisiting the Efficiency of Malicious Two-Party Computation. In: Naor, M. (ed.) EUROCRYPT 2007. LNCS, vol. 4515, pp. 79–96. Springer, Heidelberg (2007)
11. Yao, A.C.: How to generate and exchange secrets. In: FOCS 1986: Proceedings of 27th Annual Symposium on Foundations of Computer Science, pp. 162–167 (1986)

Assisting Server for Secure Multi-Party Computation

Jens-Matthias Bohli, Wenting Li, and Jan Seedorf

NEC Laboratories Europe
Kurfürsten-Anlage 36, 69115 Heidelberg, Germany
`firstname.lastname@neclab.eu`

Abstract. Distributed threats like botnets are among the most serious threats in the Internet. Due to their distributed nature, these attacks are difficult to detect in an early stage without the collaboration of several network operators. However, the exchange of monitoring data between different parties turns out to be difficult in practice, due to the desire of operators not to disclose network internals and legal data protection requirements. Secure Multi-Party Computation (SMC) for privacy-preserving sharing of network monitoring data can be a solution to the problem. As real-time performance of SMC is important for this application, we investigate ways to speed up SMC.

The focus and contribution of our work is a new model for SMC that enables to increase the performance of certain SMC primitives significantly. We introduce an assisting server which operates on dedicated, intermediate data values in plaintext. The overall rationale behind our approach is that the performance gains outweigh the slight decrease in security introduced by revealing intermediate computation results to the assisting server. We propose a new primitive for checking the equality between two values, $equal^+$, based on our new model. Through prototypical implementation we compare $equal^+$ with existing algorithms. Further, we evaluate $equal^+$ in the context of a cooperative network monitoring application, link-counting. Our results demonstrate that certain SMC applications can be computed much faster with our approach. Finally, we discuss the security implications of the new model.

1 Introduction

In today's Internet, distributed threats including malicious cooperative attacks are a tough problem to solve. In principle, coordinated attacks could be identified if the communication graph, or social graph, between nodes can be analyzed as a whole [13,7,17]. However, the communication graph is distributed across multiple network operators and every network operator is monitoring their own network only. The analysis of the communication graph will therefore require collaboration between multiple operators and the sharing of monitoring data. This seems today to be neither likely nor desirable to happen. Besides the fact that operators tend to be reluctant to share detailed monitoring information due to their own secrecy requirements, such monitoring information might well

I. Askoxylakis, H.C. Pöhls, and J. Posegga (Eds.): WISTP 2012, LNCS 7322, pp. 144–159, 2012.
© IFIP International Federation for Information Processing 2012

contain personal identifying information which is protected by data protection laws in Europe.

In this context, the EU project *DEMONS* [9] aims at providing a scalable and flexible monitoring infrastructure while ensuring user privacy of cross-domain cooperation. *Secure Multi-Party Computation (SMC)* is a cryptographic tool for privacy-preserving analysis of distributed data [19]. SMC takes private input data from multiple parties and carries out a joint computation on them, while ensuring that the input data remains private to their owners during the computation process. With the help of SMC, many cooperative computations among parties that do not necessarily trust each other can be achieved by keeping the privacy property of the data, thereby addressing a quite common problem in business and government administration.

Recently, SMC gets closer to practice. An example where SMC was applied in practice is a Danish auction of sugar beets [3]. Several frameworks for SMC have been implemented in the last years. SEPIA achieves the best performance among these frameworks and has been used for the analysis of network statistics [14]. Other frameworks are e.g. FairplayMP [1] and VIFF [6].

In this paper, we present a trade-off that increases the efficiency of SMC at the cost of a limited information leakage under the secret sharing scheme. The motivation is that to be able to detect and stop attacks before any damage is done, the solution must be extremely efficient to fulfill the real-time requirements. Specifically, we introduce a special entity, an *assisting server*, that can compute some operations on plaintext. We extend SMC based on Shamir's secret sharing; our solution is to be seen as a building block for applications implemented using such an SMC scheme.

In this new assisting server model, we realize an improved algorithm equal$^+$ for checking equality of two values. The equal$^+$ algorithm runs 20 times faster than the current algorithm for input data of 32 bits such as IP-addresses. We use this equal operation to realize a *link-counting* protocol which is an important building block in the analysis of shared monitoring data. Our equal$^+$ protocol leaks a controlled small amount of information to the assisting server. We analyze the security setting where such an information leakage can be tolerated.

2   Preliminaries

2.1   Related Work

Secure computation can be realized in various ways. Some protocols are customized for specific operations, such as [16] to sum up the input data, or [18] to realize *xor*, scalar product of vectors, and equality comparison. The data in each individual operation is processed using different techniques such as encryption or random numbers. The information exchanged among communication parties also varies for each operation or scheme. Therefore, a major drawback of these standalone protocols is that they cannot be easily combined to solve a complicated function composed of different operations, as the output of each step needs transformation for further processing.

On the other hand, much work has been done to construct a generic scheme that processes the data in a uniform representation. Yao as well as Goldreich et al. introduced the idea of a *garbled circuit* [20,12]. The function to be computed is first transformed to an encrypted circuit; then an evaluator obtains obliviously the keys for each bit of the input from the circuit creator and evaluates the circuit through partial decryption. In theory, any function can be computed in this scheme. The only concern is the performance, as public-key primitives are needed to retrieve every bit of the input. Another way for secure computation is the use of homomorphic encryption. Fully homomorphic schemes were recently proposed [11], however, the performance of these fully homomorphic schemes is currently far from being practical.

SMC based on *Shamir's Secret Sharing*, which we will build on, was introduced in [2]. Compared to the above two schemes, the distribution and reconstruction of the data is trivial. There is no need for oblivious transfer or encryption. Evaluating linear functions turns out to introduce almost no overhead. Its limitation, however, is the complexity when dealing with non-linear functions and boolean operations. Many rounds of communication among the parties that hold the shares are required to achieve such functions with state-of-the-art algorithms. Our objective is hence to improve the performance of such functions, towards using secret sharing as an efficient generic scheme for any type of computation.

We consider in this work security/efficiency trade-offs and allow a limited information leakage to an assisting server. This distinguishes the assisting server from an oblivious third party that does not gain any knowledge as used in [4] The idea of the assisting server is therefore closest to the *untrusted third party* in [18]. However, the untrusted third party is used for simple operations as a stand-alone protocol. Our assisting server operation generalizes and improves the concept towards arbitrary functions through the integration in SMC computations. Further, in [18] an equal protocol is presented based on asymmetric encryption. The equal function we propose is much more efficient as it just needs multiplication with a random number.

2.2   SMC with Shamir's Secret Sharing

An (n, k) secret sharing allows one party to distribute a secret among a set of n parties in the form of shares, such that a specified subset of the parties (k out of n) can reconstruct the secret while ensuring that less than k shares can infer no information about the secret. Shamir's secret sharing relies on the idea that it takes at least k points to uniquely define a polynomial $p(x)$ of degree $(k - 1)$. To generate shares, a random polynomial $p(x)$ is first constructed by choosing $k - 1$ random numbers $a_1, \cdots, a_{k-1}$ as the coefficients and the secret s as the free coefficient:

$$p_s(x) = s + a_1 x + \cdots + a_{k-1} x^{k-1}.$$

For SMC, we require $n > 2k$ parties to hold the shares. Every party gets assigned a coordinate x_i. We denote by $\{s\}_i = p_s(x_i)$ the share of party i. By combining any k (or more) shares together, we can rebuild the polynomial and recover the secret using Lagrange interpolation. Therefore, the distribution and reconstruction of a secret only need arithmetic evaluation, which is trivial comparing to encryption and decryption operations.

Addition in Shamir's secret sharing scheme is straightforward as it is a linear scheme. Given two secrets a and b shared by polynomials of degree $d = k - 1$, $p_a(x)$ and $p_b(x)$, the sum s is given by the polynomial $p_s(x) = p_a(x) + p_b(x)$ as $p_s(0) = p_a(0) + p_b(0) = a + b$. Therefore, the new shares of the sum can be computed by simply adding up the corresponding shares of each party: $\{s\}_i = \{a\}_i + \{b\}_i$.

The multiplication of two polynomials $p_s(x) = p_a(x)p_b(x)$, however, doubles the polynomial degree. It means that although the product result is correct: $p_s(0) = p_a(0)p_b(0) = ab$, it requires $2d + 1$ shares to reconstruct the polynomial this time. Therefore, we need $n > 2d$ parties to reduce the polynomial degree as well as restore the randomness of the coefficients, which introduces communication among the parties as a result. The protocol we adopted is described in [10] and needs one communication round to redistribute the shares after a multiplication.

Other primitives such as comparison, are mainly designed based on an algorithm build on additions and multiplications [14]. The algorithms are more complex as they invoke heavy communication among parties for such operations as multiplication or shared random number generation. Meanwhile, they should also involve as few communication rounds as possible, as each round will introduce network overhead. Therefore, we evaluate the performance of each primitive algorithm mainly according to two criteria. One is the number of multiplications it invokes, which relates to the amount of message exchanged among parties as well as local computation time[1]. The other criteria is the number of communication rounds. All messages to be exchanged are collected until no more computations can be executed. Then in one communication round, all buffered messages are exchanged. Thus, the message sent in a communication round can include the shares of several multiplications done in parallel. The efficiency of a communication round depends on the latency of the network used. For efficient protocols, in terms of computation and communication, both the multiplications and communication rounds should be minimized. The assisting server described in Section 3 aims at decreasing the number of multiplications and communication rounds in SMC.

2.3   Adversary Models

Two adversary models are commonly considered for SMC, depending on the kind of control that the adversary has over the corrupted party:

- *Semi-honest model:* The adversary has the ability to collect and read the information of a corrupted party, but still executes the protocol correctly. In

---

[1] Any operation that requires a communication round afterwards, will count as one multiplication".

other words, the adversary only intends to break the privacy of the protocol. We call this type of adversary *honest-but-curious adversary* or *passive
adversary*

 – *Malicious model:* The adversary takes full control of a corrupted party. Thus,
   the party can actively launch an attack inside the protocol and break the
   correctness of the protocol. We call this an *active adversary.*

The privacy requirement of an SMC protocol is that no one can learn any information about the input data out of his own possession during the computation
process, except for what can be inferred from the output of the function. Regarding to SMC based on secret sharing, as long as the data always remain in
the form of shares and not enough peers are colluded, the privacy of the input
data can be ensured.

For our SMC application (cooperative network monitoring), the semi-honest
model is reasonable: The various network operators involved are actually interested in the result of the joint computation and the prevention of attacks to
their networks. Therefore, we assume that all the parties will provide the correct
data and follow the protocol honestly. Meanwhile, they will not take the initiative to collude with other parties, as none of the operators would risk leaking
their own private data in exchange of those of the others. Moreover, as Shamir's
secret sharing is a threshold scheme, even when some parties are compromised
by external adversaries and collude with each other, the scheme can still resist
the collusion of a certain number of corrupted parties. In fact, out of n shares of
a k-degree polynomial, the secret remains confidential as long as no more than
$k+1$ shares are combined. Therefore, it is reasonable to assume that the parties
only behave passively and try to infer as much information as they can from the
data they obtained during the computation.

3   Assisting Server for Secure Multi-Party Computation

This section introduces the general concept of the *assisting server*, followed by
the example of equal$^+$ using an assisting server. The analysis will show an improvement in terms of computation and communication rounds.

3.1   Assisting Server Model

Traditionally, SMC is done in alternate computation and communication rounds.
In the computation rounds, each party computes locally on shares it holds. In
the communication rounds, the parties create new shares that they distribute to
other parties. With an assisting server, a new type of round is possible. In such
a round, the parties communicate with the assisting server in the following way:

 – The parties send a message to the assisting server. This message triggers the
   service requested from the assisting server, but might also include shares or
   plaintext information that can be reconstructed and used by the assisting
   server.

– The assisting server responds to the parties of the SMC. Usually, this response includes shares that the parties will subsequently use in their computation. But the response may also consist of plaintext information.

The intended efficiency gain can be achieved, if one round of communication with the assisting server can replace multiple rounds of communication between the SMC parties in the traditional model. The efficiency gains that can be achieved in the assisting server model come at a certain cost in security. The assisting server gains certain knowledge of the computation that is ongoing. Which information is revealed depends on the algorithm that is computed. We give more details in the description of the protocols for equal$^+$, and a short security discussion in the application scenarios in Section 5. As the leaked information and the impact of the leaked information is highly application dependent, setting up a SMC and choosing the right protocols becomes more difficult than with traditional multiparty computation which does not leak information. However, our use-case shows that the efficiency gain can be essential and makes it worthwhile to search for application-specific improvements.

The assisting server offers its service in a stateless way. The parties can ad hoc choose any assisting server that offers the necessary functionality, if it is required in the computation process. In case no additional information can be gained by a collusion between the assisting server and a party, one of the party could play the role of an assisting server by itself. The security assumptions concerning the assisting server are similar to the existing security assumptions. We assume that the assisting server behaves like a passive adversary. It does follow the protocol and does not collude with one of the parties in order to gain or share information. The assisting server may be interested and store all information it learns during the computation. Our requirement is not to prevent the assisting server from learning any information, but allow that a limited well-defined amount of information can be learnt. This definition needs to be evaluated and defined anew for each application where this approach is used.

3.2   Equality Comparison *Equal$^+$*

Comparing equality between two input data is one of the basic operations that SMC should provide and is used in many applications to match features in different data sets, such as evaluating conditions in privacy-preserving data mining, or aggregating data provided by different providers. The current algorithms for equality comparison under secret sharing scheme can be found in [5], [15], [14]. The protocol of [5] performs a bit-decomposition of the secret shares which is an expensive operation as well. A constant round protocol is given in [15] but requires $98l + 94l \log_2 l$ multiplications, where l denotes the bit length of p in field $\mathbb{Z}_p$ ($l = \lfloor \log_2 p \rfloor$). SEPIA [14] focuses on efficiency and aims not at constant-round communication. It adopts Fermat's little theorem (see Equation 1) and invokes $l + k - 2$ multiplications and l rounds, where k denotes the number of bits set to 1 in $p - 1$. The algorithm is

$$equal(\{a\}, \{b\}) = \{1 - (a - b)^{p-1}\}. \tag{1}$$

The efficiency of equality comparison is still not suitable for real-time applications, as l can easily exceed 32.

Therefore, we propose a probabilistic protocol referred to as $equal^+$ with the help of a shared random number and an assisting server for intermediate result evaluation.

Equal$^+$. At first, an unknown random number will be shared among the parties as $\{r\}$ using the *Joint Random Number Sharing protocol* from [15]. This is done by each party generating a local random number and distributing its shares to other parties. Then each party adds up the obtained and generated shares and the result is his share of the joint random number r. The random number r can be seen as an oblivious random number uniformly distributed over $\mathbb{Z}_p$. Its value cannot be predicted or influenced as it depends on the local random numbers generated on all parties, unless they are all colluded.

Then shares $\{c\}$ of $c = r(a-b)$ are computed by the parties by first subtracting the shares of b from the shares of a and the multiplying the shares of r and $a - b$. As we can see, c will be 0 if and only if r or $a - b$ equals to zero. With a sufficient big field size, which is usually the case, the probability $Prob(r = 0) = \frac{1}{p}$ which is negligible. Therefore, we can say that with overwhelming probability $c = 0 \Leftrightarrow a = b$.

Given that the value of r is randomly distributed, c can also be seen as a random number if $a \neq b$. Thus, c can be revealed without disclosing anything about a and b apart from $a = b$. The parties send the shares of c to the assisting server. The assisting server reconstructs c and evaluates if $c = 0$. As a result, in our solution the assisting server only has the knowledge of the equality comparison result. Nevertheless, we still need to analyze if this kind of information leakage is secure to a specific application.

What is left to complete in this function is mapping the *zero-/non-zero*-result to a binary value and sharing it back to the parties. This is done by the exponentiation using Fermat's little theorem in the previous protocol and will be done by the assisting server in our case. Therefore, our optimized equality comparison is defined as

$$equal^+(\{a\}, \{b\}) = \text{isZero}(\text{recon}(\{r \times (a - b)\})), \qquad (2)$$

where recon$(\cdot)$ denotes the reconstruction function of a secret, and isZero$(\cdot)$ is the evaluation function that maps 0 to 1 and any value $\neq 0$ to 0.

The execution of $equal^+$ in (2) takes four rounds: one for receiving the shares of r, one for the multiplication result, one for sending the message to the assisting server, and one for receiving the answer from the assisting server. Comparing to SEPIA's version with $l + k - 2$ multiplications in l rounds, our solution is more efficient, with a constant and small number of computation and communication rounds.

3.3   Applications for Cooperative Network Monitoring

We present an application protocol called *link-counting* that can be used for privacy-preserving, cooperative analysis of monitoring data between different operators. This protocol provides a database-query-like operation with two input parties. It sums up the number of matched records with specific conditions. It can for instance be used in distributed monitoring systems for Spam detection based on social graph analysis. In principle, the protocol enables two or more parties to compare and match social graphs without revealing the internal links among nodes within each network to each other.

The concept of link-counting is very similar to the *Database Query* problem described in Du's SMC problem definition [8]: Domain A has the identities of a list of users $Q = (q_1, \cdots, q_M)$, and domain B has a database of user linking records $(U, V) = \{(u_1, v_1), \cdots, (u_N, v_N)\}$; A wants to know how many records of (u_i, v_i) in B's database match the combination of (q_r, q_s), $i = 1, \cdots, N, r, s = 1, \cdots, M, r \neq s$. The privacy requirement is that B cannot know A's secret query Q or the response to that query, and A cannot know B's database contents except for what could be derived from the query result. The implemented algorithm checks for each edge (u_i, v_i), if $u_i \in Q$ AND $v_i \in Q$ and sums up the resulting values. This algorithm requires $2MN$ equality tests and N multiplications. We will see in Section 4.1 that the performance of this protocol is more acceptable when using equal$^+$ to perform the equality test.

4   Implementation and Evaluation

In this section, we present the experimental results of our performance evaluation on equal$^+$ using an assisting server as described in Section 3.2. The objective of the experimental tests is to show the consistency with our theoretical analysis and the performance advantage of our improved SMC primitive. Further, we study the running time of the link-counting protocol. The experiments will be in comparison with the *equal* algorithm in [14] because this shows the best performance among SMC frameworks and includes a comparison with the other frameworks.

We implemented our algorithms in the SEPIA framework, a Java library providing the tools for privacy-preserving aggregation of multi-domain network data [14]. The SEPIA framework adopts Shamir's Secret Sharing scheme (see Section 2.2). There are two roles in the framework, the *input peer* and the *privacy peer*. Input peers are the parties who provide private data for the joint computation. At the beginning of the computation, the input peers distribute the shares of their data among the privacy peers using Shamir's secret sharing. Privacy peers (PPs) hold the shares of the data and perform the computation on them. They will not reconstruct the inputs nor the intermediate results; they only reconstruct the final result and send it back to the input peers.

The threshold t is chosen as half of the parties: $t = \lfloor (n-1)/2 \rfloor$. Thus, the minimum number of parties is 3 when $t = 2$. With more parties, the performance will decrease as it will involve more message exchanges and synchronizations among the parties. The semi-honest adversary model suggested in SEPIA (see Section 2.3) is quite reasonable in a real application: Different business parties usually do not intend to break the protocol, but they are still interested in inferring as much information as they can during the computation to know the private data of the other parties.

4.1 *Equal*$^+$ Performance Test

The test environment of our experiments is on 3 separate PCs (Athlon XP 2800+ or better) and each runs a privacy peer process on it. The other peers including input peers and assisting peers are distributed evenly on the same group of machines. For each test, the average of 100 program executions is taken. The absolute number of equal operations per second using *equal* differs from the result in [14] because of the different test environment.

In the first experiment, we want to show that unlike *equal*, the performance of *equal*$^+$ is hardly influenced by the value of the polynomial field size p. The result confirms our theoretical analysis on the computational complexity in Section 3.2. The second experiment is a benchmark test on how many equal operations can be accomplished using each tool. The last experiment compares the performance of the link-counting protocol. The result shows that the choice of primitive operations in an application determines if the running time is acceptable or not, and that using *equal*$^+$ is a much more reasonable choice for a real-world application.

Experiment 1. Different Field Size In Section 3.2, we compared the complexity of *equal* using Fermat's little theorem and *equal*$^+$ using an assisting server by analyzing the number of multiplications and communication rounds. Our analysis shows that *equal* needs $l + k - 2$ multiplications and l communication rounds, where l is the bit length and k the hamming weight of $p - 1$. In comparison, *equal*$^+$ only requires 4 multiplications and 4 communication rounds. As a result, we can conclude that the performance of *equal* depends on the selection of the size of $\mathbb{Z}_p$, which is chosen depending on the values in the computation because any input/output or intermediate data should be smaller than p. To optimize the performance of *equal*, we choose a prime p with $k \leq 3$ which is the optimal choice to reduce the complexity.

Figure 1 shows the results of the run-time of each equal operation in relation to the size of the data space. In the test, the prime p that determines the data space is selected as the smallest prime that can cover the data space and has a weight $k \leq 3$. As expected, with increasing data space size, *equal* takes more time to accomplish one operation, while the performance of *equal*$^+$ keeps quite stable under different application data space. The sudden increase for both operations at a data space size of 32 bits is caused by the implementation of the SEPIA library. When dealing with modular multiplication, the program changes from a primitive *long* datatype ($-2^{63} \sim 2^{63}$) to a more complex data structure *BigInteger*. The impact of changing the Java data type is smaller on the performance of *equal*$^+$ because *equal*$^+$ uses less modular multiplications.

Figure 2 shows another perspective of the performance comparison. Since in principle multiplication and communication rounds are the only factors of the computational complexity, *equal*$^+$ should perform between $l/4$ and $l/3$ times faster than *equal*. We use the results from Figure 1 to plot the ratio of *equal*$^+$

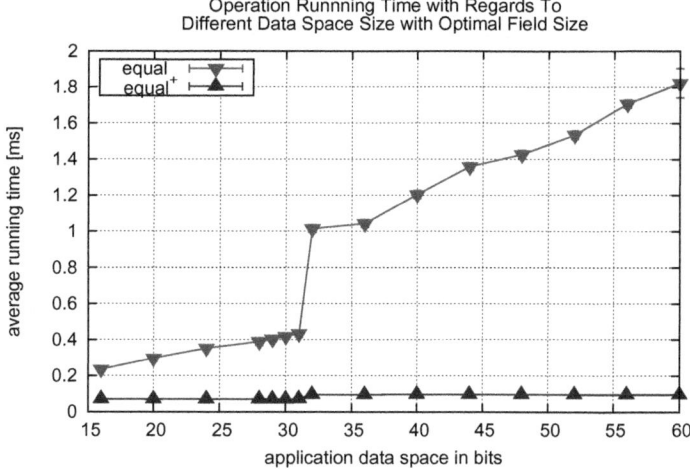

Fig. 1. Average running time of an equal operation over different application data space. The field size for each data space is selected as the smallest applicable prime number that has $k \leq 3$.

over *equal* on different values of l. Meanwhile, we also display the ideal perfor-mance ratio $l/4$ and $l/3$ (in dashed and dotted lines). We can see that most part of the experimental curve is within $l/4$ and $l/3$, which is consistent with our assumption.

Experiment 2. Benchmark for Equality Comparison. In this experiment, we fix the field size and test how many equal operations each algorithm can accomplish in one second (equals/s). Instead of giving a single result, we change some test conditions for benchmarking and discuss the outcome. In the configuration, we decide how many equal operations to run in a round by setting the test set size. We then execute the test and measure the completion time. The total number of equal operations (or the test set size) divided by the completion time is our benchmark. We run the test with different test set sizes and with different application data space sizes. The result of the benchmark is shown in Figure 3. As can be seen from the results, $equal^+$ is able to do 10-20 times more equal operations than *equal* when processing 32-bit integers, and 20-40 times more operations with 60-bit integers.

We notice that the efficiency of our equal operation increases with the test set size. The reason is that SEPIA executes the operations in parallel thus the number of communication rounds does not increase but the CPU utilization between rounds is higher. In addition, we observe in Figure 3 that both equal algorithms perform less efficiently with 60-bit integers than with 32-bit integers. This is within our expectation because computations over larger values are usu-ally slower. However, while the performance of $equal^+$ only decreases by 1.64% because of the larger data to process, the benchmark of *equal* reduces by 42.44%. This confirms that the field size is a decisive factor for the performance of *equal*.

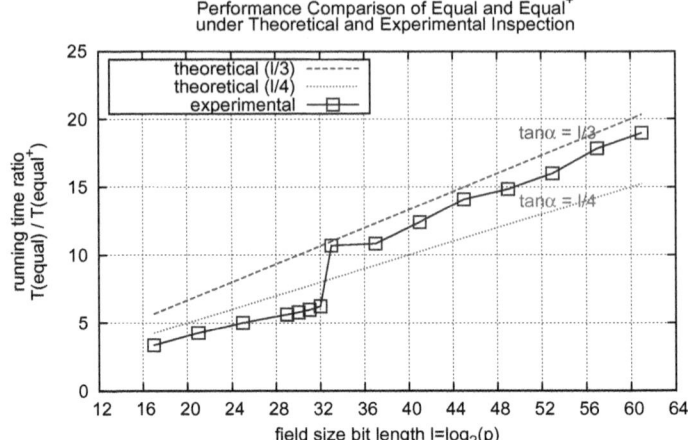

Fig. 2. Running time quotient of *equal* over *equal*+. The non-solid lines indicate the theoretical values from the computational complexity analysis.

Therefore, we can predict that if an SMC application deals with bigger data space, the advantage of *equal*+ will become more obvious.

Experiment 3. Performance in Applications. We test the performance of cooperative network monitoring using *equal* and *equal*+, respectively. We are interested to verify that link-counting will be more practical in terms of execution time with the optimized primitive *equal*+. For the link-counting protocol, the main performance challenge is the potentially large amount of records in the database. For network monitoring, a database B contains all the links between users in the network, which can easily be over a million records. However, in a real application, it is not necessary that party B provides all records to an SMC function. In fact, the query party A can provide some information regarding the range of the queried users to decrease the search space.

In the performance test, we fix the query size to 10 users, and incrementally increase the number of records in the database from 10,000 to 100,000. Figure 4 shows the performance of two implementations of the link-counting protocol, one based on *equal* and one based on *equal*+. It can be observed that using *equal*+ on 100,000 records, the query process takes less than 3 minutes, while *equal* needs to run more than half an hour.

4.2   Evaluation Summary

We used three commodity PCs in our testing environment. In a real application scenario, the absolute execution times shown in our results can be improved by using powerful machines to run the protocols. Moreover, since *equal*+ involves less communication rounds, the protocol will suffer less from a distributed and asynchronous network, and thus, profit more from powerful CPUs.

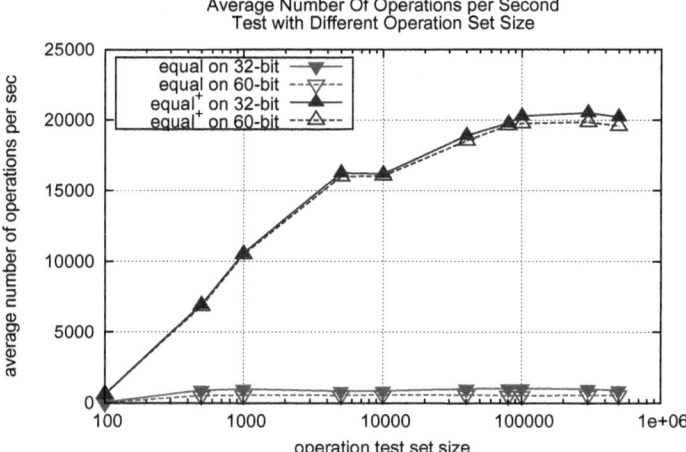

Fig. 3. Benchmark of *equal* and *equal$^+$* on number of operations per second. The benchmark runs under different test conditions: various data space size (32-bit and 60-bit) and various operation test set size.

The experimental results of the algorithm *equal$^+$* using an assisting server provide evidence of higher efficiency and stability compared to existing algorithms. The field size test shows that *equal$^+$* performs stable over different application data space. The benchmark test provides an estimate of how many equality comparisons both algorithms can accomplish in a unit of time. The result data shows that *equal$^+$* runs 10-20 times faster than the previous algorithm when dealing with 32-bit integers. The benchmark test on different operation settings also shows that - due to the parallel execution feature in SEPIA - the protocols perform more efficiently when processing data in a batch job. This is an advantage when dealing with big data sets, but we need to choose carefully how big the parallel operation set is in order to yield optimal performance.

The application protocol link-counting has been developed with cooperative network monitoring in mind. In the experimental tests of this protocol we only used data sets of medium size, e.g. the maximum size of the database is 100,000 records. Further, because SEPIA executes the operations in parallel, it will pack all operational data in a single message, which can become very large when the protocol executes a lot of operations. Nevertheless, the performance results of our protocols show that *equal$^+$* is in principle applicable on big data set operations.

In summary, our results provide evidence that the assisting server model in conjunction with the new *equal$^+$* is more efficient in execution time than existing algorithms. It is a promising solution to provide practical protocols for performance-demanding applications. We gave examples how the implementation of a protocol also affects application performance.

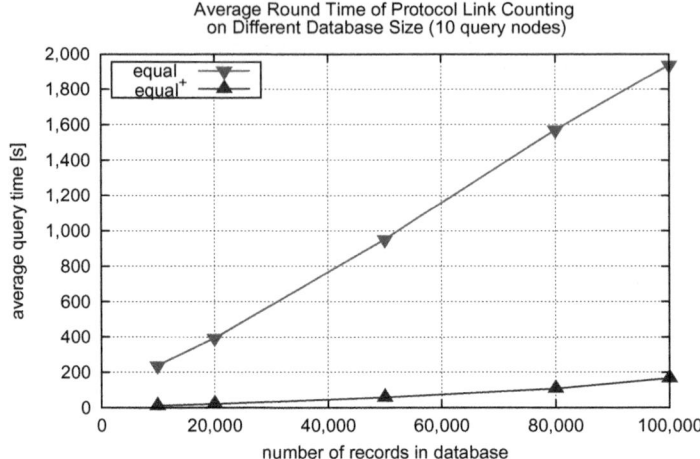

Fig. 4. Performance of link-counting protocol using *equal* and *equal*$^{+}$ test on different size of database

5   Security Discussion on the New SMC Model

We have shown that using an assisting server can make certain SMC functions much faster; we will now discuss the security implications introduced by our new model. For the parties, the security assumptions remain. In the semi-honest model, the resistant threshold for collusion still remains $n/2$, where n is the number of parties. A collusion involving at most half of the parties cannot extract any information from the computation. Certain assumptions are necessary for the assisting server: It is assumed that the assisting server does not collude with the parties and will correctly follow the protocol. The assisting server might however be curious and gather as much information as possible. The assisting server is explicitly allowed to gain some information about intermediate results of specific operations. In the case of equal^{+}, this is the result of the equality operation. The assumptions for the assisting server are clearly weaker than the assumptions for a trusted third party (TTP). A TTP would be allowed to know all the private input data, while the assisting server is only trusted to know well defined partial information of some intermediate computation steps. The limited amount of information prevents the assisting server for instance from doing large scale data mining.

Further strategies are possible to mitigate the risk of the information available to the assisting server: 1) Using an independent assisting server offering the service publicly. The server might have no context information about the origin of the evaluated data. Therefore, the assisting server will not have a relevant knowledge gain; 2) Preprocessing of the data by the parties, e.g. shuffling with the help of a different assisting server, might again help to reduce the information gained by the assisting server, under the assumption that the two assisting servers do not collude.

The assisting server model demands an application-specific security analysis. In each application using an assisting server, we need to identify whether the information leakage is acceptable by the application. Also what kind of information can be inferred through a collusion of a party with the assisting server is relevant for assessing the risk.

In many cases, the information learnt by the assisting server might be information that will finally be public anyway because it is part of the output of the parties. In that case, the intermediate results obtained by the assisting server do not give any new information even when shared with a party. In that case it is possible that one of the SMC parties plays additionally the role of the assisting server for certain functions. This scenario is in general more challenging as it corresponds to the situation of a collusion between the assisting server and a party.

Link-counting. In the link-counting protocol using $equal^+$, the assisting server learns the results of the equality comparison. The order of equal or not-equal results might leak some data about the structure of A's request and B's network that should not be disclosed to an outsider. This could be mitigated by the involved parties, e.g. by agreeing on a different random program-flow, so that the order of execution is not related to the order of elements in the input vectors.

In case one of the parties takes the role of the assisting server this is not enough. However, if the program flow is randomized in a way oblivious to the parties, e.g. by a *secret shuffle* function, this approach is still possible. Given a set of shares $\{\{a_1\}, \ldots, \{a_m\}\}$, a shuffle function produces a set of shares $\{\{b_1\}, \ldots, \{b_m\}\}$ such that $a_i = b_{\pi(i)}$ for a random permutation π. The shuffle function needs to be secret, such that no party learns the new sequence order except the one that defines the shuffle function. After the operation, even if a party knows one of the input data sets and the output of a function, it cannot be sure which of the input items corresponds to the output of the function. Therefore, the secret shuffle adds uncertainty to an SMC function, hence reducing what an adversary can learn by colluding the party with the assisting server to obtain both the input and output of a function.

Secret shuffle using an assisting server. The most straightforward way of permuting a vector is by multiplying the vector with a permutation matrix. A permutation matrix is a binary matrix with exactly one entry 1 in each column and row. If this is done by a multiplication on shares of the vector and shares of the matrix entries, the re-randomization from the share-multiplication brings the secrecy requirement of the shuffle for free. A shuffle matrix could efficiently be created and distributed by an assisting server that is not involved in any further processing steps.

6   Conclusion

We have proposed a novel model for Secure Multi-Party Computation with a new entity, an *assisting server*. Based on this model, we introduced new algorithms for the SMC primitive equality (called $equal^+$), as well as one application protocol for cooperative network monitoring, the *link-counting* protocol.

Our experimental evaluation with a prototype implementation in the SEPIA framework demonstrate that $equal^+$ can be computed much faster than previous algorithms in the traditional SMC model. Also, we showed that $equal^+$ significantly increases the performance of the link-counting protocol, and that its performance is less dependent on certain parameters than the original equal function in SEPIA. The performance gains come at the price of a certain relaxation of the security assumptions for SMC: the assisting server learns some intermediate computation results in plaintext. We have discussed options for mitigating this issue and provided concrete examples for preventing the assisting server from gaining too much insight into the overall SMC computation. Overall, we believe that algorithms can be designed in such a way that disclosing intermediate values to an assisting server is acceptable from the security perspective. In that case, the benefits of our approach, i.e. performance gains, clearly outweigh its drawbacks.

As future work, we intend to investigate other SMC primitives which can be sped up with an assisting server and to study the corresponding security implications formally.

Acknowledgment. This work was partially supported by DEMONS, a research project supported by the European Commission under its 7th Framework Program (contract no. 257315). The views and conclusions contained herein are those of the authors and should not be interpreted as necessarily representing the official policies or endorsements, either expressed or implied, of the DEMONS project or the European Commission.

References

1. Ben-David, A., Nisan, N., Pinkas, B.: Fairplaymp: A system for secure multi-party computation. In: Proceedings of the 15th ACM Conference on Computer and Communications Security, CCS 2008, pp. 257–266. ACM (2008)
2. Ben-Or, M., Goldwasser, S., Wigderson, A.: Completeness theorems for noncryptographic fault-tolerant distributed computation. In: Proceedings of the Twentieth Annual ACM Symposium on Theory of Computing, STOC 1988, pp. 1–10. ACM (1988)
3. Bogetoft, P., Christensen, D.L., Damgård, I., Geisler, M., Jakobsen, T., Krøigaard, M., Nielsen, J.D., Nielsen, J.B., Nielsen, K., Pagter, J., Schwartzbach, M., Toft, T.: Secure Multiparty Computation Goes Live. In: Dingledine, R., Golle, P. (eds.) FC 2009. LNCS, vol. 5628, pp. 325–343. Springer, Heidelberg (2009)
4. Cachin, C.: Efficient private bidding and auctions with an oblivious third party. In: Proceedings of the 6th ACM Conference on Computer and Communications Security, CCS 1999, pp. 120–127. ACM (1999)
5. Damgård, I., Fitzi, M., Kiltz, E., Nielsen, J.B., Toft, T.: Unconditionally Secure Constant-Rounds Multi-party Computation for Equality, Comparison, Bits and Exponentiation. In: Halevi, S., Rabin, T. (eds.) TCC 2006. LNCS, vol. 3876, pp. 285–304. Springer, Heidelberg (2006)

6. Damgård, I., Geisler, M., Krøigaard, M., Nielsen, J.B.: Asynchronous Multiparty Computation: Theory and Implementation. In: Jarecki, S., Tsudik, G. (eds.) PKC 2009. LNCS, vol. 5443, pp. 160–179. Springer, Heidelberg (2009)

7. Desikan, P., Srivastava, J.: Analyzing network traffic to detect e-mail spamming machines. In: Proceedings of the 2004 ICDM Workshop on Privacy and Security Aspects of Data Mining, PSDM 2004 (2004)

8. Du, W., Atallah, M.J.: Secure multi-party computation problems and their applications: A review and open problems. In: New Security Paradigms Workshop, pp. 11–20 (2001)

9. FP7-DEMONS.eu. Demons: Decentralized, cooperative, and privacy-preserving monitoring for trustworthiness, http://fp7-demons.eu/

10. Gennaro, R., Rabin, M.O., Rabin, T.: Simplified vss and fast-track multiparty computations with applications to threshold cryptography. In: Proceedings of the Seventeenth Annual ACM Symposium on Principles of Distributed Computing, PODC 1998, pp. 101–111 (1998)

11. Gentry, C.: Fully homomorphic encryption using ideal lattices. In: Proceedings of the 41st Annual ACM Symposium on Theory of Computing, STOC 2009, pp. 169–178. ACM (2009)

12. Goldreich, O., Micali, S.M., Wigderson, A.: How to play any mental game. In: Proceedings of the Nineteenth Annual ACM Symposium on Theory of Computation, STOC 1987, pp. 218–229. ACM (1987)

13. Gu, G., Perdisci, R., Zhang, J., Lee, W.: Botminer: Clustering analysis of network traffic for protocol- and structure-independent botnet detection. In: Proceedings of the 17th USENIX Security Symposium, pp. 139–154. USENIX Association (2008)

14. Martin, B., Strasser, M., Many, D., Dimitropoulos, X.: Sepia: Privacy-preserving aggregation of multi-domain network events and statistics. In: USENIX Security Symposium. USENIX (2010)

15. Nishide, T., Ohta, K.: Multiparty Computation for Interval, Equality, and Comparison Without Bit-Decomposition Protocol. In: Okamoto, T., Wang, X. (eds.) PKC 2007. LNCS, vol. 4450, pp. 343–360. Springer, Heidelberg (2007)

16. Roughan, M., Zhang, Y.: Privacy-preserving performance measurements. In: Proceedings of the 2006 SIGCOMM Workshop on Mining Network Data, MineNet 2006, pp. 329–334. ACM (2006)

17. Schatzmann, D., Burkhart, M., Spyropoulos, T.: Inferring Spammers in the Network Core. In: Moon, S.B., Teixeira, R., Uhlig, S. (eds.) PAM 2009. LNCS, vol. 5448, pp. 229–238. Springer, Heidelberg (2009)

18. Vaidya, J., Clifton, C.: Leveraging the "multi" in secure multi-party computation. In: Proceedings of the 2003 ACM Workshop on Privacy in the Electronic Society, WPES 2003, pp. 53–59. ACM (2003)

19. Yao, A.C.: Protocols for secure computations. In: Proceedings of the 23rd Annual Symposium on Foundations of Computer Science, pp. 160–164 (1982)

20. Yao, A.C.: How to generate and exchange secrets. In: 27th Annual Symposium on Foundations of Computer Science, 1986, pp. 162–167 (1986)

An Efficient Lattice-Based Secret Sharing Construction

Rachid El Bansarkhani[1] and Mohammed Meziani[2]

[1] Technische Universität Darmstadt
Fachbereich Informatik
Kryptographie und Computeralgebra,
Hochschulstraße 10, 64289 Darmstadt, Germany
elbansarkhani@cdc.informatik.tu-darmstadt.de
[2] CASED – Center for Advanced Security Research Darmstadt,
Mornewegstrasse 32, 64293 Darmstadt, Germany
mohammed.meziani@cased.de

Abstract. This paper presents a new construction of a lattice-based verifiable secret sharing scheme. Our proposal is based on lattices and the usage of linear hash functions to enable each participant to verify its received secret share. The security of this scheme relies on the hardness of some well known approximation problems in lattices such as n^c-approximate SVP. Different to protocols proposed by Pedersen this scheme uses efficient matrix vector operations instead of exponentiation to verify the secret shares.

Keywords: Secret Sharing, Lattice-based Cryptography, Shortest Vector Problem, Hash Functions.

1 Introduction

It is known from [12] that quantum algorithms could break most of number-theory based cryptosystems used in practice (e.g., RSA, DL). Indeed, such algorithms can solve both the factoring problem and the discrete log problem in finite fields and on elliptic curves in polynomial time. It may therefore be desirable to design new cryptographic primitives, such as public-key cryptosystems and secret sharing schemes, whose security depends upon problems that are not vulnerable to quantum attacks. Lattice-based systems offer a promising alternative to number-theoretic ones, and they are believed to be secure against quantum attacks since their security is based on lattice problems that in their general form are well-known NP-hard. In addition to post-quantum security, they are easy to implement and utilize only basic operations.

Motivated by the need for protecting cryptographic keys by more than one party, secret sharing schemes were first introduced independently in 1979 by Shamir [11] and Blakley [3]. The Shamir's proposal relies on polynomials with n coefficients where n is the number of parties involved to reconstruct the coefficients of polynomials with degrees at most $n - 1$. Blakley, instead, makes use

I. Askoxylakis, H.C. Pöhls, and J. Posegga (Eds.): WISTP 2012, LNCS 7322, pp. 160–168, 2012.
© IFIP International Federation for Information Processing 2012

of the fact that different hyperplanes can intersect in one point. And a certain amount of these hyperplanes is only required to specify that point. Since then several other secret sharing schemes have been developed, for example those that are based on the Chinese Remainder Theorem ([7] and [2]) or hybrid constructions [8] using the discrete logarithm problem for verification. Our construction follows a new simple approach since it uses only simple operations from linear algebra. Compared to the previous schemes it recovers a vector rather than a single value. Furthermore, the verification of the secret shares as well as the secret vector can be done via lattice-based hash functions whose security is reducible to some NP-hard problems in lattices. Previous schemes, instead, rely on the discrete logarithm problem for the verification. The main idea behind our scheme is to recover a basismatrix at first which is then required to compute the secret vector that in turn could be used as a secret key for the lattice-based LWE encryption scheme [10]. Secret sharing systems can be found in many real applications such as secure multi-party computations [4], e-voting [14], and sensor networks [6]. In the basic model of secret sharing we differ at least two major protocols: the distribution protocol in which the dealer forwards the secret shares to the participants, and the combination or reconstruction protocol in which the secret is recovered by pooling the shares of a qualified subset of the participants.

A system is called a (t, n) threshold secret sharing scheme with $t \leq n$, when at least t participants are required to recover the secret key, where n is the number of participants obtaining a secret share from the dealer. We present a (n, n) secret sharing scheme based on the difficulty to solve n^c-approximate SVP in lattices for some constant c.

2   Preliminaries

The following briefly introduces the definitions and notations used in the present paper.

2.1   Notations

The following notations and definitions will be used throughout the rest of the paper.

* $|x|$ is the length in bits of a string x.
* The Hamming weight of a string x is the number of its non-null coordinates and denoted by $\mathsf{wt}(x)$.
* $[v_1, ..., v_n]$ is the matrix composed by the column vectors $v_1, v_2, \ldots, v_n$.
* By $t_1 = (t_1^{(1)}, ..., t_1^{(n)})$ we denote a vector consisting of n elements, where $t_j^{(i)}$ identifies the i-th element of the vector t_j.
* For a finite set S, we denote by $x \xleftarrow{\$} S$ the experiment of uniformly choosing an element x from S and assigning it to x.
* With $\lceil r \rceil$ we round a real number r up to the next integer.
* $x^\top$ is the transpose of a vector x.
* $\mathsf{rot}(x)$ cyclically rotates the vector x, e.g. $\mathsf{rot}((1, 2, 3, 4)) = (4, 1, 2, 3)$.

2.2   Basics on Lattices

A lattice L is a discrete abelian subgroup of $\mathbb{R}^m$. A basis $B = [b_1, .., b_n] \in \mathbb{R}^{m \times n}$ for the lattice L consists of $d \leq n$ linearly independent vectors b_i with $\mathcal{L}(B) = \left\{ \sum_{i=1}^{n} t_i b_i \mid t_1, ..., t_n \in \mathbb{Z} \right\} \subset \mathbb{R}^m$, i.e. $\mathcal{L}$ is the set of all integer combinations of the vectors in B. The minimum distance of a lattice $\mathcal{L}(B)$, denoted $\lambda(\mathcal{L}(B))$, is the minimum distance between any two distinct lattice points, and equals the length of a nonzero shortest lattice vector.

$$\lambda(\mathcal{L}(B)) = \min\{\|x\| : x \in \mathcal{L}(B)\} \tag{1}$$

Definition 1. *(Shortest Vector Problem - SVP)*
Let $\mathcal{L}(B) \subset \mathbb{R}^n$ be a d-dimensional lattice and $B \in \mathbb{Z}^{n \times d}$ the corresponding basis matrix. An input to SVP is a lattice basis B and the goal is to find a vector x in $\mathcal{L}(B)$ such that $\|x\| = \lambda(\mathcal{L}(B))$

Definition 2. *(Approximate Shortest Vector Problem - γ-SVP)*
Let $\mathcal{L}(B) \subset \mathbb{R}^n$ be a d-dimensional lattice and $B \in \mathbb{Z}^{n \times d}$ the corresponding basis matrix. An input to SVP is a lattice basis B and the goal is to find a vector x in $\mathcal{L}(B)$ such that $\|x\| = \gamma \cdot \lambda(\mathcal{L}(B))$

3   Our Construction

In this section, we present a non-interactive verifiable lattice-based secret sharing protocol that requires all parties to participate with their shares in order to recover a secret, while at the same time enabling them to verify their secret share. In this scheme, a dealer selects different vectors of length n and weight $m > 1$ and produces secret shares of length n , where n is a positive integer. A higher weight is chosen in order to prevent the participants to get information about the basis vectors from their secret shares, because the secret share is a linear combination of the private basis vectors.

3.1   Description

This scheme works in non-interactive manner, meaning that each participant can verify its own secret share without communicating with other participants. It consists of two steps: the distribution and combination phase. On the other hand, its security relies on the hardness of solving SVP in lattices. Furthermore, it is very fast as it uses only matrix-vector multiplication to recover the secret.

The principle of our proposal is the following: the dealer generates a private lattice basis $B \in \mathbb{Z}^{n \times n}$ with low orthogonal defect and selects linearly independent vectors $\lambda_i \in \{x \in \mathbb{F}_2^n : \mathsf{wt}(x) = m > 1\}$ and publishes them together with the hashed (encrypted) secret and basis vectors. The dealer also reveals the vector $v \in \mathbb{Z}^n$ which is needed to compute the secret as $s := B \cdot v$. Here a linear hash function is used, such as Ajtai's hash function [1] or more efficient ones proposed by Lyubashevsky and Micciancio [5] or Peikert and Rosen [9], to enable each participant to verify its secret share in a non-interactive manner. It is also possible to take a semi-homomorphic lattice-based encryption scheme with additive property to achieve the same results. As next step, the dealer secretly distributes the vectors $c_i = B \cdot \lambda_i$ to each participant P_i. By doing so, n participants would be able to recover the private basis and compute the secret. In what follows, we describe the distribution and combination phase in details.

Distribution Phase

1. D chooses a private lattice Basis B and selects linearly independent binary vectors λ_i of length n and weight m > 1. Then he computes the secret shares $c_i = B \cdot \lambda_i$ and secretly forwards them to the participants.
2. Upon receipt of the own secret share, each participant P checks the hash value, in particular he verifies whether the hash value of its secret share can be written as a linear combination of the hashed basis vectors, i.e., $H(c_i) \stackrel{?}{=} \sum \lambda_{ij} \cdot H(b_j)$, since the λ_i and $H(b_j)$ as well as the secret generating vector v are public. If the hash value is valid, the participant sends its acknowledgment to the dealer back.

    Since many hash functions are fed with binary strings of a special length we can hash each component of the received vector without losing the linearity of the hash function. In this way we obtain for every input vector a matrix as hash value.

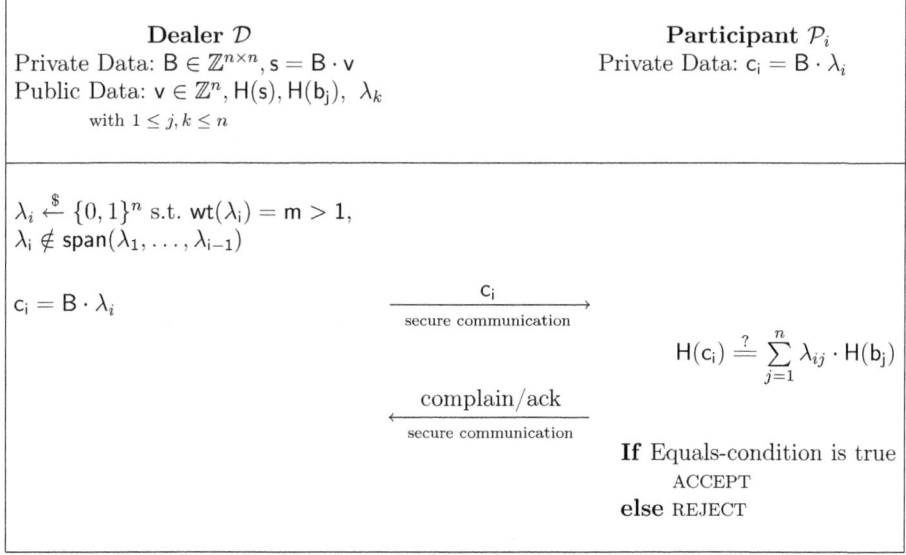

Fig. 1. Distribution Phase

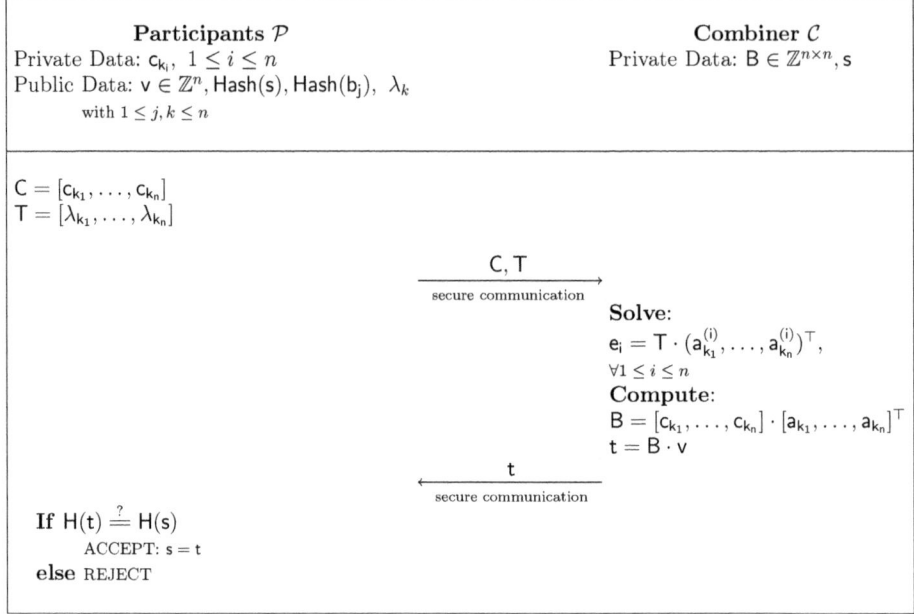

Fig. 2. Combination Phase

Combination Phase

The combination phase involves three steps to recover the secret:

1. n participants $P_{k_1}, \ldots, P_{k_n}$ secretly send their received secret shares $c_{k_1}, \ldots, c_{k_n}$ to the combiner. These secret shares $c_{k_1}, \ldots, c_{k_n}$ can be represented as square matrix of size n × n, i.e., $C = [c_{k_1}, \ldots, c_{k_n}]$. Then the combiner solves the following equations for the unkonwn vectors $a_{k_1}, \ldots, a_{k_n}$, where e_i denotes the i-th n-dimension unit vector:

$$e_i = [\lambda_{k_1}, \ldots, \lambda_{k_n}] \cdot (a_{k_1}^{(i)}, \ldots, a_{k_n}^{(i)})^\top, \; 1 \leq i \leq n \qquad (2)$$

We then obtain a matrix $A = [a_{k_1}, \ldots, a_{k_1}]$ in order to compute the private lattice basis B. The following equation shows that the private Basis can be expressed as a function of the matrices C and A:

$$\begin{aligned}
B &= [c_{k_1}, \ldots, c_{k_n}] \cdot [a_{k_1}, \ldots, a_{k_n}]^\top \\
&= [b_1, \ldots, b_n] \cdot [\lambda_{k_1}, \ldots, \lambda_{k_n}] \cdot [a_{k_1}, \ldots, a_{k_n}]^\top \\
&= [b_1, \ldots, b_n] \cdot [e_1, \ldots, e_n]
\end{aligned} \qquad (3)$$

2. The combiner computes the secret by simple matrix vector multiplication.

$$s = B \cdot v, \qquad (4)$$

The secret is then sent via a secure communication channel to each participant back.

3. The participants can then verify the secret produced by the combiner. To this end, the participant compares the hash of the received value with the hashed secret provided by the dealer which is also publicly available.

Example: n=4, wt = 3

$$[\lambda_1, \ldots, \lambda_4] = \begin{pmatrix} 1\ 0\ 1\ 1 \\ 1\ 1\ 0\ 1 \\ 1\ 1\ 1\ 0 \\ 0\ 1\ 1\ 1 \end{pmatrix}, [b_1, \ldots, b_4] = \begin{pmatrix} 7\ 9\ 8\ 4 \\ 6\ 3\ 3\ 0 \\ 5\ 9\ 0\ 5 \\ 4\ 4\ 2\ 3 \end{pmatrix},$$

$$[c_1, \ldots, c_4] = \begin{pmatrix} 15\ 22\ 10\ 12 \\ 17\ 16\ 13\ 7 \\ 18\ 21\ 11\ 9 \\ 15\ 16\ 5\ 8 \end{pmatrix}$$

3.2 Security and Performance

The security of our construction is based on the underlying hash function which is used for hiding the basis vectors as well as the secret. It is also possible to use any encryption function instead, which however needs to satisfy the additive property. The security of Ajtai's hash function (see Algorithm 1) or more efficient ones constructed by Lyubashevsky and Micciancio [5] or Peikert and Rosen [9] can be reduced to the hardness of solving approximate n^c-SVP.

Algorithm 1 Calculate A hash function following Ajtai's construction

---

1. **Parameters:** integers $n, k, p, d \geq 1$ with $n > \frac{k \cdot \log(p)}{\log(d)}$
2. **Key:** a matrix B chosen uniformly from $\mathbb{Z}_p^{k \times n}$
3. **Hash function:** $f_A : \{0, \ldots, d-1\}^n \to \mathbb{Z}_p^k$ given by $f_A(x) = A \cdot x \bmod p$

As already mentioned above many hash functions are fed with a binary input string and produce a vector. Since we operate on n dimensional vector spaces we would have to hash each component of a vector leading to a n × n-matrix as a hash value without affecting the additive property. In the distribution phase every participant verifies its secret share. The needed number of operations and transferred bits of each protocol step are depicted in the following tables. When $\mathbb{Z}^n$ is replaced by $\mathbb{Z}_q^n$, the bit size of each vector component is bounded by $\log(q)$ and the solution is unique if the determinant of $[\lambda_{k_1}, \ldots, \lambda_{k_n}]$ is coprime to q as shown in [13].

In a (n, n) scheme the dealer can efficiently generate n linearly independent vectors having length n by setting the weight to $n - 1$. If we use the vectors

Table 1. Theoretical performance in the distribution phase

	Dealer	Participant
Computation (bops)	$n^2 m \cdot \log(q)$	$\frac{n^2 \cdot \log(q)}{\log(p)}$
Communication (bits)	$n \cdot \log(q)$	1

Table 2. Theoretical performance in the combination phase

	Participants	Combiner
Computation (bops)		$n^2 \cdot (n^2 + n^{0.373} + \log(q))$
Communication (bits)	$n^2 \cdot (\log(q) + 1)$	$n \cdot \log(q)$

$\lambda_i = (\sum_{j=1}^{n} e_j) - e_i$ for $1 \leq i \leq n$ it can easily be shown that these vectors form a base due to the fact that each vector represents a vertice in a n-dimensional hypercube. These vertices are on different axial planes perpendicular to each other. So any checks in terms of linearly independence can be neglected.

Example: n = 6, wt = 5

$$[\lambda_1, \ldots, \lambda_6] = \begin{pmatrix} 1\,1\,1\,1\,1\,0 \\ 1\,1\,1\,1\,0\,1 \\ 1\,1\,1\,0\,1\,1 \\ 1\,1\,0\,1\,1\,1 \\ 1\,0\,1\,1\,1\,1 \\ 0\,1\,1\,1\,1\,1 \end{pmatrix}$$

From linear algebra we know that fewer than n participants cannot recover the private basis and thus get no information about the secret s because the secret satisfies equation (4). It is also possible to show that no unit vector can be computed in the first step of the combination phase when the number of participants is less than n. So any private basis vector remains hidden. This advantageous side effect comes from the fact that $n - 1$ of the chosen vectors λ_k span a $(n - 1)$-dimensional hyperplane connecting the $n - 1$ vertices and the origin in a hypercube. So every unit vector is outside the hyperplane.

Our secret sharing scheme has been implemented on a 2.5 GHz Intel Core i5-2520M, running Linux (Ubuntu 11.04) 32 Bit. The performance results of the implementation are reported in Table 3.

Table 3. Performance of the secret sharing scheme

Number of users (dimension)	Distribution timing (sec)	Combination timing (sec)	Verification timing (sec)
n=128	0.005864	0.006625	0.000085
n=256	0.035171	0.042033	0.00023
n=512	0.195757	0.273959	0.000676
n=1024	1.212575	1.922552	0.002577

This scheme can easily be extended to a protocol where at most n out of $\binom{n}{m}$ participants are required to recover the secret. By this means, the chosen weight would maximize the binomial coefficient and therefore the number of potential secret share holders. This is the case when m equals to $\lceil \frac{n}{2} \rceil$. To this end, the dealer selects all possible vectors with weight $wt = \lceil \frac{n}{2} \rceil$ and computes the corresponding secret shares. But the reconstruction of the secret is computational infeasible for less than $\lceil \frac{n}{2} \rceil + 1$ parties because fewer than $\lceil \frac{n}{2} \rceil + 1$ of the selected vectors cannot span a $(\lceil \frac{n}{2} \rceil + 1)$-dimensional subspace and with the same argument as above no unit vector can be computed. However, every particpant can determine which other secret share holder could involve for the purpose of computing the secret since λ_i of all participants are publicly available. As n vectors form the basis matrix B, which is not necessarily consisting of linearly independent vectors, it is required to know at least $\lceil \frac{n}{2} \rceil$ vectors in order to recover all basis vectors. One method is to use cyclic rotations of $\frac{n}{2}$ basis vectors.

Example:

1. Dimension: $n = 100, (n = 1024)$
2. Weight: $n - 2 = 98, (1022)$
3. Nr. of particpiants: $\binom{n}{n-2} = \frac{n \cdot (n-1)}{2} = 4950, (523776)$
4. Min. number of particpants to recover the secret: $n - 1 = 99, (1023)$
5. Max. number of particpants to recover the secret: $n = 100, (1024)$
6. $B = [b_1, \ldots, b_{n-1}, rot(b_{n-1})]$

4   Conclusion

In this work we present a new and efficient construction of a secret sharing scheme by making use of a lattice based hash function for the protection of the secret. Every secret share holder is enabled to verify its share due to the linearity of the employed hash function. We showed that breaking this scheme by attacking the hash function is at least as hard as solving approximate SVP. We also showed that in the (n, n)-scheme all parties have to participate in order to recover the secret. In addition, it is computationally infeasible for less than n participants to compute the basis matrix and hence the secret. Furthermore, our scheme can be extended into n out of $\binom{n}{\lceil \frac{n}{2} \rceil}$ secret sharing scheme in order to increase the number of potential secret share holders.

References

1. Ajtai, M.: Generating hard instances of lattice problems (extended abstract). In: Proceedings of the Twenty-Eighth Annual ACM Symposium on the Theory of Computing, pp. 99–108. ACM (1996)
2. Asmuth, C., Bloom, J.: A modular approach to key safeguarding. IEEE Transactions on Information Theory 29(2), 208–210 (1983)
3. Blakley, G.R.: Safeguarding cryptographic keys. In: Proceedings of the National Computer Conference, pp. 313–317. American Federation of Information Processing Societies (1979)
4. Cramer, R., Damgård, I., Maurer, U.: General Secure Multi-party Computation from any Linear Secret-Sharing Scheme. In: Preneel, B. (ed.) EUROCRYPT 2000. LNCS, vol. 1807, pp. 316–334. Springer, Heidelberg (2000)
5. Lyubashevsky, V., Micciancio, D.: Generalized Compact Knapsacks Are Collision Resistant. In: Bugliesi, M., Preneel, B., Sassone, V., Wegener, I. (eds.) ICALP 2006, Part II. LNCS, vol. 4052, pp. 144–155. Springer, Heidelberg (2006)
6. Mahimkar, A.: Securedav: A secure data aggregation and verification protocol for sensor networks. In: Proceedings of the IEEE Global Telecommunications Conference, pp. 2175–2179 (2004)
7. Mignotte, M.: How to Share a Secret? In: Beth, T. (ed.) Cryptography - EUROCRYPT 1982. LNCS, vol. 149, pp. 371–375. Springer, Heidelberg (1983)
8. Pedersen, T.P.: Non-interactive and Information-Theoretic Secure Verifiable Secret Sharing. In: Feigenbaum, J. (ed.) CRYPTO 1991. LNCS, vol. 576, pp. 129–140. Springer, Heidelberg (1992)
9. Peikert, C., Rosen, A.: Efficient Collision-Resistant Hashing from Worst-Case Assumptions on Cyclic Lattices. In: Halevi, S., Rabin, T. (eds.) TCC 2006. LNCS, vol. 3876, pp. 145–166. Springer, Heidelberg (2006)
10. Regev, O.: On lattices, learning with errors, random linear codes, and cryptography. J. ACM 56(6), 34:1–34:40 (2009)
11. Shamir, A.: How to share a secret. Commun. ACM 22, 612–613 (1979)
12. Shor, P.W.: Polynomial-time algorithms for prime factorization and discrete logarithms on a quantum computer. SIAM J. Comput. 26, 1484–1509 (1997)
13. Smith, H.J.S.: On systems of linear indeterminate equations and congruences. Philosophical Transactions of the Royal Society of London 151, 293–326 (1861)
14. Sorin, Iftene: General secret sharing based on the chinese remainder theorem with applications in e-voting. Electronic Notes in Theoretical Computer Science 186, 67–84 (2007)

On the Optimality of Correlation Power Attack on Embedded Cryptographic Systems[*]

Youssef Souissi[1], Nicolas Debande[1,2], Sami Mekki[1],
Sylvain Guilley[1], Ali Maalaoui[3], and Jean-Luc Danger[1]

[1] TELECOM ParisTech, 46 rue Barrault, 75634 Paris, France
[2] Morpho, 95 523 OSNY, France
[3] Rutgers University, NJ, USA
`firstname.lastname@TELECOM-ParisTech.fr`

Abstract. In this paper, we answer the question of what are the necessary conditions under which Correlation Power Attack (CPA), that essentially targets embedded cryptographic implementations, is optimal with regards to attacks that exploit the same leakage model. For this purpose, we offer an in-depth theoretical study which aims at determining the conditions under which the Pearson correlation coefficient is maximized. Moreover, we propose theoretical metrics to practically verify the validity of those conditions. Besides, we illustrate our theoretical study by an experiment on real electromagnetic traces acquired from a DES cryptographic implementation.

Keywords: Correlation Power Attack (CPA), Estimation theory, Security metrics, Spearman attack.

1 Introduction

Recently, E.Prouff *et al.* have shown in [1] that Side-channel distinguishers are not only asymptotically equivalent but also can be rewritten one in function of the other, only by modifying the power consumption model. In particular, they have established an equivalence between most univariate Side-channel distinguishers and Correlation Power Analysis (CPA) performed with different leakage models. Besides, based on the same statistical tool (*i.e.* Pearson coefficient), it is shown that it is possible to break protected implementations (masking countermeasure) by considering the leakage at different time samples. Such attacks, called *Higher-Order Power Correlations*, were suggested and investigated by T.Messerges in [2]. In this paper, we answer the question of what are the conditions under which CPA is optimal with regards to attacks that exploit the same leakage model. The answer we provide is principally based on *Estimation theory*. For more in-depth study about Estimation theory, we refer the reader to [3–5]. The overall goal of this study is to put the Correlation Power Analysis on a sound theoretical basis, and therefore brighten the task of an evaluator when assessing the robustness of secure embedded systems against CPA.

---

[*] This project is partially funded by the JST/ANR SPACES project.

I. Askoxylakis, H.C. Pöhls, and J. Posegga (Eds.): WISTP 2012, LNCS 7322, pp. 169–178, 2012.
© IFIP International Federation for Information Processing 2012

The rest of the paper is organized as follows: first, in Section 2, we discuss the optimality of CPA. Actually, we define the sufficient conditions to maximize Pearson correlation coefficient, thereby reaching the optimality of CPA. Second, in Section 3, we propose theoretical and practical metrics to validate those conditions. Third, in Section 4, we illustrate the theoretical study by an experiment on real electromagnetic traces acquired from a DES cryptographic implementation. Eventually, we conclude the paper in Section 5.

2   The Optimality from the Estimation Theory View Point

The Approximation Problem. Suppose we want to best approximate Y with another variable X based on their joint distribution. The approximation problem is to seek for a function $\phi(\cdot)$ of X that best fits Y among all possible forms of $\phi(\cdot)$. We write $\widehat{Y} = \phi(X)$ and we call $\widehat{Y}$ an estimator of Y. In our study, the variable X is deterministic since it is theoretically predicted from a known cryptographic process. Whereas, the variable Y is a real measure acquired by an oscilloscope. For sake of clarity, in what follows the variable X is called *the prediction* and Y *the measurement* (or the observation). Let $\epsilon = Y - \widehat{Y}$ denotes the error in estimating Y, and let $pos(\epsilon) = pos(Y, \widehat{Y})$ denotes a non negative function of ϵ. $pos(\epsilon)$ can be for instance the absolute difference or the square difference between Y and $\widehat{Y}$ (*i.e.* $|Y - \widehat{Y}|$ or $(Y - \widehat{Y})^2$ respectively). The average cost, *i.e.*, $\mathbb{E}[pos(Y, \widehat{Y})]$, is referred to as the *Bayes risk* $\Re_B$. Obviously, the approximation problem comes down to a minimization problem. In fact, minimizing the *Bayes risk* with respect to $\widehat{Y}$ for a given cost function is a proper solution of the problem. The most popular $\Re_B$ is the *Mean Square Error (MSE)*, since it is parameter free, straightforward to implement and memory-less. The MSE measures the average of the squares of the errors. In this case, it is clear that $pos(Y, \widehat{Y}) = (Y - \widehat{Y})^2$. In what follows, we will focus on the important role played by the MSE in the approximation problem. There are several ways in which the role of the MSE can be introduced. A particular way for especial convenience is to work with the L^2 space that is defined as the space of square summable variables[1]. If Z is a random variable belonging to this space, then the corresponding norm, called L_2 norm, is expressed as $\|Z\|_2 = \sqrt{\mathbb{E}[Z^2]}$; so that the distance between two elements Z_1 and Z_2 of L^2 space can be written as $\|Z_1 - Z_2\|_2 = \sqrt{\mathbb{E}[(Z_1 - Z_2)^2]}$. Z_1 and Z_2 are said to be *orthogonal* ($Z_1 \perp Z_2$) if and only if $\mathbb{E}[(Z_1 Z_2)] = 0$. Orthogonality property and mean square convergence will allow us in the following to introduce the notion of optimal estimation in the sense of L_2 norm. With these notations, the optimal estimator of Y given X, in the sense of the L_2 norm, is the function $\widehat{Y} = \phi(X)$ for which $\|Y - \widehat{Y}\|_2^2$ is a minimum [4]. But more importantly, it is proved that the conditional expectation $\widehat{Y} = \mathbb{E}[Y|X]$ is the estimator that gives such a minimum. Incidentally, using the error notation, ϵ, the MSE is written in the following form:

---

[1] The L^2 space is also often referred to as a weighted Euclidean norm.

$$MSE(\widehat{Y}) = \mathbb{E}[\epsilon^2] = \|Y - \widehat{Y}\|_2^2 .$$

Besides, in [6], it is shown that MSE can be expressed as follows:

$$MSE(\widehat{Y}) = Var(\widehat{Y}) + bias(\widehat{Y})^2 ,$$

where $Var(\widehat{Y})$ is the variance of $\widehat{Y}$ and $bias(\widehat{Y}) = \mathbb{E}(\widehat{Y}) - Y$. Note that for an unbiased estimator (*i.e. bias* = 0), the MSE is just the variance of the estimator. In the literature of estimation theory [7], two naturally desirable properties of estimators are for them to have minimal MSE and to be unbiased. Common criteria for estimation are Maximum Likelihood Estimator (MLE), Minimum Mean Squared Error (MMSE) and Maximum A Posteriori Probability (MAP [4]). From the theoretical point of view, MLE approach is more efficient than the rest of criteria. But more importantly, estimation theory says that no asymptotically unbiased estimator has lower MSE than the MLE (see *Cramer-Rao Lower Bound theory*) [8–10]. However, in practice, statisticians prefer using MMSE estimator, specifically in the linear case, which is in fact the approach that minimizes the MSE in the sense of the L_2 norm, because of its simplicity relatively to the other criteria. Additionally, later on, we will show that, under few assumptions, MMSE estimator produces the lowest MSE among all estimators, in particular unbiased ones, and can be derived as a maximum likelihood estimator.

Optimal Linear MMSE Estimation and Connection with Pearson coefficient. As stated before, the conditional expectation is the optimal estimator in the sense of the L_2 norm, which is indeed the MMSE estimator. Hence, the MSE can be rewritten as $MSE(\widehat{Y}) = \mathbb{E}[\epsilon^2] = \|Y - \mathbb{E}[Y|X]\|_2^2$. A useful property of the MMSE estimator is that the estimation error $Y - \mathbb{E}[Y|X]$ is orthogonal to every function of the variable X. This property is known as the *Orthogonality Principle* that provides a necessary and sufficient condition for the optimal estimation in the L^2 space. More formally, $\phi(X)$ is the MMSE estimator $\widehat{Y}_{MMSE}$ if and only if the error $Y - \phi(X)$ is orthogonal to every function $\gamma(X)$ that is:

$$\mathbb{E}\left[(Y - \phi(X)) \cdot \gamma(X)\right] = 0 . \qquad (1)$$

Now, the problem is that MMSE is very general; and therefore, the conditional expectation can be complicated to compute. Nonetheless, the analysis is very simple when the *linear assumption* is made (*i.e.* Linear MMSE, often termed by LMMSE). For this purpose, statisticians usually make such assumption as a first approximation. However, when the true data does not fit the linear case, we say that LMMSE is sub-optimal to the optimal estimate of MMSE. In the context of side-channel analysis, the linear case has a pure theoretical flavour for us especially when considering unprotected implementations. But it is noteworthy that even for unprotected implementations it is possible to have recourse to what we call *linear transformations* [11]; and therefore to fall into the linear case. In "Introduction to optimal estimation" book ([4] Chapter 3), using the orthogonality principle (Eqn. (1)), authors show that when the true data fits exactly the linear case (*i.e.* LMMSE is optimal) the associated MSE of $\hat{Y}_{LMMSE}$ is expressed with Pearson coefficient ρ, as follows:

$$MSE_{LMMSE} = \sigma_Y{}^2(1 - \rho_{X,Y}^2) \ .$$

In the linear case, $\hat{Y}_{LMMSE}$ is the optimal estimate in the sense of MMSE estimation. But more importantly and always from the MMSE estimation point of view, it is clear that ρ is the optimal metric to measuring the linear association between involved variables. Actually, the **maximization** of ρ^2 implies the **minimization** of MSE_{LMMSE}.

Limitations of Optimal MMSE Estimation. Up to this point, we have shown that in the linear case Pearson correlation coefficient is an optimal indicator of linearity in the sense of MMSE estimation. However, the MMSE does not make any assumption about the joint distribution. One may ask: is the Pearson correlation still the best linear indicator even if the joint distribution is not bivariate normal? Indeed, the fact that the MMSE is distribution free[2] is often seen as a weak point in the estimation literature, specifically when performing a linear estimation (LMMSE). Generally, when no assumption is made about the joint distribution, it exists two important cases in which the optimality of LMMSE, relatively to all estimators, is not guaranteed. In other words, in these cases LMMSE does not give the lowest MSE among the other estimators such as the Maximum Likelihood Estimator (MLE).

Case 1: Heteroscedasticity This basically occurs when the error of estimation ϵ depends on the prediction X. The LMMSE only states that the error of estimation ϵ is uncorrelated with the prediction X. In the linear case, this statement follows since $Cov(X, \epsilon)$ is null. However, $Cov(X, \epsilon) = 0$ does not imply the independence of X and ϵ. In other words, even if the linear estimation is optimal in the sense L_2 norm (*i.e.* $\mathbb{E}[Y|X] = \alpha + \beta X$), it could exist a relation between X and ϵ which compromises the efficiency of the LMMSE in estimating the parameters α and β of the linear model. In this case, the linear model is said to display a *heteroscedasticity*. A frequent situation of heteroscedasticity is that the error is linearly increasing with the values taken by the prediction X. For such situation, it is easy to verify that the MLE estimator is more efficient than the LMMSE as it produces the lowest MSE ([12] page 398).

Case 2: Imperfect data (*aka* outliers problem) The data, which is composed by the prediction X and the measurement Y, is often disturbed by the presence of what we call outliers. An *outlier* can vaguely be defined as an observation which shows a different behaviour with regards to observations composing the data. The reason might be due to the type of variables (continuous, discrete) and the shape of the marginal distributions of X and Y respectively.

---

[2] In statistics, a statistical criterion that does not make any assumption about the joint distribution is said to be "distribution free".

Overall Optimality of MMSE. According to **case 1** and **case 2**, the MMSE is not sufficient to **totally** characterise the dependence between X and Y, even if the true relationship between them is **linear**. More importantly, the Pearson correlation coefficient could not be considered as the best linear metric to measuring the true relationship. In statistic, several candidates exist, such as Spearman, Kendall or intra-class coefficient correlations, that are designed to be less sensitive (more robust) to outliers or heteroscedasticity and therefore they would be better than Pearson coefficient. However, the estimation theory proved that there exists one and only one condition if satisfied then the MMSE is equivalent to the MLE; and therefore considered to be the optimal estimator among all estimators, in particular unbiased ones, as it gives the lowest MSE. Thus, the Pearson coefficient ρ is the best metric for measuring a linear association. This condition requires that the joint distribution should be bivariate normal [4, 13]. In fact, under the Gaussian assumption, the true relationship is **linear**, not heteroscedastic (*i.e.* homoscedastic) and not disturbed by some undesirable effects like the outliers. Note that in this case the error of estimation follows a normal distribution. Hence, we can state that ρ is the best linear metric only when the true relationship in the MMSE sense satisfies the Gaussian assumption. If such assumption is not validated, the MMSE is less efficient than MLE; and therefore the optimality of CPA is compromised.

Sufficient Conditions for the Optimality. A common pitfall about the validity of the Gaussian assumption is to check only that X and Y are drawn from normal distributions. This is not sufficient. Indeed, if X and Y are each individually Gaussian then this does not imply that they are jointly Gaussian. Generally, a joint distribution is said to be bivariate normal if all following conditions are satisfied ([14] page 54):

1. **Linearity** The true relationship between X and Y is linear.
2. **Normal conditional distribution** The conditional distribution of Y given $X = x$ is normal.
3. **Homoscedasticity** The conditional distribution of Y given $X = x$ has a constant variance (*i.e.* the variance of the error) for each x.
4. **Normal marginal distribution** The marginal distribution of X is normal (Gaussian).

We note that, the last condition is independent from the measurements; it is only dependent on the predictions that are provided by the leakage model. Moreover, under these conditions, the error ϵ must be drawn from zero mean normal distribution. In other words, ϵ is a random variable strictly independent from X and that a linear function ϕ characterizes the dependence between X and Y, entirely. In practice, these conditions are not supposed to be strictly verified but to hold to a certain degree. Actually, in real situations, it is mostly hard to get a perfect binormal joint distribution. In such situations, the higher the departure from the Gaussian assumption is, the lower the efficiency of Pearson correlation coefficient ρ will be.

3   Practical Metrics Computation

3.1   Deviation from Linearity Metric (*DLM*)

In statistics, the *Correlation ratio* coefficient [12] between X and Y is defined as follows:

$$\eta_{Y|X}{}^2 = \frac{Var\big[\mathbb{E}[Y|X]\big]}{Var(Y)} = 1 - \frac{\mathbb{E}\big[Var[Y|X]\big]}{Var(Y)}.$$

Unlike the Pearson correlation coefficient ρ which only detects the linear dependency between two variables, the *Correlation ratio* measures the functional dependency. In other words, η quantifies the dependency strength whatever the relation between the two variables, linear or non linear. Similarly to $\rho_{X,Y}^2$, the Correlation ratio takes on values between 0 and 1. The higher the value of η is, the higher the functional dependency is. Furthermore, η is asymmetric (*i.e.* $\eta_{Y|X} \neq \eta_{X|Y}$) since the two variables fundamentally do not play the same role in the functional relationship. In the general context of this paper, the most important additional properties of η are those which characterize the relation between η and ρ. These properties are summarized as follows:

$$\eta_{Y|X}{}^2 \geq \rho_{X,Y}{}^2 .$$

$$\eta_{Y|X}{}^2 = \rho_{X,Y}^2 \quad \Longleftrightarrow \quad \exists(\alpha, \beta), \; \mathbb{E}[Y|X] = \alpha + \beta X . \tag{2}$$

From (2), we can design a new metric which aims at measuring the deviation from a perfect linear relationship. This metric that we name *Deviation from Linearity Metric (DLM)* is expressed by the ratio between the squared Pearson coefficient and the Correlation ratio as follows:

$$DLM = \frac{\rho^2}{\eta^2} \in [0,1] .$$

The *DLM* ratio takes on values between 0 when the relation is totally curved and 1 when it is perfectly linear.

3.2   Deviation from Normality Metric (*DNM*)

In the literature, there exist many variants of statistical tools (*e.g.* Shapiro-Wilk test, Lilliefors test, D'Agostino test and Jarque-Bera test [12]) that aim at measuring the deviation from a normal distribution. For sake of simplicity and convenience, we used the *Jarque-Bera* (JB) test as a "Deviation from Normality Metric" (DNM_{JB}) as it is mainly based on the computation of the skewness (S) and the kurtosis (K) ([12]). Hence, the Jarque-Bera metric can be defined as follows:

$$DNM_{JB} = \frac{n}{6}\left(S^2 + \frac{1}{4}(K-3)^2\right) ,$$

where n is the number of observations. The smaller the value of DNM_{JB}, the better the approximation by a normal distribution. Indeed, in the case of a perfect normal distribution, we have $DNM_{JB} = 0$.

3.3 Deviation from Homoscedasticity Metric (DHM)

As stated before, homoscedasticity simply requires that the conditional variances $Var(Y|X = x)$ are equals. For this purpose, we propose to compute the *Coefficient of variation* [12] based dispersion of such conditional variances to measure the deviation of data from homoscedasticity. The coefficient of variation, which is a normalized metric for dispersion, is defined as the ratio of the standard deviation to the mean. Hence, the metric proposed (DHM) can be expressed as follows:

$$DHM = \frac{\sqrt{Var(Var(Y|X = x))}}{\mathbb{E}(Var(Y|X = x))}.$$

The smaller the dispersion DHM, the better the homoscedasticity. Actually, in the case of a perfect homoscedasticity, we have $DHM = 0$.

4 Experiments on Real DES Cryptographic Implementation

In this study, we are interested in the basic attack of the Data Encryption Standard (DES), that targets the two first rounds of the encryption algorithm. For this purpose, we acquired real electromagnetic leakage traces from an unprotected DES implementation based ASIC (Secmat V1) [15] circuit (easy to attack by CPA). Recall that the DES implementation is composed of eight different Sboxes. There are thus eight secret keys to retrieve[3]. Therefore, in this case, a Hamming distance HD model can take five possible values, $HD = \{0, 1, 2, 3, 4\}$, and 2^6 key hypotheses are required to break one Sbox. Now, let us analyse the marginal distributions of the prediction X. The variable X that is represented by the values taken by HD, is a discrete type variable following a symmetric distribution [16] $\beta_{(n_b=4, p=\frac{1}{2})}$ where n_b represents the predicted bits in the targeted register R, and p is the success probability. In statistics, if n_b is large, say $n_b > 20$, and $p = \frac{1}{2}$, then the binomial distribution is approximately equal to the normal distribution [12, 17, 18]. In our case $n_b \ll 20$, therefore X can not be strictly approximated to a normal distribution. We note that for a binomial distribution, the Skewness (S) and the Kurtosis (K) are expressed by the parameters n_b, p and q [12]. In our experiment, we assume that enough traces are acquired. Thus, $p = q = 0.5$. Hence, the DNM_{JB} metric defined previously, to measure the deviation from a normal distribution, is computed as follows:

$$DNM_{JB} = \frac{n_b}{6}\left(S^2 + \frac{1}{4}(K-3)^2\right) = \frac{4}{6}\left(0^2 + \frac{1}{4}(2.5 - 3)^2\right) = 0.041.$$

Up to this point, we have only studied the marginal distribution of the prediction X and calculated theoretically its deviation from a perfect normal distribution. Therefore, three other conditions are still to be verified to assume the Gaussian

---

[3] For misuse of language, we often use the notion of "broken Sbox" to say that the secret key corresponding to the attacked Sbox is found.

case. Fig. 1 represents a CPA differential trace superposed with DNM_{JB} (for example HD = 4), DLM and DHM metrics. The idea behind calculating such metrics over the whole time samples of the real DES traces is to reveal more details, especially when the knowledge about the implementation is not total to know exactly where the secret information is happened. In this figure, we distinguish four zones ($Z1$, $Z2$, $Z3$ and $Z4$), depending on the distribution of the real leakage over the time samples. In fact, the secret information corresponds to the zones $Z2$, $Z3$ and $Z4$ in which CPA differential trace shows high values (*i.e.* peaks). But more importantly, we show that the proposed metrics are in agreement with our theoretical study, as $DLM \simeq 1$, $DHM \simeq 0$ and $DNM \simeq 0$. Therefore, CPA performance is close to the optimality (Gaussian assumption). However, $Z1$ is not suitable for CPA as the linearity metric (DLM) is virtually equal to zero. Besides, $Z4$ can not be the best zone for CPA (CPA peak is not high), because the deviations from normality DNM and homoscedasticity DHM are relatively high. In what follows, we will be interested only in the zone $Z3$ as it shows better performance of CPA than it does for $Z2$ and $Z4$. Actually, we conducted two operations: the first operation consists in performing and comparing the efficiency of two correlation attacks based on Pearson (CPA) and Spearman coefficients, respectively. We note that Spearman correlation has been developed to be more robust[4] than the Pearson correlation. Spearman correlation measures both the linear and the non-linear relationship between the two variables, as it does not require that the observations are drawn from a bivariate normal distribution. It is a *non-parametric* correlation that was first

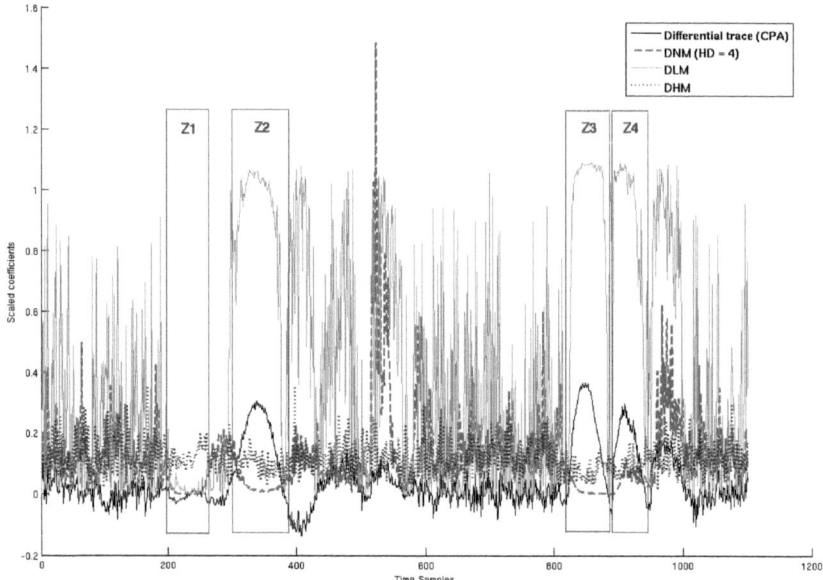

Fig. 1. Illustration of Gaussian assumption metrics on unprotected DES

---

[4] A statistical criterion that does not make any assumption about the joint distribution is said to be robust or distribution free.

applied in side-channel context in [19]. In this operation, we will show that the conditions required to maximize the Pearson coefficient (Gaussian assumption) hold to a sufficient degree, which makes the CPA more powerful than Spearman attack. The second operation consists in degrading the quality of acquired traces, by creating outliers, in order to simulate a situation in which the deviation from the Gaussian assumption is relatively high. Therefore, we show that in such case, despite the fact that the true relationship is linear, CPA becomes less powerful than Spearman attack. Recently, an evaluation metric has been proposed in [20] to assess the performance of Side-channel analysis: the *Guessing Entropy*, termed by GE. In fact, GE metric measures the average position of the secret key in a list of key hypotheses ranked by a statistical test referred to as distinguisher (*e.g.* Pearson coefficient, Spearman coefficient). According to Fig. 2, as expected, CPA outperforms Spearman attack when applied on original traces. Actually, to reach the five first ranks, we need 12 traces for CPA. Whereas, 18 traces are needed for Spearman attack. However, when the quality of original set of traces is degraded by creating outliers, Spearman attack becomes more powerful than CPA; which is in agreement with our study.

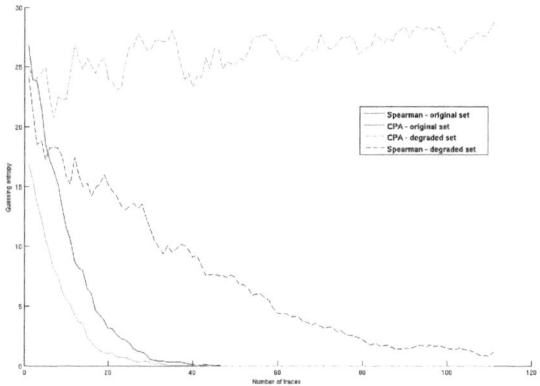

Fig. 2. GE for CPA and Spearman attacks on original and degraded traces

5   Conclusion

In this paper, we have studied the efficiency of Correlation Power Attack (CPA) from the estimation theory point of view. This study is useful in that it allows to assess the performance of CPA; and therefore to decide on the choice of an appropriate Side-channel distinguisher for the analysis. Actually, if the Gaussian assumption is satisfied, then CPA must be the best analysis to quantify the secret leakage. Besides, if these conditions do not hold to a certain degree, then CPA might not be efficient and therefore is not the best analysis anymore. In this case, more powerful attacks and distinguishers like Spearman coefficient should be investigated.

References

1. Doget, J., Prouff, E., Rivain, M., Standaert, F.X.: Univariate side channel attacks and leakage modeling. Journal of Cryptographic Engineering 1, 123–144 (2011)
2. Messerges, T.S.: Using Second-Order Power Analysis to Attack DPA Resistant Software. In: Paar, C., Koç, Ç.K. (eds.) CHES 2000. LNCS, vol. 1965, pp. 238–251. Springer, Heidelberg (2000)
3. Mendel, J.: Lessons in Estimation Theory for Signal Processing, Communications, and Control. Pearson Education (1995)
4. Kamen, E., Su, J.: Introduction to optimal estimation. Advanced textbooks in control and signal processing. Springer (1999)
5. Candy, J.: Bayesian Signal Processing: Classical, Modern and Particle Filtering Methods. Adaptive and Learning Systems for Signal Processing, Communications and Control Series. John Wiley & Sons (2011)
6. Anderson, S.: Statistical methods for comparative studies: techniques for bias reduction. Wiley series in probability and mathematical statistics: Applied probability and statistics. Wiley (1980)
7. Edward, W., Kamen, J.S.: Introduction to optimal estimation Advanced textbooks in control and signal processing Control and Signal Processing Series. Springer (1999)
8. Bar-Shalom, Y., Li, X., Kirubarajan, T.: Estimation with applications to tracking and navigation. A Wiley-Interscience Publication. Wiley (2001)
9. Bos, A.: Parameter estimation for scientists and engineers. Wiley-Interscience (2007)
10. Sorensen, D., Gianola, D.: Likelihood, Bayesian and MCMC methods in quantitative genetics. Statistics for biology and health. Springer (2002)
11. Sharma, A., Prakash, M.: Linear Transformation. Discovery Publishing House (2007)
12. Saporta, G.: Data mining et statistique décisionnelle. L'intelligence des données. Technip (2010)
13. Proakis, J., Salehi, M.: Digital communications. McGraw-Hill higher education. McGraw-Hill (2008)
14. Arnold, B., Castillo, E., Sarabia, J.: Conditional specification of statistical models. Springer series in statistics. Springer (1999)
15. Guilley, S.: Documentation technique de la conception physique (ou back-end) du circuit SECMAT (2006),
    http://perso.telecom-paristech.fr/~guilley/backend.pdf
16. Guilley, S.: Geometrical Counter-Measures against Side-Channel Attacks. PhD thesis, ENST / CNRS LTCI, 219 pages, Id: 2007 E 003 (2007),
    http://pastel.paristech.org/2562/
17. Russo, R.: Statistics for the behavioural sciences: an introduction. Psychology Press (2003)
18. Rosner, B.: Fundamentals of biostatistics. Brooks/Cole Cengage Learning (2010)
19. Batina, L., Gierlichs, B., Lemke-Rust, K.: Comparative Evaluation of Rank Correlation Based DPA on an AES Prototype Chip. In: Wu, T.-C., Lei, C.-L., Rijmen, V., Lee, D.-T. (eds.) ISC 2008. LNCS, vol. 5222, pp. 341–354. Springer, Heidelberg (2008)
20. Standaert, F.-X., Malkin, T.G., Yung, M.: A Unified Framework for the Analysis of Side-Channel Key Recovery Attacks. In: Joux, A. (ed.) EUROCRYPT 2009. LNCS, vol. 5479, pp. 443–461. Springer, Heidelberg (2009)

Impossible Differential Cryptanalysis
of Reduced-Round LBlock

Ferhat Karakoç[1,2], Hüseyin Demirci[1], and A. Emre Harmancı[2]

[1] Tübitak BILGEM UEKAE, 41470, Gebze, Kocaeli, Turkey
{ferhatk,huseyind}@uekae.tubitak.gov.tr
[2] Istanbul Technical University, Computer Engineering Department, 34469, Maslak,
Istanbul, Turkey
harmanci@itu.edu.tr

Abstract. In this paper, we improve the impossible differential attack
on 20-round LBlock given in the design paper of the LBlock cipher. Using
relations between the round keys we attack on 21-round and 22-round
LBlock with a complexity of $2^{69.5}$ and $2^{79.28}$ encryptions respectively. We
use the same 14-round impossible differential characteristic observed by
the designers to attack on 21 rounds and another 14-round impossible
differential characteristic to attack on 22 rounds of LBlock.

Keywords: LBlock, differential cryptanalysis, impossible differential
cryptanalysis, miss-in-the-middle attack.

1 Introduction

In recent years, lightweight cryptography has been getting prominent because of
the growing computation research area which uses resource constraint devices
such as RFID tags and sensor nodes. For this reason, many lightweight cryptographic algorithms have been designed such as PRESENT [3], PRINTCIPHER
[5], and LED [4].

LBlock is a lightweight block cipher introduced at ACNS 2011 [7]. The number
of rounds is 32 and the block and key lengths are 64 and 80 bits respectively. The
designers of the algorithm give a 14-round impossible differential characteristic
and attack on 20-round LBlock. To the best of our knowledge, there is only
one cryptanalytic study on the algorithm [6]. The analysis includes differential
attacks on 12 and 13 rounds and a related key impossible differential attack on
22-round LBlock.

In the impossible differential attack [1], the attacker tries to find a differential
characteristic with a probability of 0 while in the differential cryptanalysis [2] a
differential characteristic with a high probability is used.

In this paper, we improve the impossible differential attack given by the designers, using relations between rounds keys. We attack on 21-round and 22-
round LBlock in a single key model with a complexity of $2^{69.5}$ and $2^{79.28}$ encryptions. In the attack on the 21-round cipher we use only the relations in the first
4 rounds while in the 22-round attack we use all relations between the round
keys.

I. Askoxylakis, H.C. Pöhls, and J. Posegga (Eds.): WISTP 2012, LNCS 7322, pp. 179–188, 2012.
© IFIP International Federation for Information Processing 2012

This paper is organized as follows. Section 2 includes the notation we use, a short description of LBlock and an overview of the 20-round attack done by the designers. We explain the impossible differential attack technique in Section 3. In Section 4, we attack on 21-round LBlock. An attack on 22-round LBlock is presented in Section 5. Finally, we conclude the paper in Section 6.

2   A Short Description of LBlock

Notation. Throughout this paper the following notations are used.

A : a bit string
$A(i)$: i-th nibble of A. The right most nibble is $A(0)$.
$A(i, j, ..., k)$: concatenation of $i, j, ... , k$-th nibbles of A.
$A(i - j)$: concatenation of $i, (i - 1), ..., j$-th nibbles of A where $i \geq j$.
$A[i]$: i-th bit of A. The right most bit of A is $A[0]$.
$A[i, j, ..., k]$: concatenation of $i, j, ..., k$-th bits of A.
$A[i - j]$: concatenation of $i, (i - 1), ..., j$-th bits of A where $i \geq j$.
$A <<< i$: i-bit cyclic shift of A.
$A||B$: concatenation of A and B.
K_i : round key used in the i-th round.
K^i : 80-bit value calculated in the key schedule.
X_i : the leftmost 32-bit of the input of i-th round where
                  X_0 is the rightmost 32-bit of the input of the first round.

LBlock. LBlock is a block cipher with 64-bit block and 80-bit key length. It consists of 32 rounds and one round is shown on the left in Figure 1. In the F function depicted on the right in Figure 1, firstly round key K_i is exored to the input of the function. After that, 4-bit S-Boxes and finally the permutation are applied.

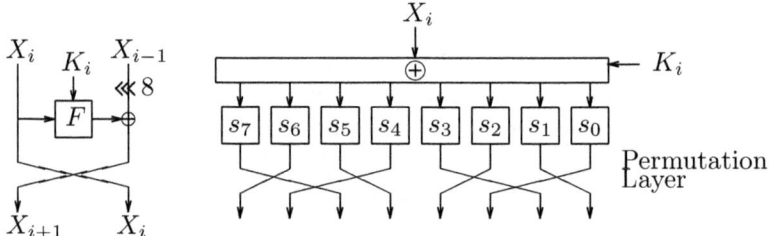

Fig. 1. *i*-th round of LBlock

The Encryption Process is as follows.

1. $(X_1||X_0) = P$
2. for $i = 1, 2, ..., 32$ do the following calculation
    $X_{i+1} = F(X_i, K_i) \oplus (X_{i-1} <<< 8)$
3. $C = (X_{32}||X_{33})$

The Key Schedule Process is as follows.

1. $K^0 = K$
2. $K_1 = K^0[79 - 48]$
3. for $i = 1, 2, ..., 31$ do the following calculations
   - $K^i = K^{i-1} <<< 29$
   - $K^i[79 - 76] = s_9[K^i[79 - 76]]$
   - $K^i[75 - 72] = s_8[K^i[75 - 72]]$
   - $K^i[50 - 46] = K^i[50 - 46] \oplus [i]_2$ where $[i]_2$ is the binary representation of the round index
   - $K_{i+1} = K^i[79 - 48]$

The S-boxes used in the encryption process and key schedule are given in Appendix B. For a complete description of the algorithm one can refer to [7].

Previous Work. In the design paper of LBlock, the designers attack on 20-round LBlock using the 14-round impossible differential characteristic $(00000000, 00 * 00000) \overset{14}{\nrightarrow} (0 * 000000, 00000000)$. They add 2 rounds at the top and 4 rounds at the bottom of the characteristic and assume that the round keys guessed in their attack are independent. This assumption doesn't change the correctness of the result but affects the complexity of the attack. The number of guessed key bits is 68 and there is a 36-bit sieving. They use 2^{63} chosen plaintexts and the complexity of the attack is $2^{72.7}$ encryptions. Using the relations between the round keys we improve the attack on 21 and 22 rounds.

3   The Impossible Differential Attack Technique

In this method, first an impossible differential characteristic is found. After finding a characteristic, several rounds are added at the top and at the bottom of the characteristic. Let E_1, E_0, and E_2 denote the encryption part which has the impossible differential characteristic, the added part before, and the added part after the characteristic respectively and the cipher $E = E_2 \circ E_1 \circ E_0$. Also, let the impossible differential be $\Delta\alpha \nrightarrow \Delta\beta$. The attack can be done in two ways. The first way is fallows. One plaintext pair P, P' is taken and guessing the keys in E_0 and E_2 the input and output differences of E_1 is calculated. In the case the input and output differences is the impossible differential characteristic, the guessed key is removed from the candidate key space. These steps are repeated using different plaintext pairs P, P' until a unique key is remained in the candidate key space. The complexity of the attack can be reduced if there is independence between guessed keys in E_0 and E_2 with the help of tables. One plaintext pair P, P' is taken and the keys which lead to the difference $\Delta\alpha$ at the end of E_0 are stored in a table whose name is A guessing the key bits used in E_0. Similarly, the keys which lead to the difference $\Delta\beta$ at the top of E_2 are stored in another table whose name is B guessing the key bits used in E_2 and partially decrypting corresponding ciphertexts. Then, the keys in $A \times B$ are removed from the candidate key space.

The complexity of the attack can be calculated as follows. Let k and l denote the bit lengths guessed for E_0 and E_2 respectively and we have n-bit elimination in total. The number of pairs m required to eliminate all wrong candidates can be calculated as

$$(1 - 2^{-n})^m \times 2^{k+l} \leq 1 \Rightarrow m \geq (k + l) \times \ln 2 \times 2^n.$$

The time complexity of the attack will be $max(2^k \times m, 2^l \times m)$.

4 An Attack on 21-Round LBlock

In this attack we use the impossible differential characteristic given by the designers of the algorithm. This characteristic is $(00000000, 00 * 00000) \xrightarrow{14} (0 * 000000, 00000000)$ which means that if there is a difference only in the 5-th nibble it is not possible having a difference only in the 14-th nibble after 14 rounds. We add 4 rounds at the top and 3 rounds at the bottom of this characteristic. Let 21-round LBlock starts with the 1-st round and ends with the 21-th round of LBlock. Attack on this 21-round LBlock can be executed using Algorithm 1.

Note that, in Algorithm 1 in Step 2, 3, 4, and 5 instead of guessing round keys we guess the bits of K^0 to use the relations between the round keys (see Table 1).

Table 1. Guessed master key bits in Step 2, 3, 4, and 5 in Algorithm 1

Step	the bits of K^0 which affect the round keys	# of guessed bits
2	$K^0[79 - 72, 51 - 48]$	12-bit
3	$K^0[63 - 56, 34 - 31, 26 - 23]$	16-bit
4	$K^0[79 - 78, 55 - 52, 22 - 19, 1 - 0]$	10-bit
5	$K^0[67 - 61, 46 - 43, 21 - 18]$	9-bit

In the attack, using 2^{50} chosen plaintext pairs we try to find 75 bits guessed and there exists 44-bit sieving. For a random key the probability of being remained in the candidate key set using only one P, P' pair is $(1 - 2^{-44})$. This probability will be $(1 - 2^{-44})^{2^{50}} \approx 2^{-92}$ when 2^{50} plaintext pairs are used which have the difference $(* * 00000*, *0 * 0 * 0 * *)$ in the plaintexts and the difference $(000 * 0 * *0, 00 * 0000*)$ in the ciphertexts. We guess 75 bits in the attack so $2^{-92} \times 2^{75} = 2^{-17}$ keys will remain in the candidate key set that means we can find the correct key with a high probability.

To have 2^{50} plaintext-ciphertext pairs which have the differences in the input and output we need $2^{50} \times 2^{44} = 2^{94}$ pairs having the input difference

$(* * 00000*, *0 * 0 * 0 * *)$. Using 2^{32} pairs having the same structure we can have $2^{32} \times 2^{31} = 2^{63}$ pairs. So we need to use $2^{94}/2^{63} = 2^{31}$ structures. Thus $2^{31} \times 2^{32} = 2^{63}$ plaintexts are required to apply the attack in Algorithm 1.

Algorithm 1. Attack on 21-Round LBlock.

1: **for all** 2^{50} plaintext pairs which have the difference $\Delta(X_1, X0) = (* * 00000*, *0 * 0*0**)$ in the plaintexts and the difference $\Delta(X_{22}, X21) = (000*0**0, 00*0000*)$ in the ciphertexts for the reduced 21-round cipher **do**

2:     **for all** $K_1(7, 6, 0)$, if $\Delta(X_2, X_1) = (0000 * 0 * 0, * * 00000*)$ then **do**

3:         **for all** $K_1(3, 2)$ and $K_2(3, 1)$, if $\Delta(X_3, X_2) = (00000 * 00, 0000 * 0 * 0)$ then **do**

4:             **for all** $K_1(1)$, $K_2(0)$ and $K_3(2)$, if $\Delta(X_4, X_3) = (00 * 00000, 00000 * 00)$ then **do**

5:                 **for all** $K_1(4)$, $K_2(6)$, $K_3(7)$ and $K_4(5)$, if $\Delta(X_5, X_4) = (00000000, 00 * 00000)$ then **do**

6:                     Insert the guessed key into the table A.

7:                 **end for**

8:             **end for**

9:         **end for**

10:     **end for**

11:     **for all** $K_{21}(5, 0)$, if $\Delta(X_{21}, X_{20}) = (00 * 0000*, *0000000)$ then **do**

12:         **for all** $K_{21}(3)$ and $K_{20}(7)$, if $\Delta(X_{20}, X_{19}) = (*0000000, 0 * 000000)$ then **do**

13:             **for all** $K_{21}(2)$, $K_{20}(1)$ and $K_{19}(6)$, if $\Delta(X_{19}, X_{18}) = (0 * 000000, 00000000)$ then **do**

14:                 Insert the guessed key into the table B.

15:             **end for**

16:         **end for**

17:     **end for**

18:     Remove the keys in the $A \times B$ from the candidate key set.

19: **end for**

The time complexity of the attack can be calculated as follows. In Step 2 in the algorithm, we make $2^{51} \times 2^{12} = 2^{63}$ partial encryptions using 2^{51} data and guessing 12-bit key values. In Step 3, the number of operations is $2^{63} \times 2^{-12} \times 2^{16} = 2^{67}$ partial encryptions because of the sieving in Step 2 and 16-bit key guessing in Step 3. In Step 4, the number of partial encryptions is $2^{67} \times 2^{-8} \times 2^{10} = 2^{69}$ due to the 8-bit sieving and 10-bit key guessing. In Step 5, we perform $2^{69} \times 2^{-4} \times 2^9 \times 7 = 2^{74} \times 7$ s-box operations. The dominant number of operations is in Step 5. As a result, the complexity will be $\frac{2^{74} \times 7}{21 \times 8} \approx 2^{69.5}$ 21-round encryptions.

5   An Attack on 22-Round LBlock

In this attack, we use the impossible differential characteristic $(00000000, 000 * 0000) \overset{14}{\nrightarrow} (000000 * 0, 00000000)$. We add 4 rounds at the top and 4 rounds at the bottom of this characteristic. In this section, we use the relations between all round keys guessed in the attack. Also, we recover K^{19} instead of the master key $K = K^0$. It is trivial to recover the master key using K^{19}. Algorithm 2 describes the attack on 22-round LBlock. In the attack, we recover 76 bits of K^{19} and there is 56-bit sieving.

Algorithm 2. Attack on 22-Round LBlock.

1: **for all** 2^{57} plaintext pairs which have the difference $\Delta(X_1, X_0) = (000*0**0, 0*0*0***)$ in the plaintexts and the difference $\Delta(X_{23}, X_{22}) = (00***0**, 0000***0)$ in the ciphertexts **do**

2:    Run Algorithm 3.

3:    Run Algorithm 4.

4:    Remove the $K^{19}[79 - 39, 37 - 10, 6 - 0]$'s which lead to the round keys returned by Algorithm 3 and 4 from the candidate keys. Table 4 in Appendix A depicts the bits of K^{19} which determine the round keys.

5: **end for**

The complexity of Algorithm 3 can be calculated as follows. In Step 2, we guess 4 bits and perform two s-box operations for one pair in each guess and on the average one guess passes the condition. Thus we perform 2×2^4 s-box operations in Step 2. Similarly the total number of operations in Step 2-15 will be $2 \times (2^4 + 2^4 + 2^4 + 2^4 + 2^8 + 2^8 + 2^{12} + 2^{12} + 2^{16} + 2^{20} + 2^{20} + 2^{21} + 2^{25} + 2^{26}) \approx 2^{27.65}$ s-box look-up's which is approximately equivalent to $2^{20.19}$ 22-round LBlock encryptions. Note that the number of guessed key bits in Step 13 and 15 is 1 because of the relations between the round keys (see Table 2).

Table 2. The number of bits of K^0 guessed in Step 2-15 in Algorithm 3

Step	round keys	the bits of K^0	# of bits	Step	round keys	the bits of K^0	# of bits
2	$K_1(4)$	$K^0[67 - 64]$	4	3	$K_1(2)$	$K^0[59 - 56]$	4
4	$K_1(1)$	$K^0[55 - 52]$	4	5	$K_1(5)$	$K^0[71 - 68]$	4
6	$K_2(4)$	$K^0[38 - 35]$	4	7	$K_1(0)$	$K^0[51 - 48]$	4
8	$K_2(2)$	$K^0[30 - 27]$	4	9	$K_1(7)$	$K^0[79 - 76]$	4
10	$K_2(5)$	$K^0[42 - 39]$	4	11	$K_3(4)$	$K^0[9 - 6]$	4
12	$K_1(6)$	$K^0[75 - 72]$	4	13	$K_2(7)$	$K^0[50 - 47]$	1
14	$K_3(5)$	$K^0[13 - 10]$	4	15	$K_4(4)$	$K^0[60 - 57]$	1

The complexity of Algorithm 4 is approximately equivalent to $2^{19.59}$ 22-round encryptions (see Table 3 for the relations between round keys guessed in Algorithm 4). Thus the complexity of Algorithm 2 is $2^{57} \times (2^{20.19} + 2^{19.59}) \approx 2^{77.92}$ encryptions. When we use 2^{57} different pairs the number of 76-bit keys in the candidate space will be $(1 - 2^{-56})^{2^{57}} \times 2^{76} \approx 2^{74.56}$ because of the 56-bit sieving. Thus the total complexity to recover 80-bit K^{19} is $2^{77.92} + 2^{74.56+4} \approx 2^{79.28}$ encryptions.

Algorithm 3. Finding the keys which lead to the difference $\Delta\alpha$.

1: A plaintext pair which has the difference $\Delta(X_1, X_0) = (000 * 0 * *0, 0 * 0 * 0 * **)$
   is given.
2: **for all** $K_1(4)$, if $\Delta S_4[X_1(4) \oplus K_1(4)] = \Delta X_0(4)$ then **do**
3:   **for all** $K_1(2)$, if $\Delta S_2[X_1(2) \oplus K_1(2)] = \Delta X_0(1)$ then **do**
4:    **for all** $K_1(1)$, if $\Delta S_1[X_1(1) \oplus K_1(1)] = \Delta X_0(6)$ then **do**
5:     **for all** $K_1(5)$ calculate $X_2(4)$ and **do**
6:     **for all** $K_2(4)$, if $\Delta S_4[X_2(4) \oplus K_2(4)] = \Delta X_1(4)$ then **do**
7:      **for all** $K_1(0)$ calculate $X_2(2)$ and **do**
8:      **for all** $K_2(2)$, if $\Delta S_2[X_2(2) \oplus K_2(2)] = \Delta X_1(1)$ then **do**
9:       **for all** $K_1(7)$ calculate $X_2(5)$ and **do**
10:       **for all** $K_2(5)$ calculate $X_3(4)$ and **do**
11:        **for all** $K_3(4)$, if $\Delta S_4[X_3(4) \oplus K_3(4)] = \Delta X_2(4)$ then **do**
12:        **for all** $K_1(6)$ calculate $X_2(7)$ and **do**
13:         **for all** $K_2(7)$ calculate $X_3(5)$ and **do**
14:         **for all** $K_3(5)$ calculate $X_4(4)$ and **do**
15:          **for all** $K_4(4)$ check if $\Delta S_4[X_4(4) \oplus K_4(4)] = \Delta X_3(4)$ then **do**
16:          Store the round keys in Table A.
17:         **end for**
18:        **end for**
19:       **end for**
20:       **end for**
21:      **end for**
22:      **end for**
23:     **end for**
24:     **end for**
25:    **end for**
26:    **end for**
27:   **end for**
28:   **end for**
29: **end for**
30: **end for**
31: Return Table A.

To have 2^{57} pairs having the input difference $(000 * 0 * *0, 0 * 0 * 0 * **)$ and the output difference $(00 * * * 0 * *, 0000 * * * 0)$ $2^{57} \times 2^{32} = 2^{89}$ pairs having the input difference $(000 * 0 * *0, 0 * 0 * 0 * **)$ are required. Using 2^{32} pairs having the same structure we can have $2^{32} \times 2^{31} = 2^{63}$ pairs. Thus $2^{89}/2^{63} = 2^{26}$ structures are needed. As a result, $2^{26} \times 2^{32} = 2^{58}$ plaintexts are required to apply the attack.

Algorithm 4. Finding the keys which lead to the difference $\Delta\beta$.

1: A ciphertext pair which has the difference $\Delta(X_{23}, X_{22}) = (00***0**, 0000***0)$
  is given.
2: **for all** $K_{22}(3)$, if $\Delta S_3[X_{22}(3) \oplus K_{22}(3)] = \Delta X_{23}(1)$ then **do**
3:   **for all** $K_{22}(2)$, if $\Delta S_2[X_{22}(2) \oplus K_{22}(2)] = \Delta X_{23}(2)$ then **do**
4:    **for all** $K_{22}(1)$, if $\Delta S_1[X_{22}(1) \oplus K_{22}(1)] = \Delta X_{23}(0)$ then **do**
5:     **for all** $K_{22}(7)$ calculate $X_{21}(3)$ and **do**
6:      **for all** $K_{21}(3)$, if $\Delta S_3[X_{21}(3) \oplus K_{21}(3)] = \Delta X_{22}(1)$ then **do**
7:       **for all** $K_{22}(5)$ calculate $X_{21}(2)$ and **do**
8:        **for all** $K_{21}(2)$, if $\Delta S_2[X_{21}(2) \oplus K_{21}(2)] = \Delta X_{22}(3)$ then **do**
9:         **for all** $K_{22}(0)$ calculate $X_{21}(0)$ and **do**
10:         **for all** $K_{21}(0)$ calculate $X_{20}(0)$ and **do**
11:          **for all** $K_{20}(0)$, if $\Delta S_0[X_{20}(0) \oplus K_{20}(0)] = \Delta X_{21}(2)$ then **do**
12:           **for all** $K_{22}(6)$ calculate $X_{21}(5)$ and **do**
13:            **for all** $K_{21}(5)$ calculate $X_{20}(2)$ and **do**
14:             **for all** $K_{20}(2)$ calculate $X_{19}(1)$ **do**
15:              **for all** $K_{19}(1)$, if $\Delta S_1[X_{19}(1) \oplus K_{19}(1)] = \Delta X_{20}(0)$ then **do**
16:               Store the round keys in Table B.
17:              **end for**
18:             **end for**
19:            **end for**
20:           **end for**
21:          **end for**
22:         **end for**
23:        **end for**
24:       **end for**
25:      **end for**
26:     **end for**
27:    **end for**
28:   **end for**
29: **end for**
30: **end for**
31: Return Table B.

Table 3. The number of bits of K^{19} guessed in Step 2-15 in Algorithm 4

Step	round keys	K^{19}	# of bits	Step	round keys	K^{19}	# of bits
2	$K_{22}(3)$	$K^{19}[5-2]$	4	3	$K_{22}(2)$	$K^{19}[79, 78, 1, 0]$	4
4	$K_{22}(1)$	$K^{19}[77-74]$	4	5	$K_{22}(7)$	$K^{19}[21-18]$	4
6	$K_{21}(3)$	$K^{19}[34-31]$	4	7	$K_{22}(5)$	$K^{19}[13-10]$	4
8	$K_{21}(2)$	$K^{19}[30-27]$	4	9	$K_{22}(0)$	$K^{19}[73-70]$	4
10	$K_{21}(0)$	$K^{19}[22-19]$	1	11	$K_{20}(0)$	$K^{19}[51-48]$	4
12	$K_{22}(6)$	$K^{19}[17-14]$	4	13	$K_{21}(5)$	$K^{19}[42-39]$	4
14	$K_{20}(2)$	$K^{19}[59-56]$	4	15	$K_{19}(1)$	$K^{19}[4-1]$	0

6   Conclusion

In this work, we have improved the attack done by the designers and attacked on 21-round and 22-round LBLock having a complexity of $2^{69.5}$ and $2^{79.28}$ respectively. In the designer's attack, it is assumed that all round keys are independent. In the proposed 21-round attack we use the relation between the rounds keys in the first 4 rounds. Also, we use all of the relations between the round keys in the first 4 rounds and the last 4 rounds to attack on 22 round-LBlock.

Acknowledgments. This work was supported by the project COGSA.

References

1. Biham, E., Biryukov, A., Shamir, A.: Cryptanalysis of Skipjack Reduced to 31 Rounds Using Impossible Differentials. In: Stern, J. (ed.) EUROCRYPT 1999. LNCS, vol. 1592, pp. 12–23. Springer, Heidelberg (1999)
2. Biham, E., Shamir, A.: Differential cryptanalysis of des-like cryptosystems. J. Cryptology 4(1), 3–72 (1991)
3. Bogdanov, A., Knudsen, L.R., Leander, G., Paar, C., Poschmann, A., Robshaw, M.J.B., Seurin, Y., Vikkelsoe, C.: PRESENT: An Ultra-Lightweight Block Cipher. In: Paillier, P., Verbauwhede, I. (eds.) CHES 2007. LNCS, vol. 4727, pp. 450–466. Springer, Heidelberg (2007)
4. Guo, J., Peyrin, T., Poschmann, A., Robshaw, M.: The LED Block Cipher. In: Preneel, B., Takagi, T. (eds.) CHES 2011. LNCS, vol. 6917, pp. 326–341. Springer, Heidelberg (2011)
5. Knudsen, L., Leander, G., Poschmann, A., Robshaw, M.J.B.: PRINTCIPHER: A Block Cipher for IC-Printing. In: Mangard, S., Standaert, F.-X. (eds.) CHES 2010. LNCS, vol. 6225, pp. 16–32. Springer, Heidelberg (2010)
6. Minier, M., Naya-Plasencia, M.: Some preliminary studies on the differential behavior of the lightweight block cipher lblock. In: Proceedings of ECRYPT Workshop on Lightweight Cryptography (2011), http://www.uclouvain.be/
7. Wu, W., Zhang, L.: LBlock: A Lightweight Block Cipher. In: Lopez, J., Tsudik, G. (eds.) ACNS 2011. LNCS, vol. 6715, pp. 327–344. Springer, Heidelberg (2011)

A   The Bits of K^{19} which Determines the Round Keys Guessed in Algorithm 3 and 4

Table 4. The bits of K^{19} which determines the round keys guessed in Algorithm 3 and 4

Round keys	The bits of K^{19}	Round keys	The bits of K^{19}
$K_1(7)$	[71-68,66-63,61]	$K_{19}(1)$	[4-1]
$K_1(6)$	[67-61,59-56,54]	$K_{20}(2)$	[59-56]
$K_1(5)$	[64-54,52-50]	$K_{20}(0)$	[51-48]
$K_1(4)$	[60-54,52-50]	$K_{21}(5)$	[42-39]
$K_1(2)$	[53-46]	$K_{21}(3)$	[34-31]
$K_1(1)$	[49-41,39]	$K_{21}(2)$	[30-27]
$K_1(0)$	[45-39,37-34,32]	$K_{21}(0)$	[22-19]
$K_2(7)$	[42-39,37-34,32]	$K_{22}(7)$	[21-18]
$K_2(5)$	[35-25,23-21]	$K_{22}(6)$	[17-14]
$K_2(4)$	[31-25,23-21]	$K_{22}(5)$	[13-10]
$K_2(2)$	[24-17]	$K_{22}(3)$	[5-2]
$K_3(5)$	[79-76,74-72,6-0]	$K_{22}(2)$	[79,78,1,0]
$K_3(4)$	[79-76,74-72,2-0]	$K_{22}(1)$	[77-74]
$K_4(4)$	[53-46]	$K_{22}(0)$	[73-70]

B   The S-Boxes Used in LBlock

x	0	1	2	3	4	5	6	7	8	9	10	11	12	13	14	15
$s_0[x]$	14	9	15	0	13	4	10	11	1	2	8	3	7	6	12	5
$s_1[x]$	4	11	14	9	15	13	0	10	7	12	5	6	2	8	1	3
$s_2[x]$	1	14	7	12	15	13	0	6	11	5	9	3	2	4	8	10
$s_3[x]$	7	6	8	11	0	15	3	14	9	10	12	13	5	2	4	1
$s_4[x]$	14	5	15	0	7	2	12	13	1	8	4	9	11	10	6	3
$s_5[x]$	2	13	11	12	15	14	0	9	7	10	6	3	1	8	4	5
$s_6[x]$	11	9	4	14	0	15	10	13	6	12	5	7	3	8	1	2
$s_7[x]$	13	10	15	0	14	4	9	11	2	1	8	3	7	5	12	6
$s_8[x]$	8	7	14	5	15	13	0	6	11	12	9	10	2	4	1	3
$s_9[x]$	11	5	15	0	7	2	9	13	4	8	1	12	14	10	3	6

Efficient Java Implementation of Elliptic Curve Cryptography for J2ME-Enabled Mobile Devices

Johann Großschädl[1], Dan Page[2], and Stefan Tillich[2]

[1] University of Luxembourg, CSC Research Unit, LACS,
6, rue Richard Coudenhove-Kalergi, L–1359 Luxembourg, Luxembourg
johann.groszschaedl@uni.lu
[2] University of Bristol, Department of Computer Science,
Merchant Venturers Building, Woodland Road, Bristol, BS8 1UB, U.K.
{page,tillich}@cs.bris.ac.uk

Abstract. The Micro Edition of the Java 2 platform (J2ME) provides an application environment specifically designed to address the demands of embedded devices like cell phones, PDAs or set-top boxes. Since the J2ME platform does not include a crypto package, developers are forced to use third-party classes or to implement all cryptographic primitives from scratch. However, most existing implementations of elliptic curve (EC) cryptography for J2ME do not perform well on resource-restricted devices, in most cases due to poor efficiency of the underlying arithmetic operations. In this paper we present an optimized Java implementation of EC scalar multiplication that combines efficient finite-field arithmetic with efficient group arithmetic. More precisely, our implementation uses a pseudo-Mersenne (PM) prime field for fast modular reduction and a Gallant-Lambert-Vanstone (GLV) curve with an efficiently computable endomorphism to speed up the scalar multiplication with random base points. Our experimental results show that a conventional mobile phone without Java acceleration, such as the Nokia 6610, is capable to execute a 174-bit scalar multiplication in roughly 400 msec, which is more than 45 times faster than the widely-used Bouncy Castle Lightweight Crypto API for J2ME.

1 Introduction

The Java programming language, introduced by Sun Microsystems in 1995, was originally designed to simplify the software engineering for consumer electronics [13,2]. Many characteristics of the Java language stem from the focus towards the consumer marketplace with its vast number of different hardware platforms and (largely incompatible) operating systems. Unlike C or C++, Java is generic and *platform-independent* because it is an interpreted rather than a compiled language. That is, when Java source code is compiled, it is not compiled into architecture-dependent "machine" instructions, but into an architecture-neutral intermediate representation consisting of generic instructions (called *bytecode*) to be executed by a *Java Virtual Machine (JVM)* [7]. The JVM can be seen as a program running on the host processor that interprets generic Java bytecodes

I. Askoxylakis, H.C. Pöhls, and J. Posegga (Eds.): WISTP 2012, LNCS 7322, pp. 189–207, 2012.
© IFIP International Federation for Information Processing 2012

and translates them to the processor's native machine instructions as they are executed. A program written in Java and compiled to generic bytecode will, in principle, run unchanged on any platform for which a JVM exists, regardless of what operating system or processor lies underneath. This "Write Once, Run Everywhere" capability has made Java the de-facto standard language for the development of cross-platform applications in the embedded domain.

The Java 2 platform is available in three different editions, each aimed at a specific area of application: J2EE (Java 2 Enterprise Edition) for developing and deploying large-scale server applications, J2SE (Java 2 Standard Edition) for the implementation of Java programs that can be executed on commodity computers, as well as *J2ME (Java 2 Micro Edition)* for creating Java applications to be run on various kinds of mobile and embedded devices[1]. These platform editions differ in terms of size (and complexity) of the class library and the capabilities of the corresponding JVM. J2ME is, roughly speaking, a stripped-down version of J2SE that contains only a small subset of the standard Java class library, in addition to J2ME-specific classes [28]. Java applications for mobile phones are called *midlets* and can be run on devices on which at least 192 kB of memory is available to the J2ME platform. Since the "conventional" interpretation of Java bytecode on such resource-restricted devices is rather slow, different techniques for speeding up the execution of midlets have emerged. For example, some JVMs feature a *Just-In-Time (JIT)* compiler that translates frequently-executed code segments ("hot spots") into native machine code at run-time (i.e. during execution of the midlet) [8]. Another approach is the provision of dedicated hardware support for the JVM through architectural extensions that allow the underlying processor to directly execute Java bytecode (e.g. ARM's Jazelle [1]).

Since J2ME is, roughly speaking, a stripped-down version of J2SE for mobile devices with restricted resources, it lacks many of the classes found in the class library of the larger editions. While the Java Cryptography Architecture (JCA) and Java Cryptography Extension (JCE) are included in J2SE/J2EE, they are absent in J2ME for both technical and legal reasons [28]. Therefore, developers of J2ME applications are forced to use third-party classes or to implement the required cryptographic operations from scratch. The latter is a tedious task, especially for Elliptic Curve (EC) cryptography, since the J2ME class library does not even contain the J2SE `BigInteger` class for multi-precision arithmetic. On the other hand, most existing EC implementations for J2ME (e.g. the Bouncy Castle Lightweight API [26] or the SIC JCE-ME [25]) do not perform very well since they aim to provide high flexibility (i.e. support of many implementation options) rather than high speed. There exist only a few performance-optimized Java implementations of EC cryptography, which is surprising given that more than three billion J2ME-enabled mobile phones have shipped to date[2]. Also the scientific literature on optimizing EC cryptosystems for the J2ME platform is

---

[1] In June 2005, Sun Microsystems renamed J2EE to Java EE, J2SE to Java SE, and J2ME to Java ME. However, since the old names are still very common and widely used today, we decided to stick with the term "J2ME" in this paper.

[2] http://www.java.com/en/about, http://java.sun.com/products/javadevice

sparse compared to the vast number of papers presenting EC implementations written in C and/or Assembly language.

In the following sections, we describe our efforts to develop a performance-optimized Java implementation of EC scalar multiplication for J2ME-enabled devices. The focus of our work was to achieve fast execution time, low memory (i.e. RAM) requirements, and small bytecode size. After a thorough evaluation of different implementation options, we decided to use a pseudo-Mersenne (PM) prime field [9] over which a Gallant-Lambert-Vanstone (GLV) curve with good cryptographic properties can be defined [12,15]. This particular choice of type of field and type of curve allows for combining fast modular arithmetic (due to the special form of the prime) with fast EC point arithmetic (thanks to an efficiently computable endomorphism). To exemplify our approach, we present an optimized Java implementation of EC scalar multiplication on the GLV curve $y^2 = x^3 - 7$ over the PM prime field $\mathbb{F}_p$ with $p = 2^{174} - 3$. The group of points on this curve has prime cardinality and offers a security level of 87 bits[3]. When using mixed Jacobian-affine coordinates, a point addition on this curve requires eight multiplications (8M) and three squarings (3S) in the underlying field (see [15] for the exact formula). The double of a point given in Jacobian coordinates can be computed using only 3M and 4S since the curve parameter a is 0. A full scalar multiplication of an arbitrary point P by an n-bit integer k represented in Non-Adjacent Form (NAF) [15] takes $5.\dot{6}n$ multiplications and $5n$ squarings on average, i.e. $5.\dot{6}$M + 5S per bit. However, the cost of a scalar multiplication on our GLV curve can be significantly reduced by exploiting the efficiently-computable endomorphism described in [12, Ex. 4]. This endomorphism allows one to accomplish an n-bit scalar multiplication $k \cdot P$ through a computation of the form $k_1 \cdot P + k_2 \cdot Q$, whereby k_1, k_2 have only half the bit-length of k. The two half-length scalar multiplications can be performed simultaneously and require $n/2$ point doublings and roughly $n/4$ additions when k_1, k_2 are represented in Joint Sparse Form (JSF) [23]. Thus, the total cost of computing $k \cdot P$ amounts to $3.5n$ multiplications and $2.75n$ squarings in $\mathbb{F}_p$, i.e. 3.5M + 2.75S per bit.

Since our implementation aims at high performance, we did not attempt to make the scalar multiplication on our GLV curve resistant against side-channel attacks such as Simple Power Analysis (SPA) [20]. However, all arithmetic operations (except inversion) in the underlying 174-bit prime field are written in a highly regular fashion without any conditional statements, i.e. branches. Such a branch-less implementation of the field arithmetic helps the VM to identify the performance-critical code sections for JiT-compilation and also eliminates the performance penalty due to branch mis-predictions. Note that, even though the field-arithmetic is SPA-resistant, our implementation of scalar multiplication is vulnerable to SPA attacks. We will address this issue in future work dedicated to SPA countermeasures for scalar multiplication on GLV curves.

---

[3] More precisely, the cardinality of the group of $\mathbb{F}_p$-rational points on said curve is a 174-bit prime. A properly implemented EC cryptosystem using this group provides a security level similar to that of a 87-bit secret-key cryptosystem, which is well above the "smallest general-purpose level" of 80 bits recommended by ECRYPT [22].

2   Prime-Field Arithmetic in Java

Our optimized Java software for EC scalar multiplication uses the prime field $\mathbb{F}_p$ of order $p = 2^{174} - 3$ as underlying algebraic structure. In the following, we explain the rationale behind choosing this particular field and elaborate on the efficient implementation of multiple-precision arithmetic in Java. Most previous software implementations of EC cryptography were written in C (or C++) and contain hand-optimized Assembly code for the performance-critical arithmetic operations. However, even though C/C++ and Java have a similar syntax, there exist also some differences which impact the implementation and optimization of multiple-precision arithmetic.

2.1   Selection of Prime Field

A major aspect when implementing EC cryptography is to find an appropriate trade-off between performance and security; this is particularly important for a Java implementation to be run on J2ME-enabled mobile phones or PDAs since (1) such devices are constrained in processing power and (2) the interpretation of platform-independent byte code is much slower than the execution of native machine code. The ECRYPT II report on algorithms and keysizes considers 80 bits as the smallest level of security that "protects against the most reasonable and threatening attack (key search) scenarios" [22, p. 32]. An 80-bit symmetric key can, under certain assumptions, be seen "equivalent" to an EC key of size 160 bits [22, Table 7.2]. In order to support 160-bit keys, an EC cryptosystem must be designed on basis of an EC group of order roughly 2^{160}, which, due to the Hasse-Weil theorem [5, page 278], requires an underlying field of (at least) 160 bits. However, GLV curves have a special structure that could reduce the time required to compute EC discrete logarithms by "a small factor" [12, Section 5], similar to Koblitz curves [29]. To account for this structure, we have to slightly increase the order of the EC group and, consequently, the order of the underlying prime field, e.g. to around 170 bits.

   A second criterion to consider when choosing a prime field $\mathbb{F}_p$ for EC cryptography is the efficiency of arithmetic operations in this field, in particular the efficiency of the reduction modulo p. Mersenne primes are special primes of the form $p = 2^k - 1$ and allow for particularly fast implementation of the reduction operation. A $2k$-bit number x can be reduced modulo $p = 2^k - 1$ by adding the higher half of x (i.e. the k most significant bits of x) to the lower half, followed by conditional subtraction(s) of p to obtain the least non-negative residue. Consequently, the reduction costs merely an addition of two k-bit numbers modulo p. Unfortunately, primes of the form $2^k - 1$ are very rare; none of the Mersenne numbers between $2^{127} - 1$ and $2^{521} - 1$ is prime [5]. The second-best option in terms of efficiency of the modular reduction are *pseudo-Mersenne (PM)* primes [9], i.e. primes that can be written as $p = 2^k - c$ where c is "small" compared to 2^k. In the ideal case $c = 3$, which allows a reduction operation to be carried out through three k-bit additions modulo p. A prime of the form $2^k - 3$ with a length of roughly 170 bits exists, namely $p = 2^{174} - 3$.

A third requirement on the prime p is the suitability to define a GLV curve with "good" cryptographic properties over the field $\mathbb{F}_p$. GLV curves of the form $y^2 = x^3 + ax$ require the underlying prime field $\mathbb{F}_p$ to contain an element of order 4 (which is the case if $p \equiv 1 \bmod 4$), whereas GLV curves defined via the equation $y^2 = x^3 + b$ need a field $\mathbb{F}_p$ with $p \equiv 1 \bmod 3$ [12]. Furthermore, the curve itself (or, more precisely, the group of points on the curve) has to satisfy certain properties, e.g. it has to contain a large subgroup of prime order. The GLV curve $y^2 = x^3 - 7$ over the 174-bit prime field specified above fulfills this property and also meets a number of other security criteria as we will show in more detail in Subsection 3.1. Taking all these considerations into account, we decided to use the prime field $\mathbb{F}_p$ with $p = 2^{174} - 3$ for our Java implementation of EC scalar multiplication.

Representation of Field Elements. State-of-the-art cryptographic libraries represent the elements of a large prime field (i.e. long integers) as arrays of single-precision words, e.g. arrays of type `unsigned int`. Most high-performance implementations written in C or Assembly language match the number of bits per single-precision word to the word-size of the target processor so as to take advantage of the full length of the datapath. Also the J2SE `BigInteger` class follows a similar idea; it uses an `int`-array as internal data structure and stores 32 bits in each element of the array. However, this approach yields sub-optimal results when the size (i.e. bitlength) of the prime field is constant and known in advance. These inefficiencies, which will be discussed in more detail below, are due to the fact that Java is a platform-independent programming language and that it does not support unsigned data types.

We conducted experiments with different representations of the $\mathbb{F}_p$-elements and found that splitting the 174-bit integers into six 29-bit words allows one to achieve the best performance. Our implementation does not store these words in an array but in six independent variables of type `int`, which are declared as `private` within the Java class that performs the $\mathbb{F}_p$-arithmetic so that they are not visible (and accessible) from "outside" [2]. Avoiding the use of an array is possible and viable in our case since the length of the operands is fixed and we implemented all arithmetic operations (except inversion) in an unrolled fashion without executing any conditional statements to achieve a maximum of performance and resistance against side-channel attacks. Formally, our implementation of $\mathbb{F}_p$-arithmetic uses a number representation radix of 2^{29}, which means that any integer $a \in \mathbb{F}_p$ can be written as

$$a = \sum_{i=0}^{5} a_i \cdot 2^{29i} \quad \text{with} \quad 0 \le a_i \le 2^{29} - 1. \tag{1}$$

However, similar to the work of Bernstein [4], we allow (i.e. tolerate) individual words a_i slightly larger than the radix of 2^{29} for reasons of both efficiency and security. Furthermore, our implementation allows incompletely reduced results in the sense that an arithmetic operation does not necessarily return the least non-negative residue modulo p, but the result is always in the range $[0, 2p]$.

2.2 Efficient Arithmetic Modulo $p = 2^{174} - 3$

In the following, we describe our Java implementation of fast arithmetic in the prime field $\mathbb{F}_p$, i.e. addition and multiplication modulo $p = 2^{174} - 3$. We will in particular explain the efficiency of our 29-bit-per-word representation of field elements versus a straightforward representation using 32-bit words.

Addition and Subtraction. Most high-speed cryptographic libraries written in C (or C++) use small Assembly-code fragments to implement performance-critical operations such as multiple-precision addition and multiplication. The former operation can be realized in a (relatively) simple yet efficient way if the underlying processor provides an add-with-carry instruction. Even though also Java features a mechanism to include Assembly code, namely the Java Native Interface (JNI), we did not follow this approach because it contradicts the idea of platform-independence. Furthermore, one has to take into account that some processors (e.g. MIPS, Alpha) do not possess an add-with-carry instruction. To perform multi-precision addition on these processors, the add-with-carry has to be emulated, e.g. by first executing the ordinary add instruction, followed by a comparison of the result with one of the two operands. If the obtained sum is smaller than either of the operands, then an overflow occurred, i.e. the addition produced a carry, which must be processed properly when adding the two next-higher words. Consequently, from the second word-pair onwards, the addition becomes more complex and time-consuming since an "incoming" carry must be considered.

High-level language implementations of multi-precision addition can follow a very similar approach as described above if the long integers are represented in such a way that the number of bits per single-precision word corresponds to the word-size of the underlying processor (e.g. 32 bits per word on a 32-bit processor). However, the performance of multi-precision addition in C/C++ or Java (or in Assembly language on processors without add-with-carry instruction) can be greatly improved by reducing the number of bits per word, e.g. to 31 when working on a 32-bit machine. In this case, the sum of two single-precision words is at most 32 bits long and, hence, fits into a 32-bit word, i.e. an overflow can not occur. The carry bit is stored in the MSB of the result-word and accessible through a right-shift by 31 bit positions. This approach was originally proposed roughly 30 years ago by Hennessy et al [16, Section 2.3.3] to demonstrate the ability of the MIPS architecture (and other architectures lacking a carry flag) to efficiently perform multi-precision addition.

Algorithm 1 shows our Java implementation of addition in $\mathbb{F}_p$; we follow, in principle, the approach of Hennessy et al [16] described above, except that we represent the long integers using 29-bit words. The variable s, which is of type int in our implementation, holds the sum of two 29-bit operand-words plus the carry bit. Even though the sum can have a length of up to 30 bits, only the 29 LSBs of s are actually assigned to the result-word z_i. The three MSBs of s are masked out via a logical AND operation using a mask value of 0x1fffffff (see line 4 of Algorithm 1). Before adding the next pair of operand-words, the sum

---

Algorithm 1. Addition in $\mathbb{F}_p$

Input: Two 174-bit integers, $A = (a_5, a_4, a_3, a_2, a_1, a_0)$ and $B = (b_5, b_4, b_3, b_2, b_1, b_0)$,
   represented by six 29-bit words.
Output: Modular sum $Z = A + B \bmod (2^{174} - 3) = (z_5, z_4, z_3, z_2, z_1, z_0)$.
   1: $s \leftarrow 0$
   2: **for** i from 0 by 1 to 5 **do**
   3:     $s \leftarrow a_i + b_i + (s \gg 29)$
   4:     $z_i \leftarrow s$ & 0x1fffffff
   5: **end for**
   6: $z_0 \leftarrow z_0 + 3 \cdot (s \gg 29)$
   7: **return** $Z = (z_5, z_4, z_3, z_2, z_1, z_0)$

---

s is shifted 29 bit positions to the right to ensure the correct alignment between a_i, b_i, and the carry bit. In fact, the shift operation yields the carry bit from the previous addition of operand words, i.e. the value of the expression $(s \gg 29)$ in line 3 of Algorithm 1 is either 0 or 1. Note, however, that our implementation does not strictly adhere to the pseudo-code shown in Algorithm 1; we unrolled the loop to maximize performance.

The sum of two 174-bit integers can be up to 175 bits long, which means a reduction modulo $p = 2^{174} - 3$ may be necessary to obtain a final result within the range of $[0, p - 1]$. Reducing the sum with respect to the prime p calls for a comparison between the sum and p, followed by a subtraction of p if the sum is greater than or equal to p. The former operation, when realized in a straightforward way, requires comparing up to six single-precision words. However, an exact comparison of the sum with the prime p can, in general, be avoided since modular arithmetic also works with incompletely reduced operands and, consequently, there is no need to fully reduce a result. Our implementation compares the sum with 2^{174} instead of the "exact" prime $p = 2^{174} - 3$, i.e. the result of a modular addition is not necessarily the least non-negative residue. The obvious advantage of performing the comparison in this way is efficiency; we just have to check whether the 174-bit addition produced a "carry-out," as described in [30, Section 3]. More precisely, after the final iteration of the loop in Algorithm 1, we simply right-shift the variable s by 29 bits to obtain the "carry out." The subtraction of the prime p is realized in our implementation by addition of the 174-bit two's complement of p to the sum, i.e. by addition of $2^{174} - p = 3$ to the least significant word z_0. Line 6 of Algorithm 1 performs the modular reduction operation, consisting of the extraction of the "carry out", its multiplication by 3, and the addition of the product to z_0. Note that, due to this addition, the least significant word z_0 can be up to 30 bits long. However, the extended size of z_0 does not require special consideration since all our arithmetic operations also work correctly with 30-bit words.

We implemented the subtraction of two elements $a, b \in \mathbb{F}_p$ through the operation $2p + a - b$, which, in turn, is carried out via word-level operations of the form $2p_i + a_i - b_i$, followed by a reduction of the result modulo p as described before. Performing the subtraction in this way (instead of a direct computation

Listing 1. Nested loop of multi-precision multiplication as implemented in the function `multiplyToLen` of the `BigInteger` class (version 1.76)

```
1  for (int i = xstart-1; i >= 0; i--) {
2      carry = 0;
3      for (int j=ystart, k=ystart+1+i; j>=0; j--, k--) {
4          long product = (y[j] & LONG_MASK) *
5                         (x[i] & LONG_MASK) +
6                         (z[k] & LONG_MASK) + carry;
7          z[k] = (int)product;
8          carry = product >>> 32;
9      }
10     z[i] = (int)carry;
11 }
```

of the difference $a - b$) ensures that the results of all word-level operations, as well as the final 174-bit result, are positive and can be calculated in a straight-forward way without the need of any conditional statements. Such branch-less execution of arithmetic operations can help to prevent implementation attacks since always the same sequence of instructions is executed, independent of the actual value of the operands. In fact, due to loop unrolling, our implementation of subtraction in $\mathbb{F}_p$ does not execute any control-flow statements at all.

Multiplication and Squaring. A multiplication of two elements $a, b \in \mathbb{F}_p$ can be accomplished by conventional integer multiplication of a and b, along with a reduction of the obtained 384-bit product modulo the prime p. There exist two principal techniques for implementing multiple-precision multiplication in software, namely *operand scanning* (also called pencil-and-paper method [19]) and *product scanning* (also known as Comba's method [6]). Both methods execute the same number of single-precision multiplications, but differ in loop structure and inner-loop operation. The operand scanning technique uses a nested loop to calculate the double-precision partial products in a row-by-row fashion [14]. In each iteration of the inner loop, an operation of the form $a \cdot b + c + d$ is carried out, i.e. two single-precision words are multiplied together and two other words are added to the product. On the other hand, the product scanning algorithm is characterized by a nested-loop structure consisting of two outer loops and two inner loops; the first outer loop calculates the lower half of the product and the second outer loop the upper half [14]. The partial products are added up in a column-wise fashion using an inner-loop operation of the form $s + a \cdot b$, i.e. two words are multiplied and the product is added to a cumulative sum.

The relative performance of operand scanning vs. product scanning depends on a range of factors such as the programming language and the representation of the long integers. Most implementations of multiple-precision multiplication written in C/C++ or Java use the operand-scanning method and represent the operands as arrays of single-precision words whose bitlength matches the word-size of the underlying processor (e.g. 32-bit words on a 32-bit processor). The inner loop of the operand-scanning method is straightforward to implement in a high-level programming language since the result of an operation of the form $a \cdot b + c + d$ is at most 64 bits long (and, therefore, fits into a C/C++ variable of type unsigned long long or a Java variable of type long) when a, b, c, and d are 32-bit words. However, a peculiarity of Java, compared to C/C++, is the lack of unsigned data types, which calls for an implementation of the inner loop as shown in Listing 1. The variables carry and product are of type long and can hold 64-bit signed integers, whereas x, y, and z are 32-bit int arrays. Java requires a type conversion (or "widening") of the operands from int to long in order to get a 64-bit result when multiplying two 32-bit integers. An integral part of this conversion process is sign extension, which means that the upper 32 bits of the 64-bit long representation are filled with the sign bit of the original 32-bit int value. These upper 32 bits have to be masked out to obtain the corresponding unsigned value; the implementation shown in Listing 1 achieves this via a logical AND operation using LONG_MASK, a final static variable of type long, which is defined in the BigInteger class and initialized with the literal 0xffffffffL. Of course, performing three such maskings in the inner loop incurs a significant performance degradation.

The product scanning method, on the other hand, performs a multiply-accumulate operation of the form $s + a \cdot b$ in its inner loop, i.e. two single-precision words are multiplied and the double-precision product is added to a cumulative sum [6]. However, the bitlength of the cumulative sum can grow beyond double precision when several double-precision products are summed up, which makes the product scanning method quite hard to implement in C/C++ or Java since high-level languages do not provide a primitive integer type whose bitlength is more than twice the length of a single-precision word. A straightforward way to circumvent this problem is to reduce the number of bits per word to less than the wordsize of the underlying processor, following the rationale discussed earlier in this section for the addition of field elements. Since most J2ME-enabled mobile devices are equipped with 32-bit processors, we can, for example, use a 29-bit-per-word representation and implement the product scanning method as shown in Algorithm 2. Having single-precision words of 29 bits means that all double-precision partial products $a_j \cdot b_{i-j}$ in Algorithm 2 consist of at most 58 bits. Consequently, we can use a 64-bit variable of type long to hold the cumulative sum s; in this case, up to $2^{64-58} = 2^6 = 64$ partial products can be added up without overflowing s. Such a reduction of the bitlength of operand words (which was first suggested by Barrett [3, p. 317] roughly 25 years ago[4]) allows for a very efficient implementation of the inner loop since masking operations as in Listing 1 can be avoided.

The result of a multiplication performed according to the first part (i.e. line $1-16$) of Algorithm 2 is a 348-bit product Z represented by an array of twelve 29-bit words, i.e. $Z = (z_{11}, \ldots, z_1, z_0)$. This product has to be reduced modulo

---

[4] Note that several other implementations of the product-scanning method, e.g. the one of Curve25519 [4], take advantage of Barrett's idea to increase performance.

Algorithm 2. Multiplication in $\mathbb{F}_p$

Input: Two 174-bit integers, $A = (a_5, a_4, a_3, a_2, a_1, a_0)$ and $B = (b_5, b_4, b_3, b_2, b_1, b_0)$, represented by six 29-bit words.
Output: Modular product $Z = A \cdot B \bmod (2^{174} - 3) = (z_5, z_4, z_3, z_2, z_1, z_0)$.

1: $s \leftarrow 0$
2: **for** i from 0 by 1 to 5 **do**
3:     **for** j from 0 by 1 to i **do**
4:         $s \leftarrow s + a_j \cdot b_{i-j}$
5:     **end for**
6:     $z_i \leftarrow s$ & 0x1fffffff
7:     $s \leftarrow s \gg 29$
8: **end for**
9: **for** i from 6 by 1 to 10 **do**
10:     **for** j from $i - 5$ by 1 to 5 **do**
11:         $s \leftarrow s + a_j \cdot b_{i-j}$
12:     **end for**
13:     $z_i \leftarrow s$ & 0x1fffffff
14:     $s \leftarrow s \gg 29$
15: **end for**
16: $z_{11} \leftarrow s$
17: $s \leftarrow 0$
18: **for** i from 0 by 1 to 5 **do**
19:     $s \leftarrow z_i + 3 \cdot z_{i+6} + (s \gg 29)$
20:     $z_i \leftarrow s$ & 0x1fffffff
21: **end for**
22: $z_0 \leftarrow z_0 + 3 \cdot (s \gg 29)$
23: **return** $Z = (z_5, z_4, z_3, z_2, z_1, z_0)$

$p = 2^{174} - 3$ to obtain a final result within the range of $[0, p - 1]$. Since p is a PM prime [9] of the form $2^k - c$, we can exploit the relation $2^k \equiv c \bmod p$ to accomplish the modular reduction in an efficient way. The reduction operation requires to split the product Z into a lower half Z_L (comprising, in our case, the six words $z_0, z_1, \ldots, z_5$) and an upper half Z_H (consisting of $z_6, z_7, \ldots, z_{11}$) so that $Z = Z_H \cdot 2^k + Z_L$. Now, Z can be reduced modulo $p = 2^k - c$ by simply substituting 2^k by c as shown in Equation (2).

$$Z \bmod p = Z_H \cdot 2^k + Z_L \bmod p = Z_H \cdot c + Z_L \bmod p \qquad (2)$$

In essence, this boils down to multiplying Z_H by c and adding the product to Z_L, which leads to a result that is at most $(c + 1)$ times larger than p (i.e. the result is just a few bits longer than p if c is small). To get a completely reduced result, one can either perform the same procedure again, or simply subtract the prime p until a final result within the range of $[0, p - 1]$ is obtained. The second part of Algorithm 2 (i.e. line 17 to 22) formally describes the reduction of the 348-bit product $Z = (z_{11}, \ldots, z_1, z_0)$ modulo $p = 2^{174} - 3$. Note that, in our implementation, the multiplication by 3 in line 19 is realized via three additions of z_{i+6}. Therefore, reducing Z modulo $2^{174} - 3$ costs, in practice, no more than adding three 174-bit integers. The for-loop in line $18-21$ is very similar to the loop of Algorithm 1 and, thus, can be implemented in Java in the same way as detailed earlier in this subsection for the addition in $\mathbb{F}_p$. Due to the 29-bit-per-word representation, it is possible to use a 32-bit variable of type `int` for the sum s and efficiently perform the additions in line 19 without overflow or loss of precision. The final result of Algorithm 2 may be not fully reduced and the least significant word z_0 may be up to 30 bits long instead of 29, similar to the result of Algorithm 1. However, as already mentioned, these "peculiarities" do not require special consideration since all arithmetic operations (bar inversion) are implemented such that they tolerate incompletely-reduced input operands and overlength (i.e. 30-bit) words. Note that Algorithm 2 is a simplified version of our actual Java implementation of multiplication in $\mathbb{F}_p$; we unrolled all loops to maximize performance. Furthermore, as stated in Subsection 2.1, we represent the field elements (i.e. 174-bit integers) by six individual variables of type `int` instead of arrays. These optimizations allow us to perform a multiplication without executing data-dependent branches or load operations, which helps to prevent certain forms of side-channel attack.

The square A^2 of a long (i.e. multiple-precision) integer A can be calculated considerably faster than the product of two distinct integers. When $A = B$, all partial products of the form $a_j \cdot b_{i-j}$ with $j \neq i - j$ in Algorithm 2 are identical to the partial products $a_{i-j} \cdot b_j$, i.e. they appear twice. However, an optimized squaring algorithm calculates each of these partial products only once and then shifts it left in order to double it. Due to our 29-bit-per-word representation, a 58-bit partial product held in a 64-bit `long` variable can be efficiently shifted to the left by one bit position without overflow. Multiplying two 174-bit integers represented by six 29-bit words requires a total of 36 word-level multiplications (i.e. `lmul` instructions in Java), whereas the squaring of a 174-bit integer costs only 21 word-level multiplications. In theory, squaring is nearly twice as fast as multiplication, but the difference in execution time decreases when taking the modular reduction into account. Modular squaring is generally only about 20% faster than modular multiplication since the reduction operation always takes the same time, regardless of whether a square or a product is reduced.

Inversion. We implemented the inversion in $\mathbb{F}_p$ according to the binary version of the Euclidean algorithm (Algorithm 2.22 in [15]) and applied some low-level optimizations such as multi-bit shifting. Even though inversion is costly, it has only little impact on scalar multiplication when using projective coordinates.

3   Point Arithmetic on GLV Curves

This section is devoted to the efficient implementation of scalar multiplication on a GLV curve and structured in a similar way as Section 2. We first explain the rationale behind choosing the curve $y^2 = x^3 - 7$ over $\mathbb{F}_p$ and then elaborate on different algorithms for scalar multiplication on GLV curves.

3.1   Selection of Elliptic Curve

At Crypto 2001, Gallant et al [12] introduced special families of elliptic curves over $\mathbb{F}_p$ that possess an endomorphism of small norm and demonstrated how to exploit this endomorphism to speed up a scalar multiplication. These so-called GLV curves can be seen as somewhat related to Koblitz curves over $\mathbb{F}_{2^m}$ since both provide a "shortcut" in the form of an endomorphism that allows one to perform a scalar multiplication significantly faster compared to random curves [15]. Gallant et al considered in [12] curves defined by the Weierstraß equation $y^2 = x^3 + ax$ (i.e. $b = 0$) and $y^2 = x^3 + b$ (i.e. $a = 0$) over a prime field $\mathbb{F}_p$ satisfying $p \equiv 1 \bmod 4$ in the former case and $p \equiv 1 \bmod 3$ in the latter. Both types of curve feature an endomorphism ϕ whose characteristic polynomial has small coefficients; in the former case the characteristic polynomial is $\lambda^2 + 1$ and in the latter case it is $\lambda^2 + \lambda + 1$ (see [15] for details). During the past ten years, the work of Gallant et al received considerable attention and the GLV method has been extended to hyperelliptic curves and recently to curves over $\mathbb{F}_{p^2}$ that are twists of curves defined over $\mathbb{F}_p$ (the so-called GLS curves [11]). However, we decided to use a Weierstraß curve of the form $y^2 = x^3 + b$ over $\mathbb{F}_p$ for our Java implementation since this choice of curve and field is more compliant with the major standards for EC cryptography (e.g. IEEE P1363 [17], SECG [24]) than hyperelliptic curves or elliptic curves over $\mathbb{F}_{p^2}$.

   GLV curves are attractive to implementers for two reasons. First, when exploiting the endomorphism as per [12], scalar multiplication on GLV curves is considerably faster than on random curves, even though the speed-up is not as dramatic as for Koblitz curves [18]. Second, the GLV method can be applied in settings where arbitrary points are used as input for the scalar multiplication (e.g. in ECDH key exchange), i.e. the GLV method does not rely on a fixed base point that is known a priori. In the next subsection, we will briefly describe the GLV algorithm for scalar multiplication on curves of the form $y^2 = x^3 + b$. As mentioned above, these curves possess an efficiently computable endomorphism ϕ with characteristic polynomial $\lambda^2 + \lambda + 1$. Thanks to this endomorphism, it is possible to calculate the scalar multiplication $k \cdot P$ as $k_1 \cdot P + k_2 \cdot \phi(P)$, whereby k_1 and k_2 have only about half of the bitlength of the original k. These two half-length scalar multiplications can be carried out in an "interleaved" fashion using Shamir's trick [15], which halves the number of point doublings and also reduces the number of point additions compared to a conventional calculation of $k \cdot P$ using the double-and-add algorithm.

   Finding a GLV curve with "good" cryptographic properties is a non-trivial task since, as mentioned in [5, Section 15.2], "the class of elliptic curves with an endomorphism of small norm is small." This task becomes harder still when one tries to find a combination of PM prime field and GLV curve so that both the field and the curve (resp. group) arithmetic can be implemented efficiently. We used the computer algebra package Magma to enumerate all PM primes of the form $2^k - c$ for $160 \leq k \leq 176$ and $c < 16$, and then search for each of them a GLV curve containing a large cyclic subgroup. Among the pairs of PM prime and GLV curve we found was $p = 2^{174} - 3$ and the curve defined through the

Weierstraß equation $y^2 = x^3 - 7$ (i.e. $a = 0$ and $b = p - 7$) over $\mathbb{F}_p$, which we finally decided to use for our Java implementation. Since a detailed description of the curve-finding methodology would go beyond the scope of this paper, we restrict ourselves to show that this specific GLV curve is suitable for use in EC cryptography. Both the IEEE standard P1363 [17] and the book of Cohen et al [5] serve as a good reference for security criteria that an elliptic curve has to fulfill; the most important ones are the following.

- First and foremost, the group of points on the curve has to contain a large subgroup of prime order n. In other words, the curve should have a small co-factor h; ideally, the co-factor is 1. Our curve $E : y^2 = x^3 - 7$ over the field $\mathbb{F}_p$ with $p = 2^{174} - 3$ has the order

$$\#E(\mathbb{F}_p) = 23945242826020951341184917212305571372738815 3314904213,$$

  which happens to be a 174-bit prime; thus, the co-factor $h = \frac{\#E(\mathbb{F}_p)}{n}$ of this curve is 1. Following the notation from Section 1, a cryptosystem using the group $E(\mathbb{F}_p)$ provides a level of security that is well above the minimum (symmetric) level of 80 bits as recommended by ECRYPT II, the European Network of Excellence in Cryptology [22, Table 7.4].
- In order to circumvent the Semaev-Smart-Satoh-Araki (SSSA) attack, the curve must not be anomalous. This is obviously the case for our GLV curve since $\#E(\mathbb{F}_p) \neq p$.
- The embedding degree of the curve must not be small (i.e. the order of the EC group n must not divide $p^k - 1$ for "small" values of k) to prevent the Menezes-Okamoto-Vanstons (MOV) attack and other attacks based on the Weil and Tate pairing. Our GLV curve clearly satisfies this condition since $p^k \not\equiv 1 \bmod n$ for any $k \in [1, 100]$.

3.2 Efficient Implementation of Scalar Multiplication

A scalar multiplication is an operation of the form $k \cdot P$ whereby P denotes an EC point of large prime order n and k is an integer in the range $[1, n - 1]$ (see [15] for more information). Scalar multiplication in an EC group is nothing else than the repeated application of the group operation (i.e. point addition) on an element of the group, similar to exponentiation in a multiplicative group. It is common practice (at least when using curves over prime fields) to represent the points in projective coordinates as they allow for performing a point addition without inversion in the underlying finite field [15]. Our implementation of the point addition (resp. point doubling) is based on the mixed Jacobian-affine co-ordinates (resp. projective Jacobian coordinates) from Section 3.2.2 in [15]. An addition of points requires eight multiplications (8M), three squarings (3S), as well as a number of less-costly operations (e.g. additions, subtractions) in the underlying prime field, whereas a point doubling takes $4M + 4S$. However, the cost of point doubling on our GLV curve can be reduced by one multiplication to $3M + 4S$ since the parameter a is 0. Note that several variants of Jacobian point addition/doubling formulae exist, some of which trade multiplications in $\mathbb{F}_p$ for squarings at the expense of an increased number of certain low-cost field operations[5]. However, none of these variants is capable to speed up our implementation due to the fact that the less-costly operations have a non-negligible execution time of between 0.1M and 0.27M (see Section 4). Thus, we decided to stick with the original formulae from [15] optimized for $a = 0$.

The most basic technique for performing a scalar multiplication $k \cdot P$ is the double-and-add method [15], which works in a similar way as the square-and-multiply method for exponentiation. Given a scalar k of a length of n bits, the double-and-add approach executes n point doublings and (in the average case) about $n/2$ point additions; the exact number of point additions depends on the Hamming weight of k. As mentioned above, a point addition on our GLV curve requires $8M + 3S$, whereas a point doubling takes only $3M + 4S$. Therefore, the overall cost of the double-and-add method amounts to $3n + 8n/2 = 7n$ multiplications and $4n + 3n/2 = 5.5n$ squarings in $\mathbb{F}_p$ (or, equivalently, $7M + 5.5S$ per bit of the scalar k). The average number of point additions can be reduced from $n/2$ to $n/3$ when the scalar k is represented in Non-Adjacent Form (NAF) [15]. In this case, the double-and-add method requires just $5.\dot{6}n$ multiplications and $5n$ squarings in the average case, i.e. $5.\dot{6}M + 5S$ per bit. However, a more significant reduction of execution time can be achieved by exploiting the endomorphism ϕ of our GLV curve as explained in [12]. This endomorphism makes it possible to obtain the scalar product $k \cdot P$ via $k_1 \cdot P + k_2 \cdot \phi(P)$, which is, in general, more efficient than a straightforward calculation of $k \cdot P$ since k_1 and k_2 have typically only half the bitlength of k and the two scalar multiplications $k_1 \cdot P$ and $k_2 \cdot \phi(P)$ can be carried out "simultaneously" (i.e. in an interleaved fashion) using Shamir's trick [15, Section 3.3.3].

In the following, we summarize some basic facts about our GLV curve and explain how to exploit its endomorphism ϕ for scalar multiplication, similar to Section 3.5 in [15]. Since the curve parameter a is 0 and the prime p satisfies $p \equiv 1 \bmod 3$, our GLV curve is of the type described in Example 4 in [12]. The underlying field $\mathbb{F}_p$ contains an element β of order 3 (because $p \equiv 1 \bmod 3$); in our implementation we use

$$\beta = 3940945791252506480086544614218081936071702723658 49$$

According to [12, Example 4], the map $\phi : E \to E$ defined by

$$\phi : (x, y) \mapsto (\beta x, y) \quad \text{and} \quad \phi : \mathcal{O} \mapsto \mathcal{O} \tag{3}$$

is an endomorphism of E defined over $\mathbb{F}_p$. The characteristic polynomial of ϕ is $\lambda^2 + \lambda + 1$. In order to exploit this endomorphism for scalar multiplication, we need a root modulo n of the characteristic polynomial, i.e. we need a solution to the equation $\lambda^2 + \lambda + 1 \equiv 0 \bmod n$; our implementation uses

$$\lambda = 7591969537352440260196679277338091599843085579298264$$

---

[5] Most of these variants can be found in the Explicit Formulas Database (EFD), an extensive repository of formulae for point arithmetic on various families of elliptic curves. The EFD is available online at `http://www.hyperelliptic.org/EFD`.

Table 1. Timings of the field arithmetic on different devices

Operation	T60	HTC	X2	6610
Addition	24.2 ns	124.2 ns	1319 ns	63.1 μs
Subtraction	24.4 ns	130.0 ns	1772 ns	64.6 μs
Multiplication	255.5 ns	994.4 ns	7256 ns	232.3 μs
Squaring	197.9 ns	860.2 ns	6702 ns	186.9 μs
Inversion	26,6 μs	191.4 μs	1479 μs	54,8 ms

The solution λ has the property that $\phi(P) = \lambda \cdot P$ for all $P \in E(\mathbb{F}_p)$ [15]. Note that computing $\phi(P)$ for a point $P = (x, y)$ requires only one multiplication in $\mathbb{F}_p$, namely $\beta \cdot x$. As stated before, the common strategy for computing $k \cdot P$ on a GLV curve is to decompose the n-bit scalar k into two "half-length" integers k_1 and k_2 (often referred to as *balanced length-two representation* of k [15]) so that $k = k_1 + k_2\lambda \bmod n$. This decomposition of k into k_1 and k_2 is described in detail in [15] and requires merely a few multi-precision multiplications if the curve and field are fixed. As $k \cdot P = k_1 \cdot P + k_2 \cdot \lambda \cdot P = k_1 \cdot P + k_2 \cdot \phi(P)$, the result of $k \cdot P$ can be obtained by first computing $\phi(P)$ (which takes one single field multiplication) and then using a simultaneous double-scalar multiplication ("Shamir's trick") to perform these two half-length scalar multiplications in an interleaved fashion. Consequently, the GLV requires only $n/2$ point doublings for an n-bit scalar multiplication, which corresponds to a 50% reduction compared to the double-and-add method. The number of point additions depends on the joint Hamming density of k_1 and k_2; in the average case (i.e. when the joint Hamming density is 0.75), a total of $0.75 \cdot n/2 = 0.375n$ point additions must be carried out. In summary, the overall cost of the GLV method amounts to $0.5n \cdot 3 + 0.375n \cdot 8 = 4.3n$ multiplications and $0.5n \cdot 4 + 0.375n \cdot 3 = 3.125n$ squarings in $\mathbb{F}_p$, i.e. $4.3M + 3.125S$ per bit. However, the Hamming density can be reduced to 0.5 (on average) by representing k_1 and k_2 in Joint Sparse Form (JSF) [23], which, in turn, cuts the number of point additions by roughly one third to $0.5 \cdot n/2 = 0.25n$. In this case, the total cost of computing $k \cdot P$ on a GLV curve is reduced to, on average, $0.5n \cdot 3 + 0.25n \cdot 8 = 3.5n$ multiplications and $0.5n \cdot 4 + 0.25n \cdot 3 = 2.75n$ squarings in $\mathbb{F}_p$, i.e. $3.5M + 2.75S$ per bit.

4   Implementation Results and Discussion

We evaluated the performance (i.e. execution time) of our Java implementation of the field arithmetic and different algorithms for scalar multiplication on an IBM Thinkpad T60 and a set of mobile phones, including an HTC Desire S, a Nokia X2, and an old Nokia 6610. The most powerful of these test devices is the Thinkpad T60; it features a 32-bit Intel T2300 ("Core Duo") processor clocked with a frequency of 1.66 GHz. At the opposite end of the spectrum is the Nokia 6610, which is equipped with an ARM 11 processor clocked at 104 MHz. Table 1 summarizes the execution times of the field arithmetic operations on the T60 and the three mobile phones. Given the differing computational power of these

Table 2. Comparison of scalar multiplication methods on different devices

Algorithm	Cost per bit	T60	HTC	X2	6610
Dbl-and-Add	$7M + 5.5S$	569.1 μs	2745 μs	19.79 ms	632.5 ms
Dbl-and-Add (NAF)	$5.\dot{6}M + 5S$	490.3 μs	2352 μs	17.24 ms	552.9 ms
GLV method	$4.3M + 3.125S$	362.5 μs	2057 μs	13.36 ms	437.4 ms
GLV method (JSF)	$3.5M + 2.75S$	326.9 μs	1885 μs	12.20 ms	400.2 ms

devices, it is not surprising that the measured execution times vary by a large extent. However, besides the differences in processing speed, one must also take into account the capabilities of the particular JVM of each device. On the T60 we used the HotSpot Client VM that comes with Sun's JDK 6 Update 27; this VM features a JiT compiler for efficient execution of bytecodes. Most modern smart phones have either a VM with JiT compilation or a processor with Java extensions. On the other hand, the old Nokia 6610 provides a conventional VM without JiT compiler or any other form of Java acceleration. In order to obtain accurate timings, we put each arithmetic function into a loop and performed a sufficiently large number of iterations so that the overall execution time was in the range of several seconds. We measured the execution time with help of the `currentTimeMillis` function, which is provided by the `System` class. Table 1 specifies the average execution time (i.e. the quotient of overall execution time and number of iterations) of the arithmetic operations.

On the Thinkpad T60, the relative execution times of the arithmetic operations are very similar to that of previous implementations (e.g. [15]) written in C and/or Assembly language. Squaring is about 22% faster than multiplication (i.e. $S = 0.78M$), whereas addition and subtraction (and similar operations like halving or negation of a field element) execute in roughly 0.1M. The inversion is slow compared to the multiplication ($I = 116M$), but this not surprising since also most C (and Assembly) implementations of prime-field arithmetic have an I/M ratio of between 50 and 100 [15]. However, the relations are different on the Nokia 6610 because addition and subtraction take more than one fourth of the execution time of a multiplication; the exact ratio of addition to multiplication is 0.27. Also the inversion is very slow compared to the multiplication; based on the results from Table 1 we have $I = 235M$. An explanation for the differences between the T60 and the Nokia 6610 can be found in the characteristics of the underlying processor. The Core Duo of the T60 is a superscalar processor able to execute several arithmetic/logical instructions in parallel, which has a positive effect on the execution time of addition, subtraction, and inversion. On the other hand, the Core Duo can execute only a single integer multiply instruction at a time, i.e. multiplication and squaring in $\mathbb{F}_p$ can take little advantage of the superscalar pipeline. In contrast, the ARM 11 processor of the Nokia 6610 has a single-issue pipeline with a relatively fast integer multiplier, which favors the field multiplication over addition, subtraction, and inversion.

Table 2 shows a comparison of the four algorithms for scalar multiplication discussed in Subsection 3.2. The actual execution times on both the Thinkpad T60 and the mobile phones roughly match with the cost-per-bit figures given in the second column when taking into account that this approximate cost model only considers multiplications and squarings in $\mathbb{F}_p$. More concretely, on the T60 the GLV method with JSF representation of k_1, k_2 is 1.74 times faster than the standard double-and-add technique, which is relatively close to the theoretical speed-up factor of 2.0 suggested by the approximate cost model. However, as stated before, the approximate cost model is based on the number of multiplications and squarings in $\mathbb{F}_p$ and ignores that the GLV method has to perform other operations such as the decomposition of k into k_1, k_2 and the calculation of the sum $P + \phi(P)$ in affine coordinates, which may involve a costly inversion in $\mathbb{F}_p$. The T60 executes the GLV method in merely 326.9 μs; this translates to over 3,000 scalar multiplications per second. In comparison, the Bouncy Castle Lightweight Crypto API [26] requires 14.95 ms for a 174-bit scalar multiplication, i.e. our implementation outperforms Bouncy Castle by a factor of 45. On the 6610, the GLV method is only 1.58 times faster than the double-and-add method, mainly because of the fact that addition/subtraction and inversion are relatively more costly (versus multiplication) than on the T60. Nonetheless, the Nokia 6610 is able to execute the GLV method in about 400 ms, which is 5.38 times faster than the Java implementation of EC scalar multiplication over the binary extension field $\mathbb{F}_{2^{191}}$ reported in [27].

The GLV method compares very well with other approaches for scalar multiplication and other forms of elliptic curves, e.g. Montgomery [21] or Edwards curves [10]. A Montgomery curve over $\mathbb{F}_p$ is defined by an equation of the form $By^2 = x^3 + Ax^2 + x$ with $(A^2 - 4)B \neq 0$ and allows for fast computation of the x-coordinate of the sum $P + Q$ of two points P, Q whose difference $P - Q$ is known. More precisely, a point addition performed according to the formula in [21, p. 261] requires four multiplications (4M) and two squarings (2S), whereas a point doubling costs 3M and 2S. However, one of the three multiplications in the point doubling uses the constant $(A - 2)/4$ as operand, which is small if the parameter A is chosen properly. Our experiments show that multiplying a field element by a small (up to 29 bits) constant costs some 0.2M. Furthermore, the point addition formula given in [21, page 261] can be optimized when using the so-called Montgomery ladder (Algorithm 13.35 in [5]) for scalar multiplication and representing the base point in projective coordinates with $Z = 1$ (see also Remark 13.36 (ii) in [5]). In this case, a "ladder"-based implementation of the scalar multiplication requires exactly $5.2n$ multiplications and $4n$ squarings in $\mathbb{F}_p$, i.e. $5.2M + 4S$ per bit, which is still a lot more than the $3.5M + 2.75S$ of the GLV method with JSF-representation of the two half-length scalars.

5   Conclusions

We introduced a Java implementation of scalar multiplication on a GLV curve over a 174-bit prime field. Our implementation supports arbitrary base points (making it suitable for ECDH key exchange) and is optimized to reach high performance, low memory footprint and small bytecode size. Furthermore, the described implementation is highly self-contained as it needs only a few classes from the standard Java class library. On a Thinkpad T60 with a 1.66 GHz Core Duo processor, our GLV method reaches a throughput of 3,000 scalar multiplications per second, which is about 45 times higher than the throughput of the widely-used Bouncy Castle library for J2ME. The scalar multiplication time on mobile phones ranges from less than 2 ms (HTC Desire S) to roughly 400.2 ms (Nokia 6610). We attribute the high performance of our GLV technique to the efficiency of both the field and group arithmetic. The radix-2^{29} representation of field elements allows for a branch-less implementation of the field arithmetic modulo $p = 2^{174} - 3$, which facilitates the execution on JiT-enabled JVMs. We also demonstrated that, when exploiting their endomorphism, GLV curves are considerably faster than ordinary Weierstraß curves or Montgomery curves. In summary, our measured results confirm the great potential of GLV curves and PM prime fields for the implementation of high-speed EC cryptography.

The full Java source code of the implementation described in this paper is available for download at `https://cryptolux.org`.

References

1. ARM Limited: Jazelle^{TM}– ARM® Architecture Extensions for Java Applications. White paper (October 2000),
   `http://www.arm.com/armtech/jazelle?OpenDocument`
2. Arnold, K., Gosling, J., Holmes, D.: The Java^{TM} Programming Language, 4th edn. Prentice Hall (2005)
3. Barrett, P.: Implementing the Rivest Shamir and Adleman Public Key Encryption Algorithm on a Standard Digital Signal Processor. In: Odlyzko, A.M. (ed.) CRYPTO 1986. LNCS, vol. 263, pp. 311–323. Springer, Heidelberg (1987)
4. Bernstein, D.J.: Curve25519: New Diffie-Hellman Speed Records. In: Yung, M., Dodis, Y., Kiayias, A., Malkin, T. (eds.) PKC 2006. LNCS, vol. 3958, pp. 207–228. Springer, Heidelberg (2006)
5. Cohen, H., Frey, G.: Handbook of Elliptic and Hyperelliptic Curve Cryptography, Discrete Mathematics and Its Applications, vol. 34. Chapmann & Hall\CRC (2006)
6. Comba, P.G.: Exponentiation cryptosystems on the IBM PC. IBM Systems Journal 29(4), 526–538 (1990)
7. Craig, I.D.: Virtual Machines. Springer (2006)
8. Cramer, T., Friedman, R., Miller, T., Seberger, D., Wilson, R., Wolczko, M.: Compiling Java just in time. IEEE Micro 17(3), 36–43 (1997)
9. Crandall, R.E.: Method and apparatus for public key exchange in a cryptographic system (October 1992), U.S. Patent No. 5,159,632
10. Edwards, H.M.: A normal form for elliptic curves. Bulletin of the American Mathematical Society 44(3), 393–422 (2007)
11. Galbraith, S.D., Lin, X., Scott, M.: Endomorphisms for Faster Elliptic Curve Cryptography on a Large Class of Curves. In: Joux, A. (ed.) EUROCRYPT 2009. LNCS, vol. 5479, pp. 518–535. Springer, Heidelberg (2009)
12. Gallant, R.P., Lambert, R.J., Vanstone, S.A.: Faster Point Multiplication on Elliptic Curves with Efficient Endomorphisms. In: Kilian, J. (ed.) CRYPTO 2001. LNCS, vol. 2139, pp. 190–200. Springer, Heidelberg (2001)
13. Gosling, J., McGilton, H.: The Java^{TM} Language Environment. White paper. Sun Microsystems, Inc., Mountain View (1996)

14. Großschädl, J., Avanzi, R.M., Savaş, E., Tillich, S.: Energy-Efficient Software Implementation of Long Integer Modular Arithmetic. In: Rao, J.R., Sunar, B. (eds.) CHES 2005. LNCS, vol. 3659, pp. 75–90. Springer, Heidelberg (2005)
15. Hankerson, D.R., Menezes, A.J., Vanstone, S.A.: Guide to Elliptic Curve Cryptography. Springer (2004)
16. Hennessy, J.L., Jouppi, N.P., Baskett, F., Gross, T.R., Gill, J.: Hardware/software tradeoffs for increased performance. In: Proceedings of the 1st International Symposium on Architectural Support for Programming Languages and Operating Systems (ASPLOS 1982), pp. 2–11. ACM Press (1982)
17. Institute of Electrical and Electronics Engineers (IEEE): IEEE Std 1363-2000: IEEE Standard Specifications for Public-Key Cryptography (August 2000)
18. Koblitz, N.: CM-Curves with Good Cryptographic Properties. In: Feigenbaum, J. (ed.) CRYPTO 1991. LNCS, vol. 576, pp. 279–287. Springer, Heidelberg (1992)
19. Menezes, A.J., van Oorschot, P.C., Vanstone, S.A.: Handbook of Applied Cryptography. CRC Press (1996)
20. Möller, B.: Securing Elliptic Curve Point Multiplication against Side-Channel Attacks. In: Davida, G.I., Frankel, Y. (eds.) ISC 2001. LNCS, vol. 2200, pp. 324–334. Springer, Heidelberg (2001)
21. Montgomery, P.L.: Speeding the Pollard and elliptic curve methods of factorization. Mathematics of Computation 48(177), 243–264 (1987)
22. Smart, N.P. (ed.): ECRYPT II Yearly Report on Algorithms and Keysizes (2009-2010). European Network of Excellence in Cryptology (ECRYPT II) (March 2010), deliverable D.SPA.13, http://www.ecrypt.eu.org/documents/D.SPA.13.pdf
23. Solinas, J.A.: Low-weight binary representations for pairs of integers. Tech. Rep. CORR 2001-41, Centre for Applied Cryptographic Research (CACR), University of Waterloo, Waterloo, Canada (2001)
24. Standards for Efficient Cryptography Group (SECG): SEC 1: Elliptic Curve Cryptography (May 2009), http://www.secg.org
25. Stiftung Secure Information and Communication Technologies (SIC): IAIK JCE Micro Edition (Version 3.04) (September 2006), http://jce.iaik.tugraz.at/sic/Products/Mobile-Security/JCE-ME
26. The Legion of the Bouncy Castle: Lightweight Cryptography API (Release 1.47) (March 2012), http://www.bouncycastle.org
27. Tillich, S., Großschädl, J.: A Survey of Public-Key Cryptography on J2ME-Enabled Mobile Devices. In: Aykanat, C., Dayar, T., Körpeoğlu, İ. (eds.) ISCIS 2004. LNCS, vol. 3280, pp. 935–944. Springer, Heidelberg (2004)
28. White, J.P., Hemphill, D.A.: Java 2 Micro Edition. Manning Publications (2002)
29. Wiener, M.J., Zuccherato, R.J.: Faster Attacks on Elliptic Curve Cryptosystems. In: Tavares, S., Meijer, H. (eds.) SAC 1998. LNCS, vol. 1556, pp. 190–200. Springer, Heidelberg (1999)
30. Yanık, T., Savaş, E., Koç, Ç.K.: Incomplete reduction in modular arithmetic. IEE Proceedings – Computers and Digital Techniques 149(2), 46–52 (2002)

Kynoid: Real-Time Enforcement
of Fine-Grained, User-Defined, and Data-Centric
Security Policies for Android

Daniel Schreckling, Joachim Posegga, Johannes Köstler, and Matthias Schaff

Institute of IT-Security and Security Law
University of Passau, Germany
{ds,jp}@sec.uni-passau.de, {koestler,schaffma}@fim.uni-passau.de
http://web.sec.uni-passau.de/

Abstract. We introduce Kynoid, a real-time monitoring and enforcement framework for Android. Kynoid is based on user-defined security
policies which are defined for data-items. This allows users to define temporal, spatial, and destination constraints which have to hold for single
items. We introduce an innovative approach to allow for the real-time
tracking and enforcement of such policies. In this way, Kynoid is the
first extension of Android which enables the sharing of resources while
respecting individual security policies for the data-items stored in these
resources. We outline Kynoid's architecture, present its operation and
discuss it in terms of applicability, performance, and usability. By providing a proof-of-concept implementation we further show the feasibility
of our framework.

Keywords: Android, security, security policies, information flow.

1 Introduction

The distribution of Smartphones to employees becomes more and more interesting for companies. They enable unified and simplified communication as well as
permanent reachability. These companies also tend to weaken their traditional
security requirements by weakening guidelines and restrictions on these devices
to avoid that users replace their business Smartphone and use other means of
communication for private purposes. At the same time, modern platforms have
seen a tremendous increase in innovative applications. They provide easy access
to web and cloud services and support the user in their daily activities. This
trend is enforced by simple and handy APIs which inspire private application
developers. As a consequence, application markets have become very popular
from a developer as well as from a consumer perspective.

1.1 Information Processing in Today's Smart-Phones

This development needs support by feasible Smartphone operating system platforms. Among other requirements, the ability to share information between applications, is essential. However, the security mechanisms which are currently

I. Askoxylakis, H.C. Pöhls, and J. Posegga (Eds.): WISTP 2012, LNCS 7322, pp. 208–223, 2012.
© IFIP International Federation for Information Processing 2012

available to control access and enforce specific security requirements are not suitable and insufficient.

Assume a very common situation in which a company distributes Smartphones to their employees. The company allows the private use of the cell phone including the installation of applications. Thus, the resources of this Smartphone, e.g. the address book, the file storage, or the browser history and bookmark database, will contain private as well as business data-items. From a privacy and from a confidentiality point of view, this is an unbearable situation in particular if we consider currently available security mechanisms protecting this information. Modern smart-phone operating systems use widely deployed access control mechanisms and sandboxing techniques. These concepts are mainly based on process privileges (capabilities) or execution profiles [1,7,8,11,18]. They grant coarse grained access to resources or processes. Once the access rights are granted to a particular process, it can perform the respective operations on the complete resource. Hence, access rights are selected for each application individually. Potentially malicious execution contexts are ignored.

Several approaches improve this situation by addressing both, the granularity of available security policies, as well as their consistency. However, they also focus on process centric security policies. As a consequence these security frameworks cannot have the level of granularity required to express security policies for individual data items. All data processed by the application is subject to the same security enforcement. Thus, it is not surprising that applications often synchronise even private or confidential contacts with inappropriate infrastructures. In our setting, an employee may install an application for a social platform. If the application gains access to a shared resource, e.g. the address book, it can accidentally start to synchronise it with the social platform, including potentially critical data.

1.2   Contribution

We define a framework which allows for the real-time tracking of fine-grained and user-controlled security policies in Android: Kynoid. We enhance the taint-tracking system TaintDroid [5] and distinguish not only between coarse grained data-sources but introduce security policies for individual data-items. In this way, a user can dynamically specify location and temporal constraints where and when data can be processed and restrict the destinations to which data-items are allowed to be distributed. Kynoid enforces these individual security policies at data sinks. In so doing, Kynoid overcomes the capability-, process-centric, and coarse grained security models implemented in todays' Smartphone operating systems. Through the implementation of a first unoptimised prototype, Kynoid further shows that it is not justified to assume that the tracking of complicated security policies during runtime is very expensive and therefore not suitable. Thus, our contribution introduces the first approach which is able to define security policies for single data items and which allows their dynamic enforcement.

We structure our contribution as follows: Section 2 explains the fundamentals of Android required to understand the work presented in this contribution. Afterwards, Section 3 gives an informal overview of our solution before Section 4 introduces the theoretical and technical details of Kynoid. Section 5 discusses the influence of Kynoid in terms of applicability, performance, and usability. Finally, Section 6 compares it with related work and Section 7 concludes this work and outlines future research.

2   Background: Android and TaintDroid

Android is a popular software stack for mobile phones developed by Google. Apart from some device drivers and the telephony stack, Android is open source. It builds on an embedded Linux and its libraries which are mainly programmed in C/C++. Android allows the use of these libraries through an application framework which is implemented in the Java programming language. Therefore, Android can be considered as a middle-ware [6] between a Linux system and the applications programmed for the Android platform.

2.1   Dalvik Virtual Machine

Applications intended to run on Android must also be written in Java and are compiled into custom byte-code. It is executed by the Dalvik virtual machine (VM) which is register-based and optimised for running on devices with limited resources[1]. Each VM instance runs in a dedicated UNIX process with an individual user and group identifier. The Dalvik EXecutable (DEX file) is zipped into an Android Package (apk file) together with application specific data, and configuration files, e.g. a manifest.

2.2   Security Architecture

The Dalvik VM is also an essential part of the security enforcement in Android. It centrally monitors security relevant activities such as the control and forwarding of intents, the access to protected APIs, the use of content providers, etc.

Applications use the manifest to specify the permissions required to run. It can request the permission to use specific API functions, forbid other applications to access activities defined by itself, define which broadcast events an application processes, etc. The respective permissions are granted at installation time. This is either done automatically by the system or requires user interaction if the permission to be granted belong to a specific protection level. All permissions must be granted, otherwise the application is not installed. During execution, if an application requested more permissions than specified in the manifest, the Android runtime environment informs the user and terminates the application execution.

---

[1] Available at http://www.dalvikvm.com/ (January 2012)

For data storage, every application possesses a separate data directory. Android uses the access control mechanisms provided by Linux to protect the data contained in this directory. Various APIs can be used to store data in files or databases. Data exchange between Android applications is accomplished by content providers or by intents. As mentioned above, access to content providers and intents is also defined in the application manifest.

2.3 Security Issues and Deficiencies

Additionally, applications can define specific access control mechanisms by delegating access to resources. An intent equipped with the correct permissions can be sent to a delegated application to grant access to a resource which is specified by a URI. Delegation is required to temporarily allow access to specific resources without granting complete access to all other resources. This security enforcement works if each developer implements his own security framework performing the correct access decisions. However, individual developers must decide at design and implementation time which security policies would fit the user and application. This generates strong dependencies among applications as applications requesting data always depend on other applications which enforce specific security policies. However, address or media databases, etc. often must offer direct access to stand-alone applications. Therefore, to not restrict the usability of his application, a developer would have to implement a multitude of access control functions or content providers. Only this will guarantee that current and future applications will be able to gain access to the appropriate data.

Thus, the process of assigning permissions in Android is not suitable. The user must decide which permissions an application should possess. From a data-centric point of view, a user has to consider which permissions assigned to an application may compromise his data. Even if the user had the ability to keep an overview of all applications installed in the system, their interaction mechanisms, and if he were aware of the security implications of all permissions, he would not be able to modify the requested permissions. Not accepting or revoking permissions would not prevent the installation of an application or require its de-installation. This coarse grained permission system results in an *all or nothing approach*. Although an application should only have access to a small fraction of data stored in a resource, it either gains access to all information or the application cannot be executed.

The situation is even worse. Permissions granted by the user or system implicitly generate trust chains between applications. In this way, applications can gain access to data items although they did not explicitly ask for it. As a consequence, the execution of an application may directly conflict with the security requirements a user implicitly expects for specific data items.

2.4 TaintDroid

TaintDroid is a taint tracking extension for Android optimized for Smartphones performance. It is mainly enabled by modifying the Dalvik VM and introducing taint tracking on the variable level. For this purpose, TaintDroid introduces shadow variables. As the VM stores local variables and arguments on an internal stack, the original taint tracking system modified this stack structure by doubling the space each variable requires on the stack. This additional space is used for a 32-bit taint value.

The 32-bits of the taint values are used to identify the privacy critical data sources which influence a data item, e.g. the contact provider or data in the telephony or location manager. To set the appropriate taint bits, TaintDroid modifies the system libraries which retrieve the requested data. These modifications modify the appropriate taint values in the Dalvik VM. These taint values are processed in a similar way at the data sinks, e.g. network sockets. Before a variable is processed by a data sink the respective taint value is retrieved. Its value is written to the system log and an appropriate warning is generated if privacy related information leaks.

Kynoid uses the infrastructure provided by TaintDroid, i.e. we use the modifications within the Dalvik VM and adjust or extend them for our purposes. The next sections describe these adaptations.

3 Approach Overview

Our work is based on the tracking framework TaintDroid [5]. TaintDroid tags data sources in Android, e.g. the address book, or the browser data, and tracks them during runtime. These tracking mechanisms are enabled by modifications of the underlying Dalvik virtual machine and the corresponding libraries which form the interface between the applications and the execution environment. The tracking capabilities can be used to log applications which gain access to the data sources of Android and misuse the information stored therein. However, this approach, even if it was used for permission enforcement, such as in AppFence [9], is far too coarse grained to effectively support a practical permission system which allows for resources containing security critical and non-critical data at the same time.

Recollect our motivating example in Section 1. A shared resource, such as the address book, contains private as well as business data. The Smartphone is open for private use and allows the installation of applications which may use this shared resource. Once granted in the Android permission system, an application may simply use all the information stored in this resource. Thus, all data items stored in this resource share the same permission. Similarly, TaintDroid and AppFence, use a one-fits-all paradigm to track and enforce the information usage, e.g. to prevent its transmission to some recipients. However, this is not feasible for real life scenarios. In fact, different data items stored within a shared resource often have different security requirements. Therefore, Kynoid extends TaintDroid to support the tracking of security policies for single data items.

TaintDroid uses an approach which is comparable to shadow variables (see Section 2.4). They only exist in the interpreter and store the taint tags associated with a variable. Special instructions which are located at the data sources set particular bits in these taint tags. Every bit accounts for a particular data source. During the run of the application, simple bit operations combine the bit fields depending on the type of instruction executed in the interpreter. At the sink, the single bits of the taint tags are evaluated and reported. In this approach, the number of different taint tags is limited to the number of bits in the shadow variable. TaintDroid currently supports a 32 bit field and thus 32 different tags, which can only cover the main data sources in Android.

We decided to use a more generic approach and use the 32 bit space of the shadow variable for identifiers (ID). In this way, we associate each variable in an Android executable with an ID which is again associated with a policy. This allows us to basically map 2^{32} variables to an arbitrary number of security policies (depending on how security policies are identified).

However, this simple change in the interpretation of the shadow variable yields some problems. The policy propagation becomes slightly more complicated in comparison to TaintDroid. Assume an interpreter instruction in the dex file, such as an addition, on two variables which carry two different taint tags in their shadow variables. The taint propagation logic in TaintDroid simply combines the shadow variables by using a bitwise OR. This sets the bits, which correspond to the appropriate data sources. Thus, the shadow variable of the result of the binary operation now indicates that the result has been influenced by both data sources.

Kynoid does not track simple taints but IDs which indirectly correspond to combinations of security policies. Thus, a simple binary operation on these IDs is not feasible. The efficiency also forbids the evaluation of the corresponding policies with their modal constraints into a new security policy during runtime. In fact, this would also induce tremendous runtime and memory overhead as the generation and registration of an instance of a data structure which stores this security policy would also be required. As a consequence, Kynoid builds a dependency graph which uses a simple graph structure to store the runtime combinations of policies. At the sink the appropriate graph is evaluated to derive the correct security policy.

4   Kynoid

Kynoid is the prototypical realisation of our dynamic, fine-grained policy tracking system. The next sections explain how this *watchdog* administrates, retrieves, tracks, and enforces security policies for data processed by an untrusted application. We introduce the Kynoid architecture and its modifications.

4.1   Framework Operation

Figure 1 gives an overview on the high-level architecture of Kynoid and sketches the modifications of the Android runtime environment to allow for the tracking of security policies. We explain the single entities of this architecture and their interaction by assuming the execution of an application. Although Google just

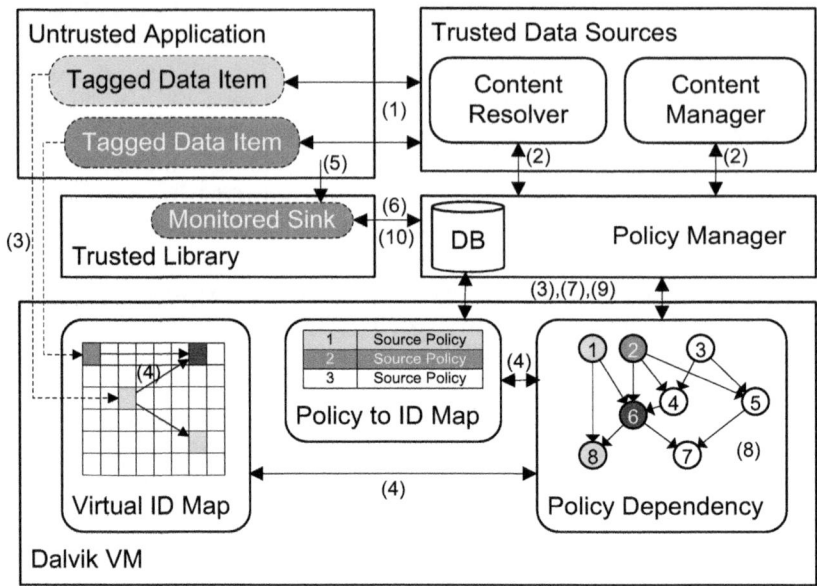

Fig. 1. Kynoid Architecture

introduced new mechanisms which allow the automatic verification of applications, we assume Android applications to be untrusted. This is particularly true for applications which stem from third-party-markets. Thus, the installed application can contain potentially malicious execution paths. It can use shared data sources (1) by using so called content providers or by accessing content managers. Content managers and content resolvers, which content providers connect to, are considered to be trusted data sources, i.e. they are delivered with the Android OS. As soon as these trusted components access data, they also query the Policy Manager (2) for a reference to the security policy associated with the requested data items. The policy manager then interacts with the Dalvik VM (3) and registers this policy reference with a unique identifier. It corresponds to the variable which contains the data item requested by the untrusted application. This association is stored in the policy to ID map.

During execution, Kynoid must correctly propagate (4) the identifiers which link the variables to the corresponding policies. For this purpose Kynoid uses a Policy Dependency graph. It stores binary dependencies among policy IDs. Every node in the graph represents a variable. A directed edge from node n to node k denotes that the information of the variable represented by node n flows into node k. Thus, the security requirement of node k depends on the security requirements for node n. More precisely, the security requirements which hold for node n must also hold in node k. Nodes without incoming edges are source nodes, i.e. their security policy is explicitly defined by the security constraints stored in the policy manager. Such policies are called *source policies*.

If an interpreter instruction or sequence of instructions combines two variables we would have to compute a new policy which holds for this variable. The computation of this policy during runtime would induce tremendous overhead as the Dalvik VM would either have to query the security policy for each item from the policy manager and administrate all newly generated policies. Using the dependency graph, such computations boil down to the creation of new nodes and their corresponding edges in the graph. Compared to the computation of a complete policy, the runtime overhead is negligible. However, depending on the execution flow and runtime of an application the memory overhead may become substantial. Therefore, Kynoid only builds dependency graphs for variables which contain information influenced by data-items which carry security policies.

Also, the complete administration of the policies by the Dalvik VM would not be feasible as the policy may change during execution. Thus, the security requirements loaded in the Dalvik VM may already be obsolete. Therefore, Kynoid postpones this computation until a data item is actually processed at a sink (5). At this point, Kynoid starts to the derive the security policy linked with this variables. For this purpose, Kynoid can assume all libraries to be trusted which are delivered with the Android system and provide writing access to resources. They basically act as policy enforcmenet points. In our prototype this is the Apache library which allows Android to send GET or POST requests to remote servers. In general, we could use any type of sink, i.e. other network sinks, e.g. sockets, can be monitored as well as other data sinks such as data base sinks, file system sinks, etc. Thus, as soon as the application tries to send a request the trusted library contacts the policy manager. The latter resolves the ID (7) delivered by the library and uses the dependency graph (8) to infer the correct policy for the processed variable. For this purpose we access the node in the graph which represents this variable and determine all of its predecessors. As soon as we arrive at source nodes a list of policy references associated with these nodes can be returned to the policy manager (9). The policy manager can now compute the correct security policy and enforce it by joining all these policies.

As an example consider node 6 of the dependency graph in Figure 1. To derive the security constraints for the variable associated with this node the source policies associated with the nodes 1,2, and 3 are required.

4.2   Policy Propagation

To correctly propagate the policy identifiers, Kynoid uses a concept which is comparable to the variable-level taint tracking within the Dalvik VM applied in TaintDroid. It mainly distinguishes in the values propagated during execution. Instead of tracking bit fields, which represent taint values, Kynoid tracks identifiers. As mentioned above, these identifiers can be associated with policies or their combinations. Thus, we have to introduce an appropriate propagation logic. This data flow logic does currently not consider implicit flows.

We assume $\mathfrak{I}$ to be the set of possible policy identifiers for our system. For efficiency reasons, the virtual memory address of a variable represents the identifier for this variable. This has the advantage that we do not have to ensure uniqueness of the identifiers within one process and several access operationscan be performed in $O(1)$. As mentioned in Section 2.4, the Dalvik VM offers five variable types. We choose the same representation as in [5] and denote local and argument variables by v_x. In the virtual machine, they represent virtual registers. Further, field variables of a class x are denoted as f_x. Without the indication of an instance object, f_x denotes a static field. If v_x denotes an instance object, $v_x(f_x)$ denotes an instance field of object referenced in v_x. Finally, $v[\cdot]$ denotes an array, where the variable v_x contains the reference to this array.

To access the policy identifiers of the variable types listed above we define the virtual identifier function ι. $\iota(v)$ returns the identifier associated with variable v. At the same time $\iota(v)$ can also assign a policy identifier to variable v. The interpretation of ι depends on its position in respect to the $\leftarrow$ symbol. Located on the right hand side of $\leftarrow$, $\iota(v)$ reads the identifier for variable v. On the left hand side $\iota(v)$ is used to set the identifier value for v. We further define the graph $G = (E, V)$ with the node set $V \subseteq \Im$ and the directed edges $E \subseteq V \times V$. It denotes the directed dependency graph used for storing the policy dependencies. To update this graph we define the function $\theta : \wp(G) \times \Im \leftarrow \wp(G) \times \Im \times \Im$ in the following way: $\theta(G', c) \leftarrow (G, a, b)$ with $a, b, c \in \Im, G' = (V \cup \{c\}, E \cup \{(a, c), (b, c)\})$. Here, $\wp(G)$ denotes all valid dependency graphs. With this definition θ creates a new node in the dependency graph and two direct edges which start at the already existing nodes a and b and end in node c and returns the modified graph and the new node, i.e. the policy identifier. Thus, $(G, \iota(v_c)) \leftarrow \theta(G, \iota(v_A), \iota(v_B))$ will modify the dependency graph by inserting the new node $\iota(v_c)$ and adding the edges $(\iota(v_A), \iota(v_C))$ and $(\iota(v_B), \iota(v_C))$.

With this information we can read the propagation logic in Table 1. To reduce redundancy and remain readable we only list the abstracted byte code versions of the instructions described in the DEX specification. Our propagation logic is very similar to the one presented in [5]. This is due to the fact that regular taint propagation is identical to policy identifier propagation if the content of the respective markings is not altered. However, as soon as there are combinations of policy identifiers, i.e. for any binary, array, or field operation, we have to modify the logic.

4.3 Inter-process Policy Tracking

Inter-applications communication is common in Android. Therefore, TaintDroid also propagates taint tags between processes (each VM runs in a separate process). To maintain overall efficiency, TaintDroid uses message level tainting, i.e. a message is assigned the upper bound of all taint tags of the variables contained in the parcel. Of course, this overestimation can generate false positives during execution. We aim at a more precise tracking system which stays on the variable level and does not decline to message-level tracking. To remain efficient, Kynoid uses a simple inter-policy-process mapping (see Figure 2). It simply maps the policy identifiers of the variables exchange between the two processes. As the policy identifiers correspond to the memory address of the variables, this mapping

Table 1. Policy Propagation Logic. Register variables and class fields are referenced by v_X and f_X, respectively. R and E are the return and exception variables maintained within the interpreter. C is a byte-code constant.

Op Format	Op Semantics	Taint Propagation	Description
$const\text{-}op\ v_A C$	$v_A \leftarrow C$	$\iota(v_A) \leftarrow 0$	Delete v_A ID
$move\text{-}op\ v_A v_B$	$v_A \leftarrow v_B$	$\iota(v_A) \leftarrow \iota(v_B)$	Set v_A ID to the ID of v_B
$return\text{-}op\ v_A$	$R \leftarrow v_A$	$\iota(R) \leftarrow \iota(v_A)$	Set the ID for the return value to v_A (0 if void)
$move\text{-}op\text{-}R\ v_A$	$v_A \leftarrow R$	$\iota(v_A) \leftarrow \iota(R)$	Set v_A ID to the ID of the return value
$throw\text{-}op\ v_A$	$E \leftarrow v_A$	$\iota(E) \leftarrow \iota(v_A)$	Set the ID of the exception taint to v_A
$move\text{-}op\text{-}E\ v_A$	$v_A \leftarrow E$	$\iota(v_A) \leftarrow \iota(E)$	Set v_A ID to the ID of the exception value
$unary\text{-}op\ v_A v_B$	$v_A \leftarrow \otimes v_B$	$\iota(v_A) \leftarrow \iota(v_B)$	Set v_A ID to the ID of v_B
$bin\text{-}op\ v_A v_B v_C$	$v_A \leftarrow v_B \otimes v_C$	$(G, \iota(v_A)) \leftarrow$ $\theta(G, \iota(v_A), \iota(v_B))$	Create new ID for v_A and store dependency on $\iota(v_A)$ and $\iota(v_B)$
$bin\text{-}op\ v_A v_B C$	$v_A \leftarrow v_B \otimes C$	$\iota(v_A) \leftarrow \iota(v_B)$	Set v_A ID to the ID of v_B
$aput\text{-}op\ v_A v_B v_C$	$v_B[v_C] \leftarrow v_A$	$(G, \iota(v_B[\cdot])) \leftarrow$ $\theta(G, \iota(v_B[\cdot]), \iota(v_A))$	Create new ID for $v_B[\cdot]$ and store dependency on $\iota(v_B[\cdot])$ and $\iota(v_A)$
$aget\text{-}op\ v_A v_B v_C$	$v_A \leftarrow v_B[v_C]$	$(G, \iota(v_A)) \leftarrow$ $\theta(G, \iota(v_B[\cdot]), \iota(v_C))$	Create new ID for v_A and store dependency on $\iota(v_B[\cdot])$ and $\iota(v_C)$
$sput\text{-}op\ v_A f_B$	$f_B \leftarrow v_A$	$\iota(f_B) \leftarrow \iota(v_A)$	Set field ID for f_B to ID of v_A
$sget\text{-}op\ v_A f_B$	$v_A \leftarrow f_B$	$\iota(v_A) \leftarrow \iota(f_B)$	Set ID of v_A to ID of field $\iota(f_B)$
$iput\text{-}op\ v_A v_B f_C$	$v_B(f_C) \leftarrow v_A$	$\iota(v_B(f_C)) \leftarrow \iota(v_A)$	Set field ID for f_C to ID of v_A
$iget\text{-}op\ v_A v_B f_C$	$v_A \leftarrow v_B(f_C)$	$(G, \iota(v_A)) \leftarrow$ $\theta(G, \iota(v_B(f_C)), \iota(v_B))$	Create new ID for v_A and store dependency on $\iota(v_B(f_C))$ and $\iota(v_B)$

process is very efficient. To resolve the security policy at the sink and allow for its evaluation Kynoid simply queries the corresponding processes to determine the identifiers of the involved source policies. The policy manager can resolve those and enforce the security policies accordingly.

Apart from this, the IPC in Kynoid communication is similar to TaintDroids' IPC. It modifies the binder library which is used by Android to accomplish inter process communication. A hook takes care of the modifications in the message exchanged between the processes and the modifications of the policy-process mapping.

4.4   Policy Derivation and Enforcement

So far we did not present the security policies defined in Kynoid. This shows another strength of our tracking system. In general, it is independent of the type of security policy to be enforced. For completeness, we consider a simple policy specification language which can describe policies with temporal, spatial, and remote host constraints. They are defined on a data-item with identifier i and consist of triples of the form $(T, S, H)_i$ where T is a set of time intervals, S is a set of circular perimeters, and H is a set of IPs of remote hosts. If a set is empty, no constraint is defined for the respective modal dimension. If a set contains more than one element, the elements are interpreted as disjunctions. We further define the operator $\wedge$ on the policies which is similar to the interpretation known from Boolean logic. $(T, S, H)_i \wedge (T', S', H')_k$ means that all constraints specified for data-items with identifiers i and k have to hold.

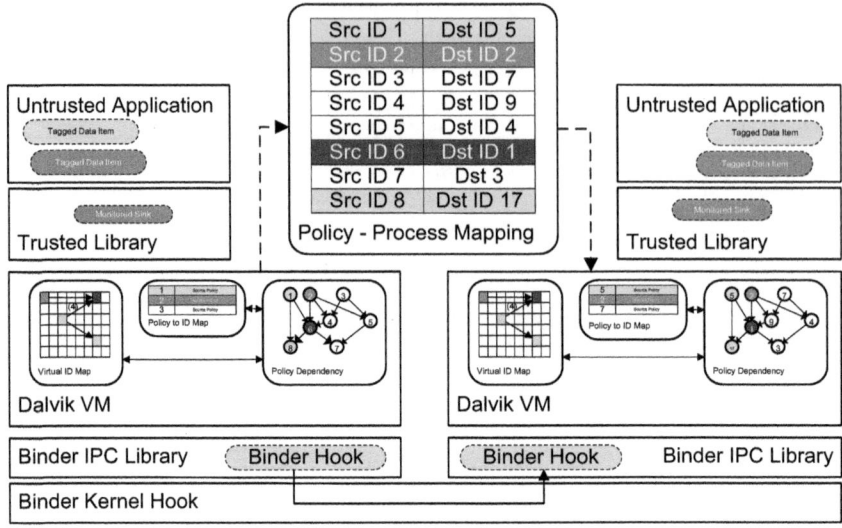

Fig. 2. Inter-Process Policy Tracking

As already sketched in Section 4.1 we use the dependency graph $G = (V, E)$ to determine the policies which have to be evaluated if a variable v is processed at the sink. For this purpose we define the function $Pred : \wp(G) \times \Im \to \wp(\Im)$ which delivers all predecessor nodes with no incoming edges, i.e. those variables for which a security policy has been defined in the policy manager. It can be used to determine the set P of variables which influenced v: $P = Pred(G, i_v)$. To determine whether variable v can be used in the execution context, the policy manager only has to verify that the policy $\bigwedge_{p \in P}(T, S, H)_p$ holds.

While our concept can be adapted to different types of sinks, we currently only consider network sinks. Thus, as soon as an application tries to send information stored in variable v using the network interface the policy $(T, S, H)_v$ is informally interpreted as: *Only send v to one of the hosts with IP addresses listed in H if the current time is in one of the time intervals specified in T, and if the phone is located at one of the locations specified in S.* In this case, the default action, if the policy does not hold, is to reject the further processing of the data item v. In fact, our proof-of-concept implementation also supports policies which have a positive default action, i.e. the further processing is only allowed if all constraints do not match. However, to maintain simplicity and due to spatial constraints we do not define these rules here.

5   Discussion

This section discusses Kynoid in terms of its added value to the existing Android platform, its performance, and in terms of its usability.

5.1   Applicability

We experimented with well known applications which tend to synchronise user data, e.g. the Facebook App. If the user does not pay attention during its first run this application may synchronise the complete address book with the facebook servers. Kynoid allows to select the contacts we like to synchronise with Facebook. Using Kynoid's administration interface, we can select our business contacts and specify that they should only be transmitted to a specific remote host. If we now start our Facebook application again it is still able to synchronise the data stored in our contacts database. However, Kynoid blocks all connections if they contain data items we marked to be business contacts. This simple example shows that even with the rudimental user interface we offer in our prototype, it is already possible to provide an added value in comparison to existing solutions.

5.2   Performance

When we started this work, the main concern was the runtime overhead induced by the tracking of complex security policies. Kynoid efficiently addresses this problem by using a graph structure which stores the flow of information between variables. It avoids policy evaluations every time more than one variable which is associated with a security policy writes into another variable. Instead of evaluating the policies during policy propagation, Kynoid only evaluates policies where they are enforced. This is done by a fast graph resolution which determines the source policies which influence a graph node. To measure this overhead we implemented a benchmark application which reads 100 entries from the bookmark database. This generates a basic dependency graph in the Dalvik VM. This benchmark was executed 50 times on a Nexus One with Android 2.2 patched with Kynoid. This delivered an average runtime of 2376 ms with a standard deviation of 89 ms. The same benchmark, was also run for our Kynoid proof-of-concept implementation with disabled tracking capabilities, i.e. no dependency graph was created. This generated an average runtime of 2292 ms with a standard deviation of 91 ms. Thus, the generation of the dependency graph for the policy IDs produces an overhead of 3.7%.

The runtime overhead produced by the propagation of policy identifiers is negligible in comparison to the TaintDroid implementation. The benchmarks applied to our proof-of-concept did not produce meaningful results in this respect. This is not surprising as the taint propagation is very similar to TaintDroid (see also Section 4.2). The memory overhead generated by the dependency graph strongly depends on the implementation of an application. An appropriate study of different applications executed by our framework can deliver appropriate estimations of the average memory overhead.

Major overhead is generated by the data base queries of the policy manager. On an Android 2.2 stock image our benchmark shows an average runtime of 740 ms with a standard deviation of 52 ms. Thus, our proof-of-concept implementation of Kynoid produces an overhead of 321% with the selected benchmark. This is also not surprising as the non-optimised policy manager induces tremendous overhead as it administrates the security policies in a database. In turn, database access is performance critical in Android. Although, the policy management was not focus of this work, we are positive to be able to reduce this overhead. We have already shown such a performance optimization for Constroid [19]. In this security policy management system, we were able to reduce the runtime overhead to $21 - 22\%$.

5.3   Usability

Most of the operations of Kynoid are transparent. In particular, the policy propagation is completely invisible for the user. Also the enforcement is mainly transparent although our prototype generates some warning messages to inform the user about blocked requests not compliant with the defined security policies.

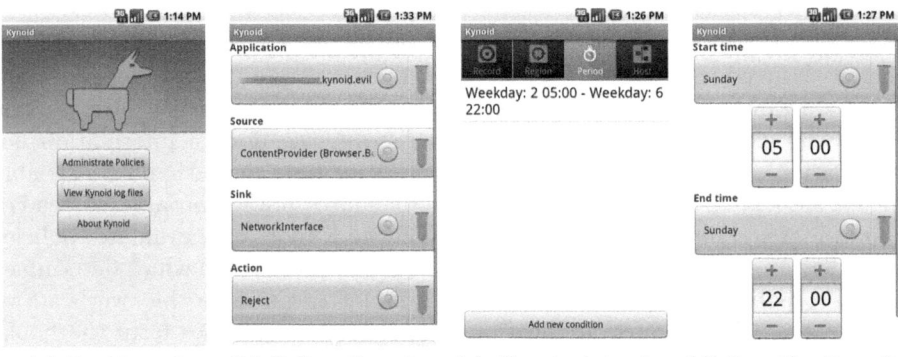

(a) Dashboard   (b) Policy Creation   (c) Constraint view (d) Specification of a
                                         for the security pol-   temporal constraint
                                         icy of a single data
                                         item

Fig. 3. Kynoid administration tool

However, for the front-end, the Kynoid proof-of-concept implementation provides a graphical user interface. Figure 3 shows some screenshots of the basic functionalities of the front-end. Through a dashboard (see Figure 3(a)) the user can administrate the security policies specified for the data-items of different data sources. To create new policies the user must first select (see Figure 3(b) the source for the data items for which policy constraints should be defined. After also selecting the type of sink for which the policy should be created in a specific application, the user can also determine the action to be performed when the policy matches. In Figure 3(b) we will define a policy for a data item in the browser database, and define a rejection policy for the network sink. On the next screen, Figure 3(c), the user can use the different tabs to define the various temporal, spatial, and host constraints for the data item he chose on the record tab. Exemplarily, Figure 3(d) show how the user can define a temporal constraint.

6   Related Work

The body of literature in the realm of taint tracking for policy enforcement is huge. Due to spatial constraints, this section focuses on the most relevant approaches.

Panorama [21], Trishul [12], TaintDroid [5], and AppFence [9] are very similar to Kynoid. This is not surprising as Kynoid is based on TaintDroid. All of these frameworks track security properties. However, the granularity of all these approaches stay on the process level and or a coarse grained resource which does not allow for much flexibility.

Porscha [15] and T-UCON [13], DRM frameworks based on TaintDroid and Trishul respectively, allow content sources to define security policies. The basic idea to protect individual data is close to our approach. However, these systems focus on DRM protected content. Secondly, Porscha and T-UCON only mediate the exchange of data between applications, Kynoid ensures compliance of data usage during execution. The European project S3MS also generated a series of publications [2,3,4,17]. They implement the concept of security by contract, specifying policies according to which an application should behave. Of course, this approach is application-centric as well.

Saint [16] and Apex [14] extend Androids permission mechanism by allowing to define rules for granting permissions and by allowing the denial of permission subsets. However, these constraints are static, enforced at runtime, and maintain the coarse granularity of the Android permission system. The same holds for Kirin [6]. It is a security service which analyses the configuration of an Android application and detects potential security issues. It does not track information to enforce security. Finally, Constroid [19] also defines a management framework for data-centric security policies of fine granularity. However, it also does not show how to track and enforce these policies.

Other platforms such as Asbestos [20], HiStar [22], Flume [10] perform information flow tracking in decentralised environments, however their architectural overhead is large compared to their granularity which also stay on the process and resource level.

Hence, Kynoid clearly distinguishes from related work by deploying data-centric and user-defined policies which can be tracked and enforced efficiently.

7   Conclusions and Future Work

The tracking of security related information in Android was limited to taint tags. For this purpose, TaintDroid provided an efficient architecture. However, TaintDroid is limited to a set of at most 32 different data sources. AppFence was the first approach based on TaintDroid which tried to abolish this coarse granularity. However, also AppFence sticks with the coarse granularity already known from TaintDroid. Kynoid, breaks with these pure taint tracking approaches and introduces finer granularity. It also defines security policies on the variable level and is the first general approach to show that the dynamic tracking of security policies of this granularity is feasible.

Although Kynoid currently only exists as a prototype implementation we can already show its potential impact on the privacy concerns of users. Smartphone owners can define security policies for single data items and specify their appropriate use. If an application does not stick to these security constraints, Kynoid can transparently block respective actions. Future implementations may also query the user for specific actions. These actions may also be used to adapt the policies of the respective items.

We also intend to couple our system with the capabilities, performance, and security characteristics of Constroid [19]. It provides a middle-ware layer which could be used to efficiently and securely retrieve the security policies required for Kynoid. The power of Kynoid will further be increased by supporting a larger number of API sources and sinks.

Finally, future work will also investigate the impact of indirect flows to the overall performance and precision of the presented policy tracking system.

Acknowledgements. We would like to thank the students Tobias Marktschef-fel, Michael Klassen, Fabian Kokot, and Steffen Kremer for their excelent work in helping to implement this framework. Without their support, we would not have been able to provide this contribution.

References

1. Apple Inc.: Security Overview. Tech. rep., Cupertino, CA, USA (2010)
2. Castrucci, A., Martinelli, F., Mori, P., Roperti, F.: Enhancing Java ME Security Support with Resource Usage Monitoring. In: Chen, L., Ryan, M.D., Wang, G. (eds.) ICICS 2008. LNCS, vol. 5308, pp. 256–266. Springer, Heidelberg (2008)
3. Costa, G., Lazouski, A., Dragoni, N., Saadi, R., Ingegneria, D.: Security-by-Contract-with-Trust for Mobile Devices. Journal of Wireless Mobile Networks, Ubiquitous Computing and Dependable Applications (JoWUA) 1, 75–91 (2010)
4. Desmet, L., Joosen, W., Massacci, F., Philippaerts, P., Piessens, F., Siahaan, I., Vanoverberghe, D.: Security-by-contract on the.NET platform. Information Security Technical Report 13(1), 25–32 (2008)
5. Enck, W., Gilbert, P., Chun, B.G., Cox, L.P., Jung, J., McDaniel, P., Sheth, A.N.: TaintDroid: An Information-Flow Tracking System for Realtime Privacy Monitoring on Smartphones. In: Proceedings of OSDI 2010, pp. 1–6. USENIX Association, Vancouver (2010), http://appanalysis.org/tdroid10.pdf
6. Enck, W., Ongtang, M., McDaniel, P.: On lightweight mobile phone application certification. In: Proceedings of the 16th ACM Conference on Computer and Communications Security, pp. 235–245. ACM Press, New York (2009)
7. Enck, W., Ongtang, M., McDaniel, P.: Understanding Android Security. IEEE Security & Privacy Magazine 7(1), 50–57 (2009)
8. Heath, C.: Symbian OS Platform Security, Software Development Using the Symbian OS Security Architecture. John Wiley & Sons Ltd. (2006)
9. Hornyack, P., Han, S., Jung, J., Schechter, S., Wetherall, D.: These aren't the droids you're looking for: retrofitting android to protect data from imperious applications. In: Proceedings of the 18th ACM Conference on Computer and Communications Security, CCS 2011, pp. 639–652. ACM, New York (2011)

10. Krohn, M., Yip, A., Brodsky, M., Cliffer, N., Kaashoek, M.F., Kohler, E., Morris, R.: Information Flow Control for Standard OS Abstractions. In: Proceedings of ACM Symposium on Operating Systems Principles (2007)
11. Microsoft Corporation: Windows Phone 7 Security Model. Tech. rep. (December 2010)
12. Nair, S., Simpson, P., Crispo, B., Tanenbaum, A.: Trishul: A Policy Enforcement Architecture for Java Virtual Machines. Tech. rep., Vrije Universiteit, Amsterdam, Netherlands (2008)
13. Nair, S., Tanenbaum, A., Gheorghe, G., Crispo, B.: Enforcing DRM policies across applications. In: Proceedings of the 8th ACM Workshop on Digital Rights Management - DRM 2008, p. 87. ACM Press, New York (2008)
14. Nauman, M., Khan, S., Zhang, X.: Apex: Extending Android Permission Model and Enforcement with User-defined Runtime Constraints. In: Proceedings of the 5th ACM Symposium on Information, Computer and Communications Security, pp. 328–332. ACM Press, Beijing (2010)
15. Ongtang, M., Butler, K., McDaniel, P.: Porscha: Policy Oriented Secure Content Handling in Android. In: Proceedings of the 26th Annual Computer Security Applications Conference. ACM Press, New York (2010)
16. Ongtang, M., McLaughlin, S., Enck, W., McDaniel, P.: Semantically Rich Application-Centric Security in Android. In: 2009 Annual Computer Security Applications Conference, pp. 340–349. IEEE Computer Society (2009)
17. Philippaerts, P.: Security of Software on Mobile Devices. PhD thesis, Department of Computer Science, Faculty of Engineering, Leuven, Belgium (2010)
18. Research in Motion Ltd.: BlackBerry Enterprise Solution, Security Technical Overview for BlackBerry Enterprise Server Version 4.1 Service Pack 6 and BlackBerry Device Software Version 4.6. Technical report, Canada (2009)
19. Schreckling, D., Posegga, J., Hausknecht, D.: Constroid: Data-Centric Access Control for Android. In: Proceedings of the 27th Symposium on Applied Computing (SAC): Computer Security Track (2012)
20. Vandebogart, S., Efstathopoulos, P., Kohler, E., Krohn, M., Frey, C., Ziegler, D., Kaashoek, F., Morris, R., Mazières, D.: Labels and Event Processes in the Asbestos Operating System. ACM Transactions on Computer Systems (TOCS) 25 (2007)
21. Yin, H., Song, D., Egele, M., Kruegel, C., Kirda, E.: Panorama: Capturing System-Wide Information Flow for Malware Detection and Analysis. In: Proceedings of the 14th ACM Conference on Computer and Communications Security, pp. 116–127. ACM Press, New York (2007)
22. Zeldovich, N., Boyd-Wickizer, S., Kohler, E., Mazières, D.: Making Information Flow Explicit in HiStar. In: Proceedings of the 7th Symposium on Operating Systems Design and Implementation, OSDI (2006)

Author Index

GPSR Compliance

The European Union's (EU) General Product Safety Regulation (GPSR) is a set of rules that requires consumer products to be safe and our obligations to ensure this.

If you have any concerns about our products, you can contact us on ProductSafety@springernature.com

In case Publisher is established outside the EU, the EU authorized representative is:

Springer Nature Customer Service Center GmbH
Europaplatz 3
69115 Heidelberg, Germany

Batch number: 09474011

Printed by Printforce, the Netherlands